S0-BSD-918

Strangers to the Law

Law, Meaning, and Violence

The scope of Law, Meaning, and Violence is defined by the wide-ranging scholarly debates signaled by each of the words in the title. Those debates have taken place among and between lawyers, anthropologists, political theorists, sociologists, and historians, as well as literary and cultural critics. This series is intended to recognize the importance of such ongoing conversations about law, meaning, and violence as well as to encourage and further them.

Series Editors:

Martha Minow, Harvard Law School
Elaine Scarry, Harvard University
Austin Sarat, Amherst College

Narrative, Violence, and the Law: The Essays of Robert Cover, edited by Martha Minow, Michael Ryan, and Austin Sarat

Narrative, Authority, and Law, by Robin West

The Possibility of Popular Justice: A Case Study of Community Mediation in the United States, edited by Sally Engle Merry and Neal Milner

Legal Modernism, by David Luban

Surveillance, Privacy, and the Law: Employee Drug Testing and the Politics of Social Control, by John Gilliom

Lives of Lawyers: Journeys in the Organizations of Practice, by Michael J. Kelly

Unleashing Rights: Law, Meaning, and the Animal Rights Movement, by Helena Silverstein

Law Stories, edited by Gary Bellow and Martha Minow

The Powers That Punish: Prison and Politics in the Era of the "Big House," 1920–1955, by Charles Bright

Law and the Postmodern Mind: Essays on Psychoanalysis and Jurisprudence, edited by Peter Goodrich and David Gray Carlson

Russia's Legal Fictions, by Harriet Murav

Strangers to the Law: Gay People on Trial, by Lisa Keen and Suzanne B. Goldberg

Strangers
to the Law

Gay People on Trial

Lisa Keen
and
Suzanne B. Goldberg

Ann Arbor
THE UNIVERSITY OF MICHIGAN PRESS

2001   2000   1999   1998   4   3   2   1

A CIP catalog record for this book is available from the British Library.

Library of Congress Cataloging-in-Publication Data

Keen, Lisa.
     Strangers to the law : gay people on trial / Lisa Keen and
     Suzanne B. Goldberg.
         p.   cm. — (Law, meaning, and violence)
     Includes bibliographical references and index.
     ISBN 0-472-10644-9 (cloth : acid-free paper)
         1. Evans, Richard G.—Trials, litigation, etc.   2. Colorado.
     Governor (1987–   : Romer)—Trials, litigation, etc.   3. Gays—Legal
     status, laws, etc.—Colorado.   4. Gay rights—Colorado.
     I. Goldberg, Suzanne B.   II. Title.   III. Series.
     KF228.E94K44   1998
     342.788'087—dc21   97-45389
                                                                  CIP

For Sheilah McCarthy,
with hope and love,
Lisa Keen

For Paula and our son Adam,
Suzanne B. Goldberg

Contents

Preface

Within the first days of the trial of Colorado's antigay initiative, known as Amendment 2, a historic moment in gay civil rights history began to unfold. As a journalist covering the trial for gay readers and a lawyer on the legal team challenging the measure, we were among a relatively small group of people in court day after day to usher this moment's entry into our history books.

Although this was not the first trial to address an antigay attack, it was the most comprehensive in its attempt to sift through all that was known about gay people—from ancient history through the latest scientific research—to determine where and how gay people fit into the body politic.

During the nine days of testimony, experts from across the country took the witness stand to offer their thoughts on the role of gay people in society and on whether and how majority rule may be limited in a democratic society.

As each day of the trial passed, it became increasingly clear that, in addition to the legal question—whether Colorado voters could deny gay people access to civil rights protections—the case was also trying to answer another question: Who are gay people? Witnesses, including a historian, a geneticist, psychiatrists, political scientists, and media experts, testified extensively about these issues. But each advanced a different answer, depending on his or her particular vantage point. To record these views, put this trial into a historical context, and explore the questions the trial raised, we agreed to write this book.

As coauthors, we, too, have viewed this case and trial from different vantage points: Suzanne Goldberg, as a lawyer for Lambda Legal Defense and Education Fund, the oldest and largest national lesbian and gay legal group, was a member of the legal team challenging Amendment 2; Lisa Keen, as executive editor for the *Washington Blade*, the oldest and largest gay newspaper in the United States, covered the trial and events surrounding the case as a journalist. This book is inevitably shaped by these two perspectives, but we have shared a commitment to record the events surrounding the trial in as full, fair, and objective a manner as possible. In doing so, we do not report every personality conflict nor every strength or weakness of the individuals involved in the case. We keep our focus on the significant conflicts about litigation strategy within the plaintiffs' legal team. We have undertaken this project independently of our affiliations with Lambda and the *Blade*. And, while we have made explicit note of Suzanne's involvement as a member of the plaintiffs' legal team, we have presented the text that follows in the third person.

Many of the key players involved in the trial and the events surrounding it have publicly identified their sexual orientation, and many have not. When the subjects of our story have made that information public—whether heterosexual, lesbian, gay, or bisexual—we indicate that. But, out of our shared belief that each person should have the right to decide for himself or herself whether to make his or her sexual orientation public, we have not attempted to report this information independently.

We also acknowledge that different people often use different terms to identify their sexual orientation, and we use those terms, too, as much as possible. But, from time to time, to keep the text readable, we use the term "gay people" to represent lesbians and gay men, as well as people who have, as Amendment 2 put it, "homosexual, lesbian, or bisexual orientation, conduct, practices, or relationships. . . ." In a similar manner, we use the term "religious right" to represent people, organizations, and movements working to advance causes, such as Amendment 2, that reflect a religiously oriented conservative political agenda. To keep the text clear, we also correct punctuation, typographical errors, and, occasionally, grammatical errors in quotations taken from the trial transcript.

We are deeply grateful for the generosity of several people who contributed to the refinement of the final manuscript by sharing with us their expertise, support, and editorial advice: David L. Chambers, Matthew A. Coles, Kathryn E. Diaz, Paula L. Ettelbrick, Chai R. Feldblum, Richard L. Goldberg, Don Michaels, Martha Minow, and Ellen Reisman; and we thank our editor at the University of Michigan Press, Charles T. Myers, for his expertise, encouragement, and enthusiasm for this work. In addition, as one of the lawyers for the plaintiffs, Suzanne thanks the plaintiffs, the legal team, and the many individuals who laid the groundwork for this victory and who continue to build upon it. Lisa thanks her colleagues at the *Washington Blade*, Don Michaels, Colleen Marzec, and Kristina Campbell, for their work to ensure that this story was reported as it happened.

Finally, we thank the colleagues, friends, and family members whose love, support, and unswerving confidence helped us in the effort to document this important moment in our history.

Lisa Keen
Washington, D.C.

Suzanne B. Goldberg
New York, N.Y.

Chapter 1

The Stakes

Over the centuries, people have been jailed, institutionalized, exiled, forced into slavery, or systematically executed for being "different." Sometimes, these severe reactions have stemmed from the majority's ignorance and fear; but, just as often, they were fueled by the desire to profit from prejudice—either economically or socially. The dangers of being targeted by this prejudice have often been so great as to drive those in a minority to take drastic measures to hide their difference—by changing their names, denying their loved ones, and even using toxic chemicals in an attempt to change the color of their skin.

Depending on the country and century, people who have been different by virtue of being homosexual have been whipped, imprisoned, hanged, banished, lobotomized, ostracized, burned at the stake, or ignored to the point of virtual extinction. For centuries they were seen as sinning against nature and, therefore, "against God," and during times and in places of "increased religious fervor,"[1] they were put to death. As conflict arose over what constituted the "laws of God," the laws of government took greater precedence. Homosexuality became condemned as both socially deviant and against nature and was penalized in the general belief that it should be discouraged, if not eradicated.

In recent years, social scientists have found strong evidence that homosexuality is a phenomenon of nature, albeit much less common than heterosexuality. With increased enlightenment, the price for being different in this way has, for the most part, lessened.

Even today, however, hostility toward people who are homosex-

---

1. Judith C. Brown, "Lesbian Sexuality in Medieval and Early Modern Europe," *Hidden from History: Reclaiming the Gay and Lesbian Past*, edited by Martin Duberman, Martha Vicinus, and George Chauncey Jr. (Ontario: New American Library, 1989), 498. In a footnote, Brown refers readers to *Ritual, Myth and Magic in Early Modern Europe* by William Monter (Athens: Ohio University Press, 1984), 116–17.

ual has persisted. It surfaced dramatically in Colorado in the early
1990s, turning gay men, lesbians, and bisexual people into fodder for a
"cultural war" in the United States. The all-out attack on the civil
rights and social status of gay people signified a new cultural war, but
not the first. In recent years, intense societal conflicts have erupted
over a range of issues, including access to contraception, the choice of
a woman to end her pregnancy, and the desire of an interracial couple
to marry. But in Colorado, the clash was over more than just this one
difference between the majority and a minority. It was also a clash
over sexual morality and over how much power the majority should
have in American democracy to translate its view of sexual morality
into law. Claiming to represent the majority, leaders of the religious
right argued that homosexuality was morally wrong, violated their
religious beliefs, and should be prohibited and discouraged. As the
minority, gay people argued that being homosexual or bisexual was as
moral as being heterosexual; that those in the majority did not have the
right to dictate such private matters as whom to love, nor to deprive
people of civil rights based on their sexual orientation. Each side called
the other "radical," and each accused the other of being "liars." One
side described the stakes in this struggle as akin to letting Satan take
over the world. The other side said the foundation of American
democracy was in jeopardy.

"We firmly believe that we're involved now in one of the most
incredible cultural wars that has ever occurred in Western civilization,"
said an activist on one side. And, he warned, "it's coming to every city,
every little town, every city council, every school. This is something
that's going to be fought out, really, all across the nation, and people
are just going to have to decide what they think about it."[2]

It was going to be fought out in a courtroom, too, through a lawsuit called *Evans v. Romer.*[3] The catalyst for the courtroom battle was an
attempt by religious right activists in Colorado to limit—through a bal-

---

2. "The New Holy War," aired November 19, 1993, on PBS's *Bill Moyer's Journal;*
Transcript No. 1003, 1.

3. The full name of the case at its inception was *Richard G. Evans, Angela Romero,
Linda Fowler, Paul Brown, Martina Navratilova, Bret Tanberg, Priscilla Inkpen, the City and
County of Denver, the City of Boulder, the City of Aspen, and the City Council of Aspen, plain-
tiffs, v. Roy Romer as Governor of the State of Colorado, defendants.* Later, the Boulder Valley
School District RE-2 also joined as a plaintiff. It was commonly referred to as *Evans v.
Romer* until it reached the U.S. Supreme Court, at which point it was referred to as *Romer
v. Evans.*

lot initiative called Amendment 2—the ability of government to address the needs of gay citizens on the same basis as the needs of other citizens. The lawsuit would not end the "war," but its ultimate resolution would have potentially enormous influence on a core issue underlying all societal disputes in a democracy: How far does the U.S. Constitution allow the majority to go in exercising its democratic power over a minority, and how far does it go in protecting that minority against what James Madison, one of its authors, called the tyranny of the majority? The answer would depend a great deal on whether the minority could find a "right" in the Constitution to protect its interests and whether the majority could prove that it was exercising democracy and not a tyranny of prejudice.

Cultural War to Court

The question was thrust into court in Denver after the people of Colorado, on November 3, 1992, voted 53 percent to 46 percent to approve a measure called Amendment 2, which had been placed on the statewide ballot through the efforts of a right-wing religiously oriented political group called Colorado for Family Values (CFV). The initiative sought to amend the state constitution to: (1) repeal any existing law or policy that protected a person with a "homosexual, lesbian, or bisexual orientation" from discrimination in Colorado and any of its cities, towns, counties, and school boards and (2) prohibit future adoption or enforcement of "any [such] law or policy." The ballot question read:

> NO PROTECTED STATUS BASED ON HOMOSEXUAL, LESBIAN OR BISEXUAL ORIENTATION. Neither the State of Colorado, through any of its branches or departments, nor any of its agencies, political subdivisions, municipalities or school districts, shall enact, adopt or enforce any statute, regulation, ordinance or policy whereby homosexual, lesbian, or bisexual orientation, conduct, practices, or relationships shall constitute or otherwise be the basis of or entitle any person or class of persons to have or claim any minority status, quota preferences, protected status or claim of discrimination.
>
> This Section of the Constitution shall be in all respects self-executing.[4]

---

4. The text of Amendment 2 as it appeared on the Colorado statewide ballot.

The majority of Colorado voters put their support behind CFV's position that laws and policies prohibiting discrimination based on sexual orientation provide "special rights" to gay men, lesbians, and bisexual people that gay people neither "deserve" nor need. The minority of voters—including gay people and those who supported civil rights laws generally—argued that Amendment 2 was both an attempt to render gay people vulnerable to discrimination and an initial step toward undermining antidiscrimination laws that protect other minorities.

The majority spoke through its vote at the ballot box. Many voters believed that, since the U.S. Constitution promises people the right to self-govern, the amendment was a reasonable exercise of their constitutional rights. And since the voters had approved Amendment 2 to become part of their state's constitution, the state government carried the responsibility of defending the initiative against any legal challenge.

The minority responded through the legal system. It expected that, since the Constitution promises that all citizens have "equal protection" under the law, the amendment would be declared unconstitutional because it sought to treat gay people unequally. The minority, however, could not count on the state to defend its rights. Instead, opponents of Amendment 2 organized a team of attorneys to mount a lawsuit against the measure. They found seven Colorado citizens, three cities, and one city council, then later a school district, within the state to serve as plaintiffs. And on November 12, 1992, they filed their lawsuit in the Colorado District Court for Denver.

It was thus left to the judiciary to referee this clash between the Constitution's principle of majority rule and its protections for the rights of minorities. Throughout the nation's history, the courts had decided that both types of constitutional provisions had some limits. With respect to minority rights, states could treat some citizens differently in some circumstances if the government could demonstrate it had legitimate or compelling reasons to do so. And regarding majority rule, the U.S. Supreme Court had also ruled that "the people may retain for themselves the power over certain subjects," but in the same decision—regarding a ballot initiative in the 1960s that discriminated against African-Americans—it also noted that the people themselves had put limits on majority power through the Constitution.[5] Thus the

---

5. *Hunter v. Erickson,* 393 U.S. 385 (1969).

majority's rule was not unchecked. It could not, for instance, vote to reestablish segregation.

The battle over Amendment 2 brought to the courts yet another national conflict over the tension between the constitutional promises of democracy and equality for all.

Decades of Division

Just as Amendment 2 was not the first ballot battle to drag those warring principles into the courtroom, it was not the first ballot measure to take hostile aim at gay people—not the first in Colorado and not the first in the United States. Before the vote on Amendment 2 in November 1992, 33 antigay initiatives and referenda had already been on local ballots in jurisdictions around the country—at least one about annually since the first in 1974. Early on, these initiatives carried a high emotional volume and profile. They were the backlash against the early surges of gay activism that followed the Stonewall Rebellion in June 1969. Though gay organizations had been active for years, the rebellion, at which gay people literally fought back against police harassment in a New York City bar called the Stonewall Inn, is commonly regarded as the starting point of modern gay political movement. As word of Stonewall spread quickly around the country, it inspired the formation of new gay political groups to seek laws to protect gay people from such harassment and discrimination. Within just a few years, these new groups succeeded in having sexual orientation antidiscrimination ordinances enacted in a number of cities and counties throughout the country, including Boulder, Colorado; Columbus, Ohio; Dade County, Florida; Detroit; Seattle; San Francisco; and Washington, D.C.

The religious right reacted strongly against this new activism. Among the most publicized of its reactions was a referendum campaign organized in 1977 by television personality Anita Bryant. The former beauty queen and well-known promoter of Florida orange juice sought votes to overturn the new Dade County ordinance and quickly captured national headlines and attention. The gay community fought back, mounting its own highly publicized and successful boycott of Florida orange juice. Despite those efforts, voters repealed the ordinance in Dade County, and Bryant moved ahead, establishing a national office in Washington, D.C., and taking her campaign to Wichita, Kansas; St. Paul, Minnesota; and other cities that had recently enacted ordinances prohibiting discrimination based on sexual orientation. Her efforts inspired a number of religious right activists to enter the political arena, and many would later play key roles in the campaign for Amendment 2.

The activism and backlash seen around the country were also being played out during the early 1970s inside Colorado. The first battle there took place in 1974 in Boulder where the city council approved a law prohibiting discrimination based on sexual orientation in employment. The issue had triggered such a volatile debate between supporters and opponents that the city council put the ordinance on the ballot and let the voters decide. The majority voted overwhelmingly to repeal the antidiscrimination law. But while most voters in a number of cities opposed such laws, they also seemed opposed to negative political campaigns aimed at a minority group. Bryant's organized "crusade" against gay people across the country quickly fizzled, and by 1987, when Boulder voters were again asked to vote on whether they wanted a law to prohibit discrimination based on sexual orientation, they voted yes. The turnaround in Boulder was a sign that the gay civil rights movement had made some gains in the 13 years since that first referendum.

But the movement was also riding a political seesaw in Colorado. In November 1988, voters in Fort Collins, Colorado, rejected a ballot initiative that gay activists had proposed in hopes of amending the town's human rights ordinance to prohibit discrimination based on sexual orientation. Two years later, the Denver city council approved such an ordinance. Right-wing activists put a referendum on the ballot and pressed voters to repeal the new law, but, in 1991, Denver voters decided to keep protections in place.

The political seesaw for gay people could be seen around the country, too. Supporters of equal rights for lesbians and gay men would win passage of laws; opponents would win ballot referenda to repeal them. But while opponents of such laws won 17 out of 22 square-offs around the country in the 15 years between 1974 to 1989, the two sides began to split victories thereafter, and, even when the progay campaigns lost, their margins of defeat were narrower than they had been in the early 1970s.

The level of activity by gay people to establish civil rights protections had expanded dramatically in the late 1980s, too. In 1982, only one state, Wisconsin, had a statewide law prohibiting discrimination against gay people. No other state passed such a law until 1989. But by 1992, seven states had them, and governors in ten states had issued executive orders banning sexual orientation discrimination in state employment and services.[6]

In the midst of this surge of activity, Colorado governor Roy Romer, in 1989, issued an executive order prohibiting discrimination against people with AIDS, many of whom were gay men. And, in July 1991, the Colorado Civil Rights Commission recommended that the state adopt a law prohibiting discrimination based on sexual orientation.

That same year, the idea of an antidiscrimination law was also put on the agenda of the city council in Colorado Springs, a much more politically conservative town than Boulder or Denver. Colorado Springs was home to a large number of religiously oriented conservative groups, including many of the largest and most powerful right-wing organizations in the country. These groups fought the proposed law in Colorado Springs, and the council dropped the idea.

But stopping the proposed law in Colorado Springs was not enough for some activists of the religious right. Three of them—David Noebel, Tony Marco, and Kevin Tebedo—formed a new organization called Colorado for Family Values. They enlisted a local car dealer, Will Perkins, as their chairperson and began a campaign for a statewide initiative. They wanted not only to block the antidiscrimination ordinance in Colorado Springs but also to repeal the governor's executive order and sexual orientation antidiscrimination laws that were on the books in other cities—Aspen, Boulder, and Denver. And they wanted to prevent any future efforts to pass antidiscrimination laws protecting gay people anywhere else in the state. Their inspiration, as the *Denver Post* put it, was their feeling that "America has deteriorated because it has turned away from literal interpretations of the Bible, and fundamentalist church teachings must play a bigger role in government."[7]

---

6. Massachusetts enacted its law in 1989, followed by Connecticut and Hawaii in 1991, and New Jersey, Vermont, and California in 1992. Governors in the following states issued executive orders between 1975 and 1992: Pennsylvania, California, New York, Ohio, New Mexico, Rhode Island, Washington, Minnesota, Oregon, and Louisiana.

7. Michael Booth, "Colorado: Gay-Rights Battlefield," *Denver Post*, September 27, 1992, A-7.

The Role of Religion

This desire for church teachings to have a greater role in government
had recently become a highly visible part of the national agenda for the
religious right, which was regrouping after having suffered an embarrassing series of sex scandals involving prominent television evange-
lists and a decidedly negative public reaction to the televised speeches
of some of its leaders at the 1992 Republican National Convention—
speeches that derided gay people and attacked other vulnerable people, such as unmarried mothers. Suffering this tarnished image on the
national level, the religious right turned its focus to the local level. Borrowing from a history of tactics used against the black civil rights
movement, the religious right began seeking victories state by state.
This time, instead of literacy tests and poll taxes to limit the power of
African-Americans to vote, religious right activists sought to repeal
laws prohibiting discrimination, to stop legal recognition of same-sex
relationships, to bar even a neutral discussion of homosexuality in the
classroom, and—in a preemptive strike through Amendment 2 and like
initiatives—they sought declarations that lesbians, gay men, and bisexuals could not even ask the government to address their specific needs
on the same terms as other citizens.

Pat Robertson, head and host of the Christian Broadcasting Network, had galvanized a comeback for such activists through a
national cable television program that discussed newsworthy events
with a religious perspective, through the creation of the national
Christian Coalition to inform and motivate voter support for conservative, religious-based viewpoints, and with his bid for the Republican
presidential nomination in 1992. He and others, such as James Dobson, head of the Focus on the Family organization in Colorado
Springs, were using the powerful reach of television and radio programs to sign up millions of supporters and contributors around the
country at the grass roots level and to mobilize them to the polls for
important issues or races. Gay people were just one of their targets,
for they were also organizing to prohibit women from obtaining abor-
tions, to win government support for church-run schools funded by
public money through school vouchers, and to promote prayer and
religiously based views on sex education in the schools. Often, they
blurred the lines between their target issues to get the maximum
punch for their attacks. For instance, in opposing an equal rights

amendment measure for women in Iowa, Robertson sent out a letter claiming that the real motive of the "feminist agenda" was to encourage women to become lesbians.[8]

When Colorado for Family Values was formed, its organizers modeled their efforts on those of the national groups and put representatives from those groups onto CFV's board, including individuals from Lou Sheldon's Traditional Values Coalition, Dobson's Focus on the Family, the antifeminist Eagle Forum, and Concerned Women for America.[9] CFV's strategy for the campaign to promote Amendment 2 echoed that of a handbook called *How to Defeat Gay Rights Legislation*, written by an attorney for Concerned Women for America. That handbook urged its readers to warn voters that antidiscrimination laws must be repealed because they were just the tip of the iceberg of the "homosexual agenda."[10] An attorney for another right-wing group, the National Legal Foundation, founded by Pat Robertson, coached CFV on the specifics of language for Amendment 2 that would help avoid legal pitfalls. Focus on the Family, Dobson's multimillion-dollar organization, gave CFV in-kind support and, in alliance with a right-wing think tank called the Family Research Council, distributed a publication that detailed how to start an initiative against the "Homosexual Agenda."[11]

While Amendment 2 was the first statewide test of a new prototype for antigay initiatives resulting from the collaboration of national and local conservative organizations seeking to secure a role for religion in government, the very first tests had been at the local level, in two California cities—Riverside and Concord—in 1991. The Riverside initiative had sought to repeal existing ordinances prohibiting discrimination based on AIDS and sexual orientation and to forbid any future laws protecting people on either of those grounds. It was proposed by a group called Citizens for Responsible Behavior, loosely affiliated with Traditional Values Coalition leader Lou Sheldon. But the Riverside

8. Aras van Hertum, "ERA Encourages Witches and Lesbians, Says Pat Robertson," *Washington Blade*, August 28, 1992, 6.

9. *Anti-Gay Ballot Initiatives: An Analysis of Colorado's Amendment 2—Strategies to Defeat Other Initiatives*, a briefing book prepared and published by the American Civil Liberties Union Lesbian and Gay Rights Project, 1993, 43.

10. Lisa M. Keen, "Ballot Box Fights Are Far from Knock-Outs," *Washington Blade*, December 8, 1989, 1.

11. "Constructing Homophobia: Colorado's Right-Wing Attack on Homosexuals," *The Public Eye*, March 1993, published by Political Research Associates, 5.

City Council voted to keep the measure off the ballot, and a Riverside Superior Court judge and a California appellate court agreed that the measure violated the constitutional guarantee of equal protection because it lacked a rational justification and was motivated by prejudice. The Citizens group did not appeal further. The initiative in Concord, called Measure M, did get onto the November 1991 ballot due to the efforts of another Traditional Values Coalition affiliate called Concord United for Fair Law. Similar to initiatives in other cities in the 1960s that required popular votes on laws that prohibited racial discrimination, the Concord initiative sought to prevent the local government from passing any law involving sexual orientation. Measure M also sought to repeal an existing law prohibiting discrimination against gay people and people with AIDS. The initiative was narrowly approved by voters in November 1991 but was challenged in court. A trial court judge declared it unconstitutional, and, again, the initiative's supporters did not appeal.

In May 1992, a group called Oregon Citizens Alliance (OCA) put a somewhat similar initiative on the ballot in two Oregon cities, Springfield (where it passed) and Corvallis (where it failed). Those initiatives, and a statewide version in November 1992, asked voters to ban laws that "promoted" homosexuality, pedophilia, sadism, and masochism. OCA leader Lon Mabon said he was unaware of the Colorado initiative until after he began his campaign and that his organization "linked up" subsequently with the Christian Coalition and got $20,000 from it. But beyond that, Mabon's 1992 effort was an independent one, and his measure was defeated at the ballot box by a margin of 57 to 43 percent. The true test of the cooperative effort of national and local right-wing organizations took place in Colorado with Amendment 2, under the banner of fighting "special rights."

"Special Rights"

The term *special rights* was first used by opponents of laws prohibiting discrimination based on race. Characterizing these laws as conferring "special rights" or "special privileges" gave the public the sense that those of minority races were getting rights that people of the majority race were not getting. In truth, the laws simply ensured that minorities would have the *same* rights the majority already had, to participate in society without fear of discrimination based on their race. But the "special rights" distortion took hold in the public's mind, particularly around the development of specific efforts to address race discrimination—such as affirmative action programs. Perhaps the terminology "affirmative" action contributed to the confusion. Rather than seeing the programs as attempts to remedy the damage of the past—the educational and economic inequities that racial minority groups faced as a result of decades of discrimination—many people in America's white majority began seeing these efforts and civil rights laws generally as giving racial minorities a special advantage in such competitive arenas as the workplace.

In political parlance, "special rights" became a code word that expressed hostility toward such civil rights programs. And that was apparent in a June 13, 1991, letter about Amendment 2's text, written to CFV founder Tony Marco, from Brian McCormick, staff counsel for Pat Robertson's National Legal Foundation. McCormick's letter coached CFV to keep the term *special rights* out of the initiative's language but to use it in the campaign for voter support. "If language denying special privileges to homosexuals is in the amendment," explained McCormick, "it could possibly allow homosexuals to argue that they are not asking for any special privileges, just those granted to everyone else. I believe that 'No Special Privileges' is a good motto for the amendment's public campaign, but I fear the possible legal ramifications if it is included in the amendment itself."

Elsewhere in the letter he explained that, "while homosexuals do not get far by asking the electorate for special privileges, they do get a good deal of sympathy by asking to be 'treated just like everyone else.' "

In its campaign, CFV pounded in the "special rights" message with great effect. Civil rights supporters tried to convince voters that laws prohibiting discrimination based on sexual orientation were not about "special rights" but rather about access to equal rights for gay people. Without these antidiscrimination laws, they said, people could be thrown out of jobs, hotels, restaurants, or apartments just because they are gay; gay youth could be refused counseling in public schools for issues related to their being gay; lesbians and gay men in relationships could be denied the right to attend to their loved ones in a hospital emergency room; and gay people would lose the basic right to petition their own elected officials to create laws or policies to meet their needs.

"By singling out homosexual, lesbian, and bisexual persons in the state constitution and effectively denying them potential remedies for discrimination, the amendment denies them the same equal protections under the United States Constitution as other citizens," said the Legislative Council of the Colorado General Assembly, which prepared "An Analysis of 1992 Ballot Proposals" to explain the potential impact of the initiative. The council routinely prepares such analyses for voters, summarizing the arguments made on both sides of an issue. While the council's analysis also noted the argument of Amendment 2's proponents that the initiative supported "the original purpose of legislation enacting civil rights protections," a voter pamphlet prepared by the League of Women Voters of Colorado said just the opposite: that "nothing this negative against basic civil rights . . . has ever been tried in the United States."

The aspect of Amendment 2 that sought to stop gay people from seeking any future legislative action in response to their needs was one that especially worried many civil rights activists. If CFV and others could convince the public that laws prohibiting discrimination against lesbians and gay men amounted to "special rights," it would be easier, then, to characterize existing antidiscrimination laws protecting other minorities the same way. A large number of groups representing minorities and working to preserve civil rights laws publicly declared their opposition to Amendment 2, including the Colorado Hispanic League, the Anti-Defamation League of B'nai B'rith, Colorado Black Women for Political Action, and the National Organization for Women.

The Colorado Hispanic League issued a statement opposing Amendment 2, making its concern explicit: "If the civil rights, privacy, privileges and protections of citizens can be restricted because of sexual orientation, what protects Hispanics from similar initiatives based on equally arbitrary reasons?"

The religious right knew it had to assuage this fear. If it did not, racial minorities and others would join forces with gay people and CFV's efforts would be jeopardized. Not surprisingly, then, CFV's Will Perkins often stated during his Amendment 2 campaign that he had no objections to people getting "special rights" based on race or gender but that he did not want them given to people "because of what [they are] doing in their bedroom."

CFV also had to be mindful of the Constitution's separation of church and state and, at times, would couch its points carefully so as

not to appear to be trying to convert its religious beliefs about homosexuality into law. The group had mixed success. "In its public campaign, the family values group has tried to steer the debate over
Amendment 2 towards a discussion of civil rights and what groups
deserve protection," noted the *Denver Post* in September 1992. "But in
less publicized talks at churches statewide, it becomes clear that the
activists' arguments are rooted in the philosophy of the religious
right."[12] The *Post* reported that CFV cofounder Kevin Tebedo told one
church group gathered to discuss Amendment 2 that "we say that we
should have separation of church and state, but, you see, Jesus Christ is
the king of kings and the lord of lords. That is politics, that is rule, that
is authority. So whose authority is going to rule?"

Using a "rule" like that as a public campaign slogan might alienate
many Coloradans—not just those who believed in the privacy of bedroom activity, but also those whose faiths did not include Jesus Christ
and those who believed the Constitution's guarantee to freedom of religion included the freedom *from* religion. To the extent that proponents
of Amendment 2 discussed the religious aspects of their motives, they
tried to convince voters that antidiscrimination laws protecting gay
people violated the freedom of religion of people who believe homosexuality is a sin. In CFV's view, the Bible condemned homosexuality
as a sin, thus laws that prohibited discrimination based on homosexuality interfered with the ability of those who read the Bible that way to
exercise this religious belief.

For lesbians, gay men, and bisexual people in Colorado, Amendment 2 was not an attempt to exercise religious freedom but an attempt
to codify that particular religious view of homosexuality and, in so
doing, enable anyone to discriminate against gay people for any reason. The intended effect of this "special rights" and "religious freedom" approach to the law, as the plaintiffs' lawsuit stated, was to rele-
gate "gay men, lesbians and bisexuals to a second-class citizenship."

The Political and Personal

To some extent, gay people in 1992 had already been legally designated
second-class citizens in the United States for six years. In 1986, through
its decision in the landmark case *Bowers v. Hardwick*, the U.S. Supreme

---

12. Booth, *Denver Post*, September 27, 1992.

Court had upheld as constitutional a Georgia law that had been applied to prohibit consensual sexual relations between two men in the privacy of one of their homes. The law in question had also prohibited sodomy between heterosexual couples, but the Supreme Court had chosen to address the law only as it applied to same-sex couples. It said simply that gay people had no "fundamental right" under the constitution to engage in "homosexual sodomy."

In the years following the *Hardwick* ruling, many courts and governments had interpreted this decision liberally to authorize a wide variety of bans and limitations on the lives of gay people, including the ability to parent children, serve in the military, and secure financial and legal protections for their relationships.

In light of this history, both gay activists and those who opposed equal rights for gay people were watching closely when the lawsuit against Amendment 2 came to trial in 1993. The case seemed almost certain to reach the U.S. Supreme Court for an ultimate resolution, and that resolution was expected to have a profound impact on what other rights and freedoms gay citizens would or would not have.

But as high as the legal stakes riding on *Evans v. Romer* were, the political stakes were perhaps even more significant—for gay people, for religious activists, for all Americans and American society. As one expert witness at trial explained, in reflecting on his own career litigating against racial discrimination, there is "bound to be some rip in the fabric of civility from trying to eliminate by law discrimination that is otherwise the social norm or the economic norm, or the political norm."

Discrimination against gay people had long been a social norm; the Supreme Court's decision in *Hardwick* dramatically reflected the general acceptance of antigay hostility. But despite that 1986 ruling— maybe because of it—the momentum for creating laws that prohibit such discrimination had grown. By the time the Amendment 2 trial began in October 1993, an eighth state (Minnesota) had passed a law prohibiting sexual orientation discrimination, as had more than 100 towns, cities, and counties. A national public debate was raging over whether gay people should be permitted to serve in the military, and the controversy had prompted the U.S. Congress to pass a law to secure that ban. The controversy had also undercut the popularity of newly elected president Bill Clinton, who had promised gay people during the campaign that he would end the military's ban. While a Gallup poll in June 1992 had shown 57 percent of Americans *favored* allowing gay people in the military, in 1993, it showed 53 percent *opposed*. The sudden turnabout dampened Clinton's enthusiasm to speak in support of strengthening civil rights protections for gay people, and the raucous debate put considerable media attention on everything gay and kept it there.

At the same time, although the religious right had been winning at the ballot boxes with its antigay initiatives (winning 60 out of 80 campaigns in 22 years), the gay civil rights movement was making some gains in the public sphere with increased national visibility and organizing. A national march for gay civil rights in April 1993 had drawn to Washington, D.C., one of the largest gatherings ever for a political demonstration. The massive march captured front-page media attention nationwide. With the increased coverage came more public discussion of gay people and a greater understanding of and familiarity with what it means to be gay. While the percentage of Americans who believed that "homosexual relations are always wrong" was still high in 1993 (66 percent said so), it had dropped significantly from its highest point in 1987 (when 77 percent said so) and was at its lowest point in 24 years.[13] The AIDS epidemic, which during its first decade from 1981 to 1991 struck primarily gay men, had inspired a surge in gay people coming out of the closet, identifying as gay, and funneling their money and time into various activities to care for their loved ones.

When the Amendment 2 case reached the U.S. Supreme Court in the spring of 1996 as *Romer v. Evans,* another national debate was erupting—this time over whether states should offer the same legal recognition through marriage to gay couples as they offer to heterosexual couples. President Clinton, who was now up for reelection, voiced his opposition to equal marriage rights for gay people. And although the president had stated publicly that he was against discrimination against gay people, his administration did not file a brief with the Supreme Court in opposition to Amendment 2.

Lingering in the background of the Amendment, the trial, and the national debates surrounding gay people was the question of who is a "heterosexual" or a "homosexual" or a "bisexual" and how one defines these terms. While such terms were used frequently and easily in com-

---

13. "What Americans Think: 1996 Report: A Guide to Trends in Public Opinion, 1972–1996," a report from the National Opinion Research Center at the University of Chicago, October 1996. The survey is conducted annually.

mon discourse, they were, in practice, quite difficult to define—as difficult as attempts a century before to define who was "white" and who
was "black" and who was "mulatto." People do not always fit clearly
into one definition or another. And if the law was going to turn on such
distinctions, could the courts find answers to these underlying questions?

Chapter 2

Prelude to a Trial

Tensions ran high around the conference table on a sunny but cold Denver afternoon in early December 1992. Although the roomful of lawyers were all on the same side of the case they were about to launch, the group, at that moment, seemed more divided than united.

The group's goal was to arrive at the best litigation strategy for defeating the newly adopted amendment to Colorado's state constitution. Now that Amendment 2's fate had passed through the political process, where voters had approved it by a close margin, the legal challenge was critical. A couple of the team's attorneys had sketched out a lawsuit during the previous weeks, just in case the amendment passed. However, in light of polling data showing strong disapproval of the measure among voters, few had expected Amendment 2 actually to garner the necessary votes, and a firm strategy to stop the amendment from taking effect had not yet been agreed upon.

Around the table sat about a dozen Colorado attorneys. Some represented the cities in Colorado that had already decided to be plaintiffs in the lawsuit because the amendment threatened their own governmental prohibitions against sexual orientation discrimination. Lawyers for the individual lesbians and gay men and the Boulder Valley school district who would also be plaintiffs in the suit were present, further enriching the mix of experience and perspectives around the table.

Jean Dubofsky, a former Colorado Supreme Court justice, had been asked by an in-state gay activist group that had been planning for the lawsuit, the Colorado Legal Initiatives Project (CLIP), to take the lead in representing the individual plaintiffs in the suit.

A well-respected Colorado attorney with strong political connections, Dubofsky was, after stepping down from the Colorado high court and serving a stint as a law professor, working as a solo practitioner handling mainly appellate cases out of her Boulder office. In private practice, Dubofsky represented some gay and lesbian clients in various civil actions, including adoption and divorce cases, but she had little experience in cases that would have a broad impact on the lesbian and gay civil rights movement.

Dubofsky was friends with a couple who had a gay son and who were active in opposing Amendment 2. "They called me up one day and said, 'We just want you to know that we're really involved in this and have talked about you'" to CLIP as a possible attorney to handle the legal challenge, recalled Dubofsky.

Dubofsky said that she had some concerns about taking the lead—although not because people might think she was a lesbian and discriminate against her. Instead, Dubofsky said, her concern was that attorneys often become "the face of a case," and that a heterosexual person should not be the "face" on this prominent gay civil rights case, a feeling she believed many gay people would share. But CLIP, she said, "wanted a heterosexual attorney to take the lead for a bundle of reasons"—including, primarily, that they felt Colorado's conservative climate would respond better to a lawsuit led by a well-known and respected heterosexual.

"It was their sense that our chances of prevailing in the courts of Colorado might be greater" by having a heterosexual lead attorney, said Dubofsky. In addition, according to plaintiff and gay activist Richard Evans, "It was always our intention that this be a locally controlled case with a local attorney. We saw this as a Colorado problem and we were going to provide a Colorado solution."

Still, even before Amendment 2 passed, the national gay legal groups were already involved in an advisory capacity in preparing the legal strategy. Lambda Legal Defense and Education Fund and the ACLU's Lesbian and Gay Rights Project joined forces with Dubofsky and with the Colorado ACLU, which had also offered its services.

Suzanne Goldberg, a staff attorney with Lambda's national headquarters in New York, was also present at the meeting on behalf of the individual lesbian and gay plaintiffs. The only representative of the national groups in Denver at that time, she was to bring to the table the perspective of both Lambda and the ACLU's Lesbian and Gay Rights Project, two long-standing national groups focused on lesbian and gay legal issues. Goldberg was sent to represent Lambda as Lambda attorney Mary Newcombe, who had contributed early work on the case, was leaving the Lambda staff. Goldberg had been at Lambda just over a year, working on various lesbian, gay, and HIV-related civil rights cases. She was just two years out of law school, but she was in close communication with Newcombe as well as other Lambda and ACLU colleagues and was representing the views of some of the most experienced lesbian and gay civil rights attorneys in the country.

Lambda, the nation's oldest and largest legal group to focus specifically on sexual orientation and HIV-related discrimination, was founded in 1973 and had been involved with most of the major gay civil rights litigation in the United States, including challenges to sodomy laws and discrimination in the military and efforts to secure rights for lesbian and gay families. The ACLU's Lesbian and Gay Rights Project, also headquartered in New York, was founded in 1986 and was similarly involved in the major gay civil rights cases throughout the country. Matt Coles of the ACLU's Northern California office, Bill Rubenstein, legal director of the ACLU's Project, and Ruth Harlow, another of the ACLU's Project's attorneys, were all actively involved in the case on the ACLU's behalf. Although the organizations generally handled different cases, they sometimes took on cases together and frequently collaborated on litigation strategies.

Also representing the ACLU was David Miller, legal director of the Colorado ACLU, which was the state's chief organization dedicated to protecting civil rights and civil liberties. Miller, who was not gay himself, had handled a couple of lesbian and gay cases during his ACLU tenure as well as a wide variety of other matters in the state.

Darlene Ebert, Joe DeRaismes, and Jed Caswall, attorneys for Denver, Boulder, and Aspen, respectively, were also at the table and all strongly committed to the case as advocates for their local governments. For the cities, the battle was joined because Amendment 2, in effect, allowed the state's voters to overrule each city's own determination as to which antidiscrimination protections were necessary. For example, if voters in Colorado Springs and elsewhere could forbid Boulder from prohibiting discrimination against some of Boulder's residents, the city's leaders feared not only for their civil rights laws but also for their power to legislate generally. In fact, voters in Boulder, and in Denver and Aspen, had overwhelmingly rejected Amendment 2 at the ballot box while a majority of Colorado Springs voters had supported the measure.

The group at that December meeting had only a short time together to discuss case strategy before their scheduled meeting with attorneys for the state of Colorado. Amendment 2 was to take effect in mid-January, according to Colorado law regarding the effective date of voter-initiated measures. A short period of time after voter results were certified by the state elections board, Colorado's governor, Roy Romer, would be legally bound to declare the amendment part of Colorado's governing charter. To stop Amendment 2 from taking effect, the plaintiffs' legal team had two choices—to persuade the state to refrain voluntarily from enforcing the measure while a legal challenge proceeded or to ask a court, in a proceeding for a preliminary injunction, to ban enforcement by official order.

Sitting around the table in the plain conference room of the Denver city attorney's office, the choices created some early tensions on the plaintiffs' side. Dubofsky felt strongly that the team should try to persuade the state to hold off enforcement voluntarily. Attorneys for the ACLU, Lambda, and Aspen were committed to the preliminary injunction route. The others, perhaps ambivalent about the options, did not take sides at that time.

Dubofsky feared that the legal standard for winning a preliminary injunction order from the court was too high for the plaintiffs to meet—the plaintiffs would have to show that they would be irreparably harmed by the amendment taking effect and that they would likely win on the merits of the case. If they lost this argument, they would suffer an early and potentially devastating setback to the overall challenge. The case would be more compelling, Dubofsky maintained, if the legal team could show some real-life personal injury in addition to the more theoretical or abstract harm to constitutional rights.

Dubofsky was also concerned that presenting a preliminary hearing on such short notice, and then a trial shortly after, would be difficult and possibly duplicative. "I thought we needed a couple of months [to prepare for the hearing] and I wanted the state to agree to put the whole thing on at once," she said.

Lambda and the ACLU, on the other hand, were concerned that the state's attorneys lacked the authority to stay the amendment's enforcement. Further, they were concerned that the state lacked the will to hold off on enforcement in the face of the measure's approval by a majority of voters. Despite the difficult legal standard that must be satisfied to win a preliminary injunction, it was, in their view, the only reasonable strategy. On behalf of Lambda and the ACLU, Goldberg also illustrated the double standard that the two groups felt was being applied in deciding which strategy to pursue.

"If this was a case where the state's voters decided to ban protections for African-Americans or establish an official religion," she argued, "we would not be afraid of lacking sufficient enough evidence to show irreparable harm. The very fact that the state's powers were being used to single out African-Americans for harm or to privilege one religion above all others would be enough. The situation here is not materially different."

And among other concerns, Caswall, Aspen's attorney, was fearful about reports that gay activists would intensify their call for a boycott of conferences or tourist travel in Colorado because of the antigay amendment's passage. A boycott could destroy Aspen's upcoming "Gay Ski Week," a profitable annual event that drew hundreds of lesbian and gay skiers from across the country. Only a quick resolution of the conflict, Caswall believed, could be acceptable for Aspen. If the other plaintiffs did not come along, Aspen, with a reputation for independence, might consider breaking from the team and pursuing a preliminary injunction on its own.

Agreeing at least to broach the voluntary restraint option with the state, the plaintiffs' attorneys proceeded into the meeting with the state's attorneys. After greetings and introductions, though, the meeting did not last long in the state's well-appointed conference room. It quickly became apparent that, absent a court order, the state could not be counted upon to withhold enforcement. Dubofsky repeatedly pressed the state to stay Amendment 2's enforcement, but the request was persistently refused. When the meeting ended, the debate for the plaintiffs' team went back to whether to seek the preliminary injunction.

The debate swung back and forth over the next week and included a number of tense conference calls that pulled in the other ACLU and Lambda attorneys, including Matt Coles, Mary Newcombe, and Bill Rubenstein. While not on site, these lawyers, too, were intensely focused on blocking, as quickly and firmly as possible, the serious risk presented by Amendment 2 for gay people nationwide. If Amendment 2 were to take effect, similar measures would surely be introduced throughout the country. At several points over the course of this round of decision making, the fragile coalition of attorneys who were committed to bringing one united challenge to Amendment 2—rather than several separate challenges that the courts might or might not consolidate—appeared to be on the verge of collapse. Most of the Colorado attorneys wanted a wait-and-see strategy and felt they knew what was best for the state; the Lambda and ACLU team wanted to move immediately for an injunction and believed they knew what would best protect the gay community.

Ultimately, Dubofsky shifted positions and a decision was reached: the team would ask the Denver district court to issue a preliminary injunction against enforcement of Amendment 2. United in the decision, the legal team set to work. But the tensions that surfaced during these early days would set the stage for debates to come, with the lesbian and gay civil rights lawyers struggling to insert their view of the best legal strategy and of what was best for lesbians and gay men throughout the country and the Colorado attorneys pressing their views of what was best for the lawsuit and those living in the state. Much of the time, the team managed to agree. But the stress of reaching agreement took its toll early on and would continue to exact a price during the next three and a half years as the case wound its way up and down the Colorado legal system and ultimately to the U.S. Supreme Court.

The Legal Theories

Still, for the time being, a decision had been made, and the team focused on the next steps in the case. It now had to decide which legal theories to pursue. A complaint filed by the plaintiffs just over a week after election day afforded plenty of choices—it included every theory that might be a basis for success. Among these theories were claims that the amendment violated the federal Constitution's guarantees of equal protection of the laws, freedom of association and expression, freedom from establishment of an official religion, the right to petition government for redress of grievances, the right to be free from enforcement of vague laws, the right to have a republican form of government, the right of access to courts, and the right to have the U.S. Constitution be considered the supreme law of the land. It also included claims based on Colorado's constitution: violations of limits on voter initiatives, unlawful restrictions on cities' home-rule authority and the power of local school districts, and overstepping of limitations on amendments to the state constitution.

To keep the preliminary injunction action streamlined and clear, since the judge would be asked to take quick action, the team picked its best theories to present in this first round of litigation—that Amendment 2 violated the rights guaranteed by the U.S. Constitution to equal protection of the laws and to freedom of association and expression.

These theories led to three main arguments. The first argument alleged that the state, by disabling gay people from obtaining governmental protection against discrimination, infringed the fundamental right of lesbians, gay men, and bisexuals to participate in the political process on an equal footing with other Colorado citizens. To restrict a fundamental right, a government must satisfy the highest legal standard—known as the "strict scrutiny" test. This test requires the government to demonstrate that the law infringing on the fundamental right is "narrowly tailored" to serve a "compelling governmental interest."

The second argument maintained that the state's singling out of gay people for differential treatment lacked a legitimate purpose and therefore also violated the Constitution's equal protection clause. By singling out gay people for discriminatory treatment, the plaintiffs argued, Amendment 2 violated that clause's most basic guarantee— that laws may not arbitrarily discriminate against a group of people. This argument requires a court to scrutinize the discriminatory law under a less stringent legal standard known as "rational basis review." Under this standard, a court must decide whether a law's singling out of a group can be rationally explained by a legitimate government interest. This is the easiest test for a government to meet; the Supreme Court has explained that any reasonably *conceivable* government interest will do—the legislators need not actually have had that interest in mind when enacting the law.[1]

Third, the plaintiffs argued that Amendment 2 violated the First Amendment's guarantee of free expression and association. Any person who expressed his or her identity as gay or lesbian would be exposed to heightened risk of discrimination and retaliation for efforts to seek protection against antigay discrimination.

Succeeding with any of these arguments would mean that the amendment would be stopped.

---

1. *Heller v. Doe,* 113 S.Ct. 2367, 2643 (1993).

Getting Ready for Court

In addition to selecting the primary legal theories, the plaintiffs' legal team had immediately to resolve other strategy questions regarding presentation of the case. A preliminary injunction proceeding is somewhat unusual. It does not require a court to make a final determination on the merits of the issues in a case. Instead, the court takes a look at the evidence and decides, based on that evidence and any legal arguments presented, whether the party asking for the injunction would suffer irreparable harm if the injunction is not granted, whether the party is likely to succeed on the merits of its legal arguments, and whether granting the preliminary injunction is in the public's best interests. The plaintiffs prepared their most succinct, compelling evidence and wrote legal briefs that would put the evidence and arguments in context.

A date was set. On January 11, 1993, both sides were to report to the courtroom of Denver district court judge Jeffrey Bayless.

Bayless, 47, had been a judge on the Colorado District Court for the Second Judicial Circuit for six years, having been appointed in January 1987 by then-governor Richard Lamm, a Democrat. Bayless grew up in Galesburg, Illinois, the site of Illinois's first antislavery society and of the Lincoln–Douglas debates. During the Vietnam war years, he served in the Army Reserve while earning a bachelor of arts degree from a small Iowa liberal arts college affiliated with the United Methodist Church and a law degree from the University of Denver. Following law school, Bayless clerked for U.S. District Court judge Sherman Finesilver (a Nixon appointee) in Denver. He then worked for six years as a Deputy District Attorney in Denver's District Attorney's Office, and for four years in private practice in two different law firms, before returning to become Chief Deputy of the Denver District Attorney's office. In light of his experience as a prosecutor, Bayless was known, not surprisingly, as a political conservative.

During the weeks leading up to the hearing, the team of plaintiffs' attorneys actively involved in the case grew larger. Dubofsky added two experienced Colorado trial lawyers to handle the presentation of evidence to the court. Jeanne Winer, a Boulder resident, was first considered as a potential plaintiff. But Dubofsky, who was not a trial attorney, heard from a Boulder district court judge that Winer was "the best lawyer who ever appeared in [his] courtroom."

"I had in mind specific kinds of people to meet specific needs," said Dubofsky. "It was nice that Jeanne was a lesbian," she said, but made clear that she brought Winer onto the team for Winer's legal skills and experience. Winer was a longtime public defender who had extensive trial experience, chiefly in representing indigent criminal defendants. Her straightforward style and her good humor would prove to be a great asset. Apart from Lambda and ACLU Lesbian and Gay Rights Project attorneys, Winer was also the only other openly gay person on the plaintiffs' legal team. Dubofsky's other choice for a trial attorney, Gregory Eurich, also brought important assets to the team in addition to his well-honed trial skills. Eurich was a litigation partner at Holland & Hart, one of Denver's leading law firms, and he volunteered to help. His presence lent not only the cachet and credibility of a major firm to the plaintiffs' efforts, but also gave the plaintiffs' team access to the firm's extensive administrative staff and resources to help coordinate the voluminous exhibits and attend to the multitude of tasks required to put on a trial.

And the Proceedings Begin

On a bright and frosty Monday morning, January 11, 1993, both legal teams reported to Judge Bayless's courtroom, ready to proceed. The dark paneled courtroom was packed with lawyers, witnesses, and courtroom personnel, and with activists from all places on the political spectrum. Many lesbians, gay men, and other opponents of Amendment 2 came to show their support for the challenge. And Amendment 2's proponents were likewise present to support the defense, including representatives of the National Legal Foundation, the organization that had helped draft the antigay amendment. Television cameras and a bevy of reporters from news organizations also filled the room. The implications of this case were no longer in doubt. Should Amendment 2 take effect, it would be only a matter of time before Amendment 2 clones would spread across the country.

After addressing several preliminary matters, plaintiffs' attorney Gregory Eurich stood at the podium to make the plaintiffs' opening argument. "May it please the court," he began, "This Friday, absent an order of this court, an amendment of the Colorado Constitution will take effect which selects out a group of our fellow citizens for special treatment. And that special treatment is that, absent a statewide referendum repealing this amendment, gays, lesbians, and bisexuals cannot be afforded the same nondiscriminatory treatment as the rest of us are entitled to."

Eurich sketched out the framework of the plaintiffs' challenge and described in brief how each witness's testimony would help to meet the rigorous legal standard for the requested preliminary injunction. He focused, too, on three reasons the state had offered, in its written briefs filed with the court, to justify the antigay amendment: (1) that Amendment 2 would promote freedom of religion and association; (2) that it would limit "special protections" only to characteristics for which there was statewide consensus; and (3) that it would avoid "dilution" of existing civil rights protections. Eurich offered brief arguments for why the court should reject each.

Jed Caswall then offered a short additional statement on Aspen's behalf, making the point that Amendment 2 called into question Aspen's long-standing prohibition against sexual orientation discrimination.

"What it comes down to, Your Honor," Caswall said, "is that we would like to know whether or not on Friday our 15-year-old antidiscrimination ordinance disappears from the books."

John Dailey, Colorado's deputy attorney general, made the opening argument for the state. He criticized the plaintiffs' arguments, saying that the plaintiffs were asking the court "to do a very extraordinary thing"—to go "against the will of the majority wishes in this state." He urged the court to reject the plaintiffs' arguments in the case, which he described as coming down to a "legal tussle."

For four days, attorneys for the plaintiffs and the state called numerous witnesses to testify. Among the plaintiffs' witnesses were experts in psychology and in the workings of the religious right. Both were called to provide the court with the context for evaluating the amendment's true purposes and its real life consequences.

The plaintiffs called John Gonsiorek, a clinical psychologist who specialized in sexual orientation and sexual identity issues, to define sexual orientation. He described it as "the erotic and/or emotional preference for the same or opposite gender or both." He testified that most psychologists believe sexual orientation is set early in life, and that efforts to change an individual from homosexual to heterosexual are generally unsuccessful and questionable from an ethical standpoint. He also testified that being in a minority causes lesbians and gay men significant stress, and that Amendment 2 posed serious psychological dangers to Colorado's gay population. All of his testimony was aimed to inform the court about sexual orientation generally and the impact of Amendment 2 in particular.

Jean Hardisty, director of Political Research Associates, a group with expertise in monitoring right-wing and religious right activities, focused her testimony on describing the religious right. She identified the links between Colorado for Family Values and the national network of religious right organizations that have, as part of their agenda, the condemnation of homosexuality. Hardisty noted that CFV's use of the "no special rights" slogan further illustrates the connections between Amendment 2 in Colorado and a national campaign to cut back the rights of lesbians and gay men. She also testified that the material about homosexuality supplied by CFV to the public distorts information about gay people. Her testimony aimed to show the court that Amendment 2 was a deliberate attempt to enshrine antigay bias into law.

The material about homosexuality that CFV has used, she said, "is not taken seriously by anyone outside the religious and political right, yet it is promoted as a kind of pseudoscientific evidence to prove that homosexuals really should not be permitted to have any rights in society."

Several of the individual plaintiffs took the stand, too, to put a human face on the effect of Amendment 2. In selecting plaintiffs, Colorado Legal Initiatives Project attorneys had looked for individuals who could best illustrate both the devastating impact of antigay discrimination generally and the ways that Amendment 2's specific ban would interfere with gay people's ability to advocate for their own equality. One plaintiff, Angela Romero, testified about her fears of rejection by her family when she realized that she was a lesbian. She told the court about her lifelong dream of serving as a school resource officer for the Denver police where she could be a role model for young Latino children and other children living in the inner city of Denver. As she recounted the story of her removal from that position when her supervisor discovered that she was a lesbian, Romero broke into tears, giving everyone in court that day a glimpse into the pain caused by antigay discrimination. Romero also described her advocacy within the Denver police department that ultimately resulted in a policy forbidding officers from discriminating based on sexual orientation and from making derogatory remarks over the police radio about lesbians and gay men. Under Amendment 2, she said, all of her efforts would be wiped out and her safety would be endangered.

Richard Evans, the "Evans" in *Evans v. Romer,* also testified. He described his experience of coming out as a gay man and his work as the liaison between Denver's mayor and the lesbian and gay community. Evans described the efforts he had made to protect himself from danger after the passage of Amendment 2, including asking his apartment manager to remove his name from the building directory.

John Miller, a professor at the University of Colorado in Colorado Springs, and father of three children, testified about his role as a resource person for gay students on campus. He described, too, his unsuccessful efforts to have the University of Colorado include sexual orientation in its antidiscrimination policy. If Amendment 2 was upheld, Miller testified, he would cease his advocacy because the university would be unable to authorize the protections he sought. Miller also explained that, under Amendment 2, he would not continue to advocate for Colorado Springs to enact protections against sexual orientation discrimination "because it would be a waste of our time and energy."

Plaintiff Paul Brown told the court about his experience of learning, as a young child, that he was gay, and feeling "very isolated" because of that. He described his experiences of being harassed on the job for being gay, including having one of his coworkers paint "Paul is a fag" in very large letters across the wall facing the employees' parking lot of the office building where he worked. He told of hostile anti-gay calls received by his friends after Amendment 2 passed, and his own fears about his personal safety and that of his pets and his property. When asked whether Amendment 2 would affect his ability to work for changes in the political system, Brown said it would because it was clear to him that the amendment proscribed government from providing protections to gay people.

Although the other individual plaintiffs did not take the stand, each had his or her own compelling story to tell. Linda Fowler, for example, was a Denver resident and worked in the construction industry. She would immediately lose protections under Denver's antidiscrimination ordinance were the amendment to take effect. Likewise, Priscilla Inkpen, a Boulder resident and an ordained minister, would immediately lose protections under Boulder's antidiscrimination ordinance. Brett Tanberg, although not a gay man, had joined the lawsuit because he had AIDS and had been subjected to discrimination by people who believed he was gay. Martina Navratilova, Aspen resident and world-class tennis champion, joined the suit as a plaintiff, motivated in part by her experience growing up in Czechoslovakia and witnessing the machinery of government used to oppress disfavored groups of people in society. In addition, one plaintiff joined the suit under the pseudonym "Jane Doe." An employee of Jefferson County, Doe feared loss of safety and employment under an Amendment 2 regime.[2]

The plaintiffs rested their case on Wednesday afternoon, day three of the hearing. Next, the state attempted to show why the court should not block Amendment 2 from taking effect. To make their case, the defendants called upon several witnesses, each of whom urged that Amendment 2 was not a weapon of hatred but rather was a reasonable response to perceived threats to civil rights laws in the state—threats posed by the small but growing number of measures prohibiting discrimination based upon sexual orientation. Among the state's witnesses, and the first to take the stand for the state, was Joseph Nicolosi. A psychologist who specialized in the "treatment" of male homosexuality, Nicolosi testified that he considered homosexuality to be a developmental disorder that can be corrected through "reparative therapy." He also testified that gay people represent a much smaller segment of the population than commonly thought.

John Franklin, a former Colorado civil rights commissioner, testified that Colorado for Family Values was not an extremist group targeting gay people but was instead a group legitimately concerned about the risks of including sexual orientation protection in civil rights laws. Blind since birth, Franklin told the court that, because of the difficulty of identifying sexual orientation, protections against sexual orientation discrimination were significantly different from civil rights protections for disabilities and other traits that could more easily be identified.

Paul Talmey, a well-respected Colorado pollster, also testified on the state's behalf. His firm's polling, he said, showed that "the vast majority of those who voted for Amendment 2 are not particularly prejudiced against gay people," despite much popular rhetoric labeling Colorado the "hate state." Instead, he explained, voters supported Amendment 2 because they believed it necessary to "stop special rights."

---

2. Ultimately, Tanberg, Navratilova, and Doe each were dismissed as plaintiffs—Tanberg died, Navratilova had scheduling concerns should the state try to depose her during the discovery process, and Doe feared revelation of her identity.

Closing Arguments

After Talmey's testimony, the state rested its case. Plaintiffs' attorney Dubofsky then gave the plaintiffs' closing argument late Thursday afternoon. Before she started, though, Dubofsky requested that the court issue a temporary restraining order to prevent Amendment 2 from taking effect that night. Tensions had been mounting throughout the day as it became clear that if the court took no action by midnight Thursday, Governor Romer would be duty-bound to declare Amendment 2 in force and the plaintiffs' effort to bar the amendment from ever taking effect would be dashed. Bayless was clearly frustrated, asking why the plaintiffs had not moved more quickly to avoid the need for a restraining order. Dubofsky explained that the plaintiffs had tried unsuccessfully in early negotiations to have the state voluntarily stay enforcement of the amendment.

She then reviewed the plaintiffs' arguments for the court. Thirty years ago, she said, voters had sought to eliminate civil rights advances of racial minorities by amending California's constitution to bar protections against housing discrimination. Here, Dubofsky urged, the situation was "remarkably similar." Through Amendment 2, Colorado for Family Values was attempting to roll back the limited protections won by the individual plaintiffs and others and "embody the right to discriminate immune from redress at any level." She summarized some of the witnesses' testimony, described Amendment 2's impact, and walked the court through the plaintiffs' two equal protection arguments—that Amendment 2 violated a fundamental right of equal political participation and that its purpose in singling out gay people was to harm them, which was not a rational or legitimate explanation for the discrimination. Dubofsky also explained the plaintiffs' argument, based on the First Amendment to the U.S. Constitution, that Amendment 2 would have a chilling effect on the plaintiffs' freedoms of association and expression. As an example, she pointed to plaintiff Romero's testimony about losing her job as a school resource police officer after she was identified by her coworkers as a lesbian.

"I think that shows there is a substantial risk of engaging in expressive conduct," said Dubofsky.

Dubofsky also offered several specific examples of what would happen immediately if the amendment took effect: (1) the plaintiffs and other lesbians and gay men would lose the ability to lobby the government to outlaw antigay discrimination; (2) gay people would lose the protection of existing antidiscrimination measures with a potentially devastating impact, as Romero's and Brown's experiences illustrated; (3) lesbians and gay men would be at increased risk of public and private discrimination if they self-identified as lesbian or gay; (4) cities would lose the power to remedy discriminatory practices; and (5) programs to protect against teen suicide and to educate people about HIV would be ended.

In addition, Dubofsky said, a preliminary injunction was necessary to preserve the status quo, to provide the plaintiffs with a speedy and adequate remedy, and to serve the public interest. Hundreds of thousands of people in the state would assume second-class citizenship status if the amendment became effective, she argued. Dubofsky urged the court to grant the preliminary injunction.

Dailey, as counsel for the state, stood up next. "What is not at issue," he said, is Colorado's status as a hate state, the views of the religious right, or the desirability of particular social, economic, or political policy. The plaintiffs' entire analysis is flawed, he said, because the amendment would prohibit only "special rights." It would not affect private employers' antidiscrimination policies nor was it "designed to deprive homosexuals and bisexuals of basic civil rights." Nothing in the amendment encourages the violation of First Amendment rights, said Dailey. Amendment 2 simply did not address speech, nor did it provide a license to commit attacks against gay people. With respect to the Equal Protection Clause, he argued, the plaintiffs misunderstood their rights. Earlier cases protecting the right to participate in the political process all involved race discrimination. It was race discrimination, not a basic denial of political rights, that had triggered the heightened judicial scrutiny in those cases.

Further, Dailey continued, there is a "moral value component" that justifies Amendment 2. There is a difference between irrational prejudice and moral judgment, he said, and it is proper for a law to embody a "cultural moral value." The moral component in Amendment 2, he said, involved the right to be left alone *and* the right to raise children according to the parents' wishes. The moral judgment of society, Dailey said, can be taken into consideration "in determining whether or not to grant people rights that were not otherwise existing under state law" to protect existing civil rights laws from "dilution."

The First Ruling

As the closing arguments concluded at 5:25 P.M. on Thursday, January 14, Judge Bayless did not look happy. "In six hours and 35 minutes, a provision adopted by a majority of voters . . . will become effective. . . . I am supposed to come to some conclusion in six hours and 35 minutes. The court is not comfortable being placed in that situation. . . ." He said that he would grant the plaintiffs' motion to temporarily restrain Governor Romer from executing and implementing Amendment 2 for roughly 24 hours—until 5 P.M. the next day. That small victory brought cheers from opponents of Amendment 2 who were seated behind the attorneys in the public gallery. Just as quickly, the judge's face turned red, and he hammered his gavel several times. "Oh, stop it," he demanded, in response to the cheers. "We are not going to have any of that in here." He told all parties to return the next afternoon and retired from the courtroom.

Although rebuked for their joyous outburst, anti–Amendment 2 onlookers filed out of the room with grins on their faces while the amendment's supporters consoled themselves with the knowledge that the order was only temporary and would expire the next day without further action by Bayless.

Friday was a tense day for both sides. At just before 4 P.M., everyone filed back into court, talking nervously in hushed voices and taking up familiar seats as they prepared to be launched by the court's ruling into the litigation's next phase. Court was called to order. The packed room stood as Bayless entered and then settled back into their seats as he sat down behind the bench to deliver his ruling.

Bayless reviewed the arguments of each side, noting that the plaintiffs bore the burden of satisfying the heavy legal requirements for a preliminary injunction. He emphasized that he was not ruling on the constitutionality of Amendment 2 at this time, but was instead ruling only on whether the plaintiffs had a reasonable probability of success. As Bayless spoke, deliberately and at length, explaining each step of his own deliberation, the tension in the courtroom grew more palpable. He then reached the crux of his opinion: "There is a fundamental right . . . not to have the state endorse and give effect to private biases." Bayless said the amendment targeted an identifiable class and appeared to violate a fundamental right. In future proceedings, said Bayless, the state would have to meet the high "strict scrutiny" legal standard to save

Amendment 2. With that, Bayless announced that the plaintiffs' motions for a preliminary injunction were granted and that the governor and the attorney general were enjoined from enforcing Amendment 2 until further order of the court.

Silently but visibly fighting both tears and applause, both sides filed out of the courtroom. This first crucial step toward victory for the plaintiffs was realized. Out in the hallway, with television lights blazing and camera flashes glaring, Amendment 2's opponents enjoyed the first moments of victory, and the state and Amendment 2's supporters vowed to appeal the injunction order. News of Amendment 2's temporary demise flashed around the country. And attorneys for both sides went quickly back to work, preparing for the state's appeal of Bayless's ruling to the Colorado Supreme Court.

After receiving extensive briefs from both sides, the Colorado Supreme Court heard argument in July 1993 on the state's appeal of Bayless's preliminary injunction and upheld his ruling shortly thereafter. Taking a different analytic tack from Bayless and following an approach suggested by the plaintiffs as well as a friend-of-the-court brief from the Colorado Bar Association, six of the seven justices of the Colorado Supreme Court held that the amendment appeared to violate the fundamental right of lesbians, gay men, and bisexuals to participate in the political process on an equal footing with other Coloradans. Relying on a series of U.S. Supreme Court cases going back to the high court's "one man one vote" ruling, the Colorado Supreme Court determined that, by barring gay Coloradans from seeking antidiscrimination protection from their government (except through a new constitutional amendment), Amendment 2 impermissibly interfered with the right of gay citizens to equal access to government. Because Amendment 2 violated a "fundamental" constitutional right, it would have to be subjected to strict scrutiny, the most searching form of judicial review. Again, under this standard, Amendment 2 could survive only if the state proved it had a "compelling" governmental interest for treating gay citizens this way and that Amendment 2's ban was "narrowly tailored" to achieve that interest.

Only one justice on the court sided with the state. Justice William Erickson dissented, arguing that the amendment did not infringe any fundamental right and that numerous rational and legitimate government interests justified its limitation on the rights of gay people to obtain protection against discrimination.

The state then appealed the Colorado high court's ruling to the U.S. Supreme Court by filing a special brief, known as a petition for a writ of certiorari. The U.S. Supreme Court has absolute discretion to grant or deny review in most cases; grants of review are rare and will typically be given, if at all, only after a case has been finally resolved on the merits and not on a preliminary motion. In mid-October, the plaintiffs filed their opposition brief with the Court, arguing that the case was still in the *preliminary* injunction phase and therefore premature for review. As expected, the U.S. Supreme Court denied the state's petition on November 1, 1993.

While the state's appeal of the injunction was pending, however, the case on the merits continued to move forward in the Colorado court system. With Bayless's preliminary injunction ruling upheld by the Colorado Supreme Court, the plaintiffs' attorneys again had two options: they could take the case to trial and bring in witnesses and exhibits to prove facts in support of their legal theories, or they could argue that the amendment, on its face, deprived gay people of their constitutional rights and should be struck down as a matter of law. This second option, known as moving for "summary judgment," requires a court to decide whether there are any material facts in dispute and, if not, whether the challenged action should be invalidated based purely on the moving party's legal arguments.

For the plaintiffs' legal team, the decision about whether to go to trial or move for summary judgment aggravated familiar tensions that had emerged during the preliminary injunction strategy debate. The ACLU and Lambda attorneys urged that there was no need for a trial to "prove" that sexual orientation was genetically rooted, that gay people were politically powerless, or any other fact. The amendment's ban on equal access to government for gay people was, in their view, unconstitutional as a matter of law. They also believed a trial would distract the court from the core question of whether the Constitution permitted voters to bar one group of citizens from obtaining antidiscrimination protections from government.

Dubofsky and the other Colorado attorneys, on the other hand, believed a trial was necessary to demonstrate all of these facts, just in case Bayless or a judge hearing the appeal of the case considered them important to the legal claims. Dubofsky told the group that Bayless "is known for liking to hear testimony" and that this case would be more persuasive with the people most affected by Amendment 2 "being there, in person" before the judge. In addition, the Colorado attorneys saw a trial as an important educational opportunity for the public at large. After a prolonged debate, Dubofsky ultimately stuck by her own instincts and announced the team would go to trial. And, with another difficult decision reached, the team began to prepare for trial.

The Suspect Classification Argument

Then a third major debate surfaced for the legal team. Relying upon the Equal Protection Clause of the U.S. Constitution, the team intended to continue making the two arguments it had advanced at the preliminary injunction stage: that Amendment 2 violated a "fundamental right" and that it lacked a legitimate purpose to justify its discrimination. Within equal protection theory, the plaintiffs also had a third argument available: that Amendment 2, by treating people differently according to sexual orientation, created a "suspect classification."

When laws make suspect classifications, they appear to courts to treat one group of people differently than other people based on prejudice and outmoded stereotypes. A court, thus, is said to be "suspicious" of the motivation behind the law that classifies the group for discriminatory treatment and will apply extra-close review of the government's justifications for the discrimination if that law is challenged. Put another way, a court will apply the same "strict scrutiny" standard to assess the need for a law that makes a suspect classification as it applies when a law violates a "fundamental" right: the government must show that the law is narrowly tailored to serve a "compelling" interest. This legal test stems from a famous footnote in a 1938 Supreme Court ruling, *United States v. Carolene Products,* which said that "prejudice against discrete and insular minorities may be a special condition which tends seriously to curtail the operation of those political processes ordinarily to be relied upon to protect minorities, and . . . may call for a correspondingly more searching judicial inquiry."[3] In this simple statement, the Court recognized that prejudice in society is sometimes reflected in the law, and that laws that single out certain groups for negative treatment should be carefully scrutinized for such prejudice or bias.

Through several cases in recent decades, the U.S. Supreme Court

---

3. *United States v. Carolene Products Co.,* 304 U.S. 144 (1938).

has held that laws singling out people based on race, ethnicity, or national origin are typically motivated by prejudice and must be treated as making suspect classifications. In a 1985 case, the Court explained that race, ethnicity, and national origin are

> so seldom relevant to the achievement of any legitimate state inter-est that laws grounded in such considerations are deemed to reflect prejudice and antipathy—a view that those in the burdened class are not as worthy or deserving as others. For these reasons and because such discrimination is unlikely to be soon rectified by legislative means, these laws are subjected to *strict scrutiny* and will be sustained only if they are suitably tailored to serve a *compelling state interest*.[4]

The Court has also held that classifications by other characteristics—gender and illegitimacy—are "quasi-suspect." Under this standard, a government must demonstrate an *important* governmental interest sub-stantially related to the law's classification for the law to be upheld.

Although the Supreme Court has never defined a single test for determining whether a classification is suspect or quasi-suspect, it has identified certain factors for courts to consider in making that determi-nation. These include whether a group has had a history of "purpose-ful unequal treatment" based on the characteristic in question,[5] whether the classification is either based on circumstances beyond the individual's control[6] or on a characteristic that is "obvious, immutable, or distinguishing,"[7] and how much political power the group has to ensure its rights are protected and to defend against attacks in the mainstream political process.[8] For example, in 1986, in *Lyng v. Castillo*,[9] the Supreme Court ruled that a law that disadvantaged close blood rel-atives was not "suspect" or even "quasi-suspect" because, "as a histor-ical matter, [close relatives] have not been subjected to discrimination; they do not exhibit obvious, immutable, or distinguishing characteris-

---

4. *City of Cleburne v. Cleburne Living Center,* 473 U.S. 432, 440 (1985) (emphasis added).

5. *Massachusetts v. Murgia,* 427 U.S. 307, 313 (1976).

6. *Plyler v. Doe,* 457 U.S. 202, 216 n.14 (1982).

7. *Bowen v. Gilliard,* 483 U.S. 587, 602 (1987), (quoting *Lyng v. Castillo,* 477 U.S. 635, 638 [1986]).

8. *Frontiero v. Richardson,* 411 U.S. 677, 686 (1973).

9. *Lyng v. Castillo,* 477 U.S. 635 (1986).

tics that define them as a discrete group; and they are not a minority or politically powerless."

Lesbians and gay men challenging discrimination have long argued that the trait of sexual orientation should be considered a suspect classification both because it is irrelevant to individuals' abilities and because it satisfies the other factors identified by the high court. Winning suspect classification review for laws classifying people by sexual orientation would mean that any law singling out gay people for discrimination or harm—from the federal government's ban on military service by openly gay people to state laws barring gay couples from marrying—would come under the most rigorous judicial scrutiny.

While even the courts most hostile to gay claimants have conceded that gay people have been historically subjected to discrimination, many of those same courts have also ruled that sexual orientation classifications fail to satisfy the other elements identified by the high court. Often, a stumbling block for courts has been the nature of sexual orientation. Rather than see it as a characteristic that is "obvious, immutable or distinguishing" and irrelevant to the "ability to perform or contribute," many have seen sexual orientation as a choice to behave in a way that is disapproved by society. Some of these courts have also rejected strict scrutiny of sexual orientation discrimination after concluding that gay people have sufficient political power to challenge discriminatory laws so that such laws do not need additional close review by courts.

Among members of the plaintiffs' legal team, trial strategies aimed at "proving" the suspect classification factors—in particular regarding immutability and political power—raised difficult questions. With respect to the "immutability" factor, the latest genetic research provided strong support for the argument that sexual orientation had biological origins. Some team members, as well as gay leaders, maintained that this evidence would help end discrimination by people who believed homosexuality was a "life-style choice." Other gay activists were concerned that such research would prompt efforts to find a "cure" for homosexuality. Still others believed the gay civil rights movement should defend a person's right to have a same-sex partner, even if it was a choice for that person. And some maintained that the research was far too preliminary and limited to provide any conclusive indication at all.

Providing proof of the "political powerlessness" element also posed complex and controversial questions. By trial time in October 1993, the gay movement was gaining national recognition as a political force. Its growing power had stirred active opposition, its limited advances had been dealt severe setbacks in Congress, and its efforts to achieve equal treatment for gay people were under constant challenge. But the movement was, beyond question, at its most powerful point in history. It was ironic, at the least, that a legal team representing gay people would attempt to show that the gay movement was politically powerless.

The plaintiffs' legal team debated vigorously whether the Supreme Court's suspect classification analysis even demanded such scientific or political proof. After all, laws singling out people based on national origin are considered suspect, even though national origin is neither genetically based nor a fair proxy for political power. The Lambda and ACLU advocates argued that the core question was whether sexual orientation affected individuals' abilities and maintained that the Supreme Court's cases did not require the plaintiffs to put on evidence on that point. Other attorneys on the team believed that proving these points at trial would enable them to make the strongest possible case. Again, after much debate and no consensus, Dubofsky made the call. The plaintiffs' team would try to prove these suspect classification factors.

On this issue, as well as a couple of other key strategy questions, including whether to go to trial, the ACLU and Lambda lawyers sensed that Dubofsky did not fully consider their perspectives or value their collective experience in gay civil rights litigation. On disputed issues, there was a sense, too, that Dubofsky did not take fully into account the broader implications of the Amendment 2 challenge for lesbians and gay men nationally. CLIP board members, who had selected Dubofsky as their counsel, disagreed. And on the question of how a heterosexual attorney from Colorado came to make some of the most important decisions in a case that had enormous consequences for the entire gay civil rights movement nationally, they insisted that Dubofsky's being a heterosexual attorney with no previous ties to the gay civil rights movement did not affect her decision-making ability on crucial strategies. "I disagree that Jean didn't understand the issues that gay people wrestle with," said CLIP board member Pat Steadman. "You don't have to be gay to understand. We were simply turning the case over to the most competent and capable attorney we could find, and that was Jean."

On to Trial

The key decisions—to go to trial and to attempt to prove the facts supporting the suspect classification argument—were now made. Setting aside their disagreements once again, the entire team geared up for the enormous task of preparing for trial. Witnesses had to be identified, exhibits had to be selected, and briefs had to be written.

Identification of expert witnesses to prove each of the plaintiffs' contentions was a challenging task. Although scholars, scientists, and psychologists have increasingly focused, in recent years, on a wide range of issues related to lesbians and gay men, few have amassed the authority that comes with lengthy study. However, in each of several areas, at least one or two individuals had spent a significant portion of his or her career examining lesbian and gay issues from a particular professional vantage point. Consulting with the gay attorneys on the team, Dubofsky and Roderick Hills, a scholarly young lawyer who was working as an associate in Dubofsky's law practice before beginning his career in law teaching, amassed a list of potential experts and began to contact them. Few of the witnesses had experience testifying at a trial, since the topics of their testimony were not usual fare in lawsuits. Still, generally speaking, those contacted were eager to help in whatever way they could, including by testifying at trial or providing their expertise to assist the legal team in preparing its arguments.

The state faced challenges finding its own experts, too. The pool of credentialed scholars and researchers who were likely to testify that gay people are politically powerful, historically well-treated, or psychologically unhealthy was even smaller. Consequently, the state relied on academics and activists who had only recently turned their attention to gay issues.

Following Colorado's rules of civil procedure, each side identified its experts and provided a general description of its witnesses' anticipated testimony to the other.

The state's experts were to help prove that Amendment 2's discrimination was motivated by compelling government interests and therefore permissible. In the course of pretrial motions and briefing filed with the court, the state had expanded upon the interests it advanced at the preliminary injunction stage, arguing that Amendment 2 was necessary to accomplish six government aims:

1. to deter factionalism and promote statewide uniformity by eliminating "city-by-city and county-by-county battles over the political issue of homosexuality and bisexuality," or, as the state also put it, to ensure that "the deeply divisive issue of homosexuality does not serve to fragment Colorado's body politic";

2. to preserve the integrity of the state's political functions by allowing a voter-approved initiative to take effect. The state rested this "preservation of governance powers" argument, in part, on the Tenth Amendment to the U.S. Constitution, which provides that "the powers not delegated to the United States by the Constitution, nor prohibited by it to the States, are reserved to the States respectively, or to the people." In essence, the state contended, once the people had decided to change their constitution by voting for the amendment, that should "end the discussion";

3. to preserve the ability of the state to remedy discrimination against suspect classes by not requiring the state to expend resources prohibiting discrimination based on traits not considered suspect for purposes of judicial scrutiny;

4. to prevent the government from interfering with personal, familial, and religious privacy (presumably, of those who preferred not to associate with gay people). To illustrate why Amendment 2 was necessary to protect such rights, the state submitted to the trial court an affidavit from a Wisconsin resident found guilty of violating a prohibition against sexual orientation discrimination when she refused to sublet a room in the house she rented because the prospective tenant was a lesbian. The state argued that "preventing this sort of intrusion into personal matters of the utmost privacy is a compelling interest." In later stages of the litigation, this justification also came to refer to the state's interest in having "the people themselves establish public social and moral norms," including the disapproval of homosexuality;

5. to prevent the government from subsidizing the political objectives of a special interest group. In its brief, the state wrote: "The public is deeply divided over the issue of homosexuality; by adopting Amendment 2, the people have sought to ensure that

government will not attempt to coerce, either explicitly or implicitly, a belief about the morality of homosexuality"; and

6. to promote the physical and psychological well-being of children. In its trial brief, the state argued that it had a compelling interest in "supporting the traditional family because without it, our children are condemned to a higher incidence of social maladies such as substance abuse, poverty, violence, criminality, greater burdens upon government, and perpetuation of the underclass."

Although the state (and other parties filing friend-of-the-court briefs in support of Amendment 2) varied the description of these interests as the case proceeded after trial to the Colorado Supreme Court and then the U.S. Supreme Court, all were advanced, in one form or another, as justifications for Amendment 2's discrimination.

To get ready for trial, each side had the opportunity to take the deposition of each of the other's experts. A deposition is a question-and-answer session, in which the witness has to answer a lengthy series of questions by the other party's attorney about his or her intended testimony, background, and experience. The deposing lawyer's goal is to obtain enough information to prepare the questions for cross-examination at trial. Although no judge is present and the session typically takes place in a law office conference room, the witness takes an oath to tell the truth and can be charged with perjury for lying. The lawyer representing the expert may object to inappropriate questions and is permitted to question the witness as well, usually after the opposing counsel has concluded his or her questioning.

The state's attorneys traveled around the country to complete a tightly packed schedule of expert witness depositions in Chicago, New York, and California, as well as Colorado, while the plaintiffs' team worked with cooperating attorneys in each location who represented the plaintiffs' interests at the depositions. For example, Kathryn Emmett was the personal lawyer of Burke Marshall, an expert for the plaintiffs, and represented Marshall at his deposition. In addition, members of both teams handled in-state depositions of local witnesses.

As the depositions were taking place, both sides were also busily gathering evidence, working with their witnesses, preparing numerous motions on various issues that would arise, and drafting briefs to guide Judge Bayless through the voluminous material that would be introduced in support of various legal arguments at trial. And on October 12, 1993, the two teams of lawyers, loaded down with trial notebooks and examination plans, reported to Judge Bayless to begin the trial of Amendment 2.

Chapter 3

The Science of Sexuality

In one of its most controversial strategic decisions, the plaintiffs' legal team decided to try to show that sexual orientation is immutable, and, once again, the team was split.

In addition to the legal debate about whether it was necessary to prove that sexual orientation was immutable in order to establish sexual orientation as a suspect classification, there were nonlegal factors influencing the decision for the legal team. While Dubofsky and the Colorado attorneys could focus squarely on trying this case, the attorneys for the gay legal groups had to weigh the impact that arguments made in this case might have on future litigation on gay civil rights issues. Pinning civil rights protection on the immutability of a characteristic seemed risky to most of the gay attorneys. If scientists someday concluded that sexual orientation was not strictly immutable, gains won through such an argument would be vulnerable. But there was a personal discomfort in the argument for many of the gay attorneys as well. The gay people on the legal team had each experienced firsthand how complex being gay is and how the experience of being gay can vary from person to person.

With classic decorum, very little about these debates spilled into public view at that time. During the trial, Peter Cicchino, a gay attorney who represented the ACLU's Lesbian and Gay Rights Project on the team, made one of the few comments that revealed the disagreement publicly. He told a newspaper only that he considered it unfortunate that gay civil rights supporters had to argue that gay people have an "immutable" trait in common because taking that strategy seemed to focus the court's scrutiny on gay people instead of the anti-gay initiative.

"It's gay people who are on trial here," said Cicchino, who also noted that he resented the argument because "I've always thought

about the movement as being about the freedom to choose."[1]
Cicchino's comments highlighted the role of the gay civil rights movement as part of a larger social movement toward sexual liberation,
which also included the liberation of women from gender stereotypes
and the pursuit of reproductive freedom. But for most gay people, the
freedom to choose meant primarily the ability to decide whether to
express one's feelings for people of the same sex openly. Many people in
the gay civil rights movement had been carefully choosing their language to avoid giving the impression that *having* those feelings was a
choice. The term *sexual preference*, with all its connotations that homosexuality is a "choice," was consistently dismissed as inaccurate. The
generally accepted term was *sexual orientation*.

The Troubling Question

Regardless of its legal and social consequences, the question about the
origins of sexual orientation was one that many people were searching
to answer through scientific research. In the year leading up to the trial,
four important new studies had been published. In fact, just three
months before the Amendment 2 trial began, a scientist at the National
Institutes of Health, a biomedical research agency of the U.S. Department of Health and Human Services, published a study showing that
genes are probably one factor determining whether a person is homosexual, heterosexual, or bisexual. That study, and others before it, had
triggered unprecedented media interest in homosexuality in general
and its "cause" in particular. On National Public Radio's *All Things
Considered*, commentators discussed how finding the cause of homosexuality might lead to the development of a test that parents could use
to determine the sexual orientation of their child before birth. ABC
Nightline host Ted Koppel took this inquiry a step further, pondering
the concept that if a "cause" for homosexuality could be found, one
might also find a "cure."

It was that type of discussion, of course, that made many gay people uncomfortable, and not just because it was simplifying something
that many had experienced as complicated. For some, there was the
fear that the scientific discoveries that would help society understand
gay people better would also enable it to "cure" gay and bisexual peo-

---

1. Lisa M. Keen, "Gay People Are Put 'On Trial' in Colorado Case," *Washington
Blade,* October 15, 1993, 27.

ple right out of existence, as Koppel had pointed out. For others, it was simply the wrong question.

"I don't think it's an argument worthy of our energy," said one national gay leader in 1986, when one of the first studies came out reporting that a biological marker had been found that might, through measuring hormone levels in the blood, distinguish gay men from heterosexual men. "The problem is not what *we* are. It's what *they* are. . . . If people stopped asking why we're homosexual and would ask why they're homophobic—that would be a step forward."[2]

For many gay people, attempting to prove the biological or genetic origins of a homosexual sexual orientation also reeked of the implication that gay people had some physical defect as compared to the heterosexual majority. One lesbian journalist characterized the argument as thinking that "the road to gay rights runs through the thicket of gender dysfunction" and that homosexuality is "a sort of tumor on the body politic."[3]

But while the discussion was considered counterproductive politically by many gay people, it was considered useful legally by Dubofsky and others on the plaintiffs' legal team. They believed it would strengthen the legal argument that sexual orientation fit the "obvious, immutable and distinguishing" indicia of suspect classification analysis. Dubofsky and others also felt that both the courts and the general public would be more opposed to Amendment 2 if they understood that sexual orientation was an inborn characteristic rather than a "lifestyle choice." Since the case against Amendment 2, they knew, would be widely reported in the press, they believed the trial would be a good opportunity to make their case in court and in the country. Also, as Dubofsky explained, it was important that this trial lay down as complete a record as possible on all issues involving homosexuality to prepare for further appeals. "If we end up at the U.S. Supreme Court," said Dubofsky, "we want to be sure we have everything in the record that we might possibly need or want to argue."

---

2. Virginia Apuzzo, executive director of the National Gay Task Force, as quoted in "Biological Marker Found in Gay Men," by Dave Walter, *Washington Blade,* September 28, 1984, 1, 10, in reference to a study, "Neuroendocrine Response to Estrogen and Sexual Orientation," by Brian Gladue, Richard Green, and Ronald Hellman, published in September 28, 1984, issue of *Science* magazine, about the effect of a female hormone on luteinizing hormone levels in men. The study found that the female hormone triggered higher levels of the luteinizing hormone in gay men than in straight men.

3. Donna Minkowitz, "Trial by Science: In the Fight Over Amendment 2, Biology Is Back—And Gay Allies Are Claiming It," *Village Voice,* November 30, 1993, 27–29.

The Educated Guess

Of the 35 hours of testimony at trial, about 20 percent was devoted to the biological and genetic origins of sexuality. The testimony around the issue became both a primer in sexuality and an exercise in educated guessing under oath.

On the second day of the trial, plaintiffs called the first of three expert witnesses to the stand: Richard Green. Green, a sex researcher and professor of psychiatry at the University of California in Los Angeles, was involved with some of the first studies that sought concrete evidence that homosexual sexual orientation originates in some biological factor. One of Green's studies, published in September 1984,[4] claimed to be the first valid[5] study to show clearly that a biological *marker* exists for homosexuality. It did not, however, claim to identify a "cause" for homosexual sexual orientation. That distinction was a big one—it was one thing to find a biological trait that people with a homosexual sexual orientation seemed to share in common; it was quite another to suggest that that trait was the cause of the homosexual orientation.

Green, who also held a law degree, taught courses covering the intersection of psychiatry and law. His specialty was human sexuality, in particular, how children develop their sexual identity or, as Green put it, "what their sexual orientation is."[6] Green had been working in the field for 23 years, authoring more than 100 professional papers on the subject of sexuality. He estimated that he had been used as an expert witness in about 30 trials.

But by some standards, he was an odd choice. Over the previous seven years, Green had annoyed some gay people with studies claim-

---

4. Brian A. Gladue, Richard Green, and Ronald E. Hellman, "Neuroendocrine Response to Estrogen and Sexual Orientation," *Science*, September 28, 1984 (vol. 225), 1496–99.

5. There were several earlier studies, but Green and his colleagues said these predecessors were "not convincing." Among these was one published in the *Archives of Sexual Behavior* in 1975 (vol. 4, no. 1) by Gunther Dorner et al., researchers in what was then East Germany. This report, "A Neuroendocrine Predisposition for Homosexuality in Men," included a suggestion that tests should be developed to measure the hormone levels of the fetus. In fetuses without the "proper" level of hormones for a male or female, the authors theorized, "a preventive therapy of sexual differentiation disturbances could be accomplished during these critical prenatal organizational periods."

6. Most scholars in this area, including Green, are very careful about their terminology. Sexual identity is not sexual orientation, as Green would soon explain.

ing that many gay men, as children, were likely to have behaved as "sissy boys"[7] and that they could be identified through a simple blood test for hormone levels. The "sissy boy" profile was a stereotype that few gay people cared to have perpetuated, much less given any credence by the appearance that it had a scientific basis. And many worried about the consequences of Green's hormone test. "Gay people have a right to be worried that some people will go around saying, 'If you don't want a queer son, get this injection,'" commented one gay researcher about Green's hormone study.[8]

Prior to trial, Green advised plaintiffs' attorney Jeanne Winer about his various studies and which ones he believed would be best for her to ask him about to make the plaintiffs' case that there is some biological basis to homosexuality. His testimony covered three basic areas—genetics, hormones, and brain anatomy—and examined how each affects sexual orientation.

Elements of Identity

In court, Winer asked Green to start with some basic definitions. A person's "sexual identity" or "gender identity," he said, has three elements:

> awareness of oneself, anatomically, as either male or female;
> awareness of how one's culture defines being "masculine" or "feminine"; and
> awareness of one's own "sexual orientation."

"Sexual orientation," said Green, is measured across three areas:

> physical arousal,
> fantasy, and
> self-identification.

According to Green, a person's sexual orientation can be discerned through "extended interviews" about these elements. He

---

7. Richard Green, *The 'Sissy Boy' Syndrome and the Development of Homosexuality,* Yale University Press, New Haven, Conn., 1987.

8. James Weinrich, a sex researcher at the Boston University Medical Center, quoted in *Washington Blade,* September 28, 1984 (vol. 15, no. 39), 1, 10.

explained the "Kinsey scale" commonly used for measuring a person's sexual orientation. The scale, he noted, ranges from zero to six. A person who rates a zero is exclusively heterosexual in both his or her fantasy life and behaviors, a person who rates a six is exclusively homosexual, and in between are conditions Green characterized as "various bisexuality."

Although Green did not go into great detail on the witness stand, it bears noting that the "Kinsey scale" was developed by sexual researcher Alfred Kinsey in the 1950s and was originally intended to measure only sexual behavior—not fantasies, attractions, or self-identification. At a symposium sponsored by the Kinsey Institute in 1986, experts generally agreed that a person's Kinsey scale rating could change over his or her lifetime and that separate ratings should be gauged for behavior, fantasy, and self-identification. In other words, a person's sexual fantasies could be exclusively about a person of the same sex (making him or her a Kinsey 6) but that same person's behaviors—for various reasons, including opportunity and the level of concern about societal conformity—could be limited to persons of the other sex (a Kinsey 0).

The *Kinsey Institute New Report on Sex: What You Must Know to Be Sexually Literate*[9] notes:

> Thoughtful scientists have come to question whether labels such as homosexual or bisexual tell us very much about the way a person actually behaves sexually. In many past studies, once a person described himself or herself as homosexual, the researcher did not ask any questions about behavior with the opposite sex, assuming these questions would not apply to a homosexual; they also did not ask people who called themselves heterosexual about same-sex partners. But in a recent Kinsey Institute study of a group of lesbians from across the United States, 43 percent of even the women who had always referred to themselves as lesbian had had sex at least once with a man since age 18; of the total group of lesbians, 74 percent had experienced heterosexual sex.

---

9. June Reinisch with Ruth Beasley, *The Kinsey Institute New Report on Sex: What You Must Know to Be Sexually Literate*, edited and compiled by Debra Kent; St. Martin's Press, 1990, 141.

A Riddle of Numbers

These complications were not discussed during the trial. As she had planned out with Green ahead of time, plaintiffs' attorney Winer simply asked Green, "What percentage of the population is homosexual?"

The answer, explained Green, is riddled with "controversy and some uncertainty." Accurate estimates, he said, were made difficult because sexual activity between two people of the same sex is a "stigmatized behavior," one that many people surveyed are reluctant to acknowledge to an interviewer or even in filling out a questionnaire.

"But having said that," said Green, "the numbers which appear to be in the majority of studies indicate that somewhere between two and three to four percent of males and perhaps one to two to three percent of females are exclusively or predominantly homosexuals as adults, but this may represent an underreporting."

Even though on cross-examination Green was careful to emphasize a difference between *behavior* and *orientation,* under Winer's questioning, he did not choose to make these distinctions in explaining various estimates. Winer asked Green to explain the commonly heard estimate that lesbians and gay men make up about 10 percent of the population; Green said 10 percent referred to "the number of males who were at least predominantly homosexual for a three-year period after age 16." In fact, that answer represented only one theory.

Zeroing in on an estimate of *how many* people have a homosexual or bisexual orientation was as difficult, it seemed, as zeroing in on *why* they had such orientations. Still, in court, an estimate was important to the plaintiffs in making for Judge Bayless the first broad sketch of who gay people are and what their power might be as a minority. But it was only a tentative sketch because, as Green noted, "there isn't really an accurate estimate" available.

There had been many attempts to gauge what part of the population is homosexual, but nearly every survey was different from the others in some significant way—either in its execution or interpretation—making all of them difficult to compare or to use to show any one number as being most representative. Some surveys had asked questions that provided information about behavior, some about self-identity, and even a few about attractions and fantasies; but, among them, there was no clear agreement about what represented "homosexual-

ity." Should the survey takers, for instance, count as homosexual a person who had sex only with a person of the other sex but who was a Kinsey 6 in fantasy and arousal? Should they count a person who identified as "gay" but who had never had sex with anyone? How should
they count a person who had an equal number of same-sex and oppo-
site-sex partners and who felt an equal attraction to both?

Lost in most discussions of the numbers was the important influence the wording of the questions had in determining the answers. For
instance, a survey looking for men at risk for AIDS might find fewer
men acknowledging they had had sex with another man than a survey
that asked men to indicate first what types of sexual activities they had
engaged in and then asked them to indicate the gender of their partners.

In addition to the variations in how questions were asked, there
were variations in how the answers were interpreted. For instance,
when Kinsey was interpreting his own results in the 1950s, he wrote:
"At least 13 percent of the male population would have to be institutionalized and isolated if all persons who were *predominantly* homosexual were handled in that way." But on the witness stand in Denver in
1993, Green testified that Kinsey had "indicated that approximately
four percent of adult males were predominantly to exclusively homosexual throughout their lives."

For women, said Green, "about two percent . . . would have been
predominantly or exclusively homosexual."

Somehow, in popular currency, the 10 percent figure Green discussed had come to represent something much broader than "the number of males who were at least predominantly homosexual for a three-
year period after age 16." Sometimes, the 10 percent was cited as an
estimate of both lesbians and gay men in the United States; sometimes
it was referred to as an estimate of people who had ever acknowledged
engaging in sex with a partner of the same sex. While Green's testimony implied that the 10 percent figure was generated out of the Kinsey study of men, it is not entirely clear either that that is true or how
the 10 percent estimate had acquired such acceptance. But it seems
obvious that the number did have its origins in Kinsey's famous sexual
behavior studies conducted in the 1940s and 1950s. Those studies—one
on men and one on women[10]—found that 13 percent of men and 7

---

10. Alfred C. Kinsey, Wardell Pomeroy, Clyde E. Martin, and Paul H. Gebhard,
"Sexual Behavior in the Human Male" and "Sexual Behavior in the Human Female."

percent of women reported having sex with persons of the same gender during the three years prior to the study. Many believe the 10 percent figure was simply an average of those two figures.[11]

Studies between then and 1994 found widely disparate percentages—as low as 1.2 percent[12] and as high as 22 percent.[13] Predictably, the lower estimates tended to come out of surveys designed for AIDS-related studies that focused on behaviors only, while the higher estimates tended to come out of surveys that asked questions about sexual attractions and fantasies.

Green also testified that while Kinsey's studies had been subsequently criticized for including an "overrepresentation" of male prostitutes and prisoners, a later analysis of the data by Kinsey coauthor Paul Gebhard "upheld" the finding that "close to 10 percent of males were predominantly homosexual for a significant period of years after age 16."

So which was it—13 percent, 4 percent, or 10 percent?

While attorneys challenging Amendment 2 had reasons to try to establish this point, it was an exercise as complicated as trying to estimate the number of people in the United States with easygoing personalities. And, in truth, it did not matter. Amendment 2 did not target only those people who were "predominantly" or "exclusively" gay. It did not target only those people who had this orientation for life or for only brief periods of time. It targeted everyone with "homosexual, lesbian, or bisexual orientation, conduct, practices, or relationships."

The Growing Evidence

After having Green set out what sexual orientation is and estimating how many people might have a homosexual orientation, attorney Winer asked him to discuss what scientific research has revealed thus far about the origin of homosexual orientation. Green began by

---

11. In *The Social Organization of Sexuality: Sexual Practices in the United States,* by Edward Laumann, John Gangnon, Robert Michael, and Stuart Michaels (University of Chicago Press, 1994), the authors note that gay activist Bruce Voeller, once head of the National Gay Task Force, took credit for coming up with the average.

12. John Billy, "Sexual Behavior of Men in the United States," in *Family Planning Perspectives* magazine of the Alan Guttmacher Institute, 1993.

13. Cynthia and Samuel Janus, *The Janus Report on Sexual Behavior,* John Wiley and Sons, 1993.

explaining that neither he nor most experts in the field believe sexual orientation can be "consciously chosen."

"At this time," he said, "I believe there is a growing body of biological research pointing to prenatal origins of sexual orientation." In making this statement, Green said, he relied on studies about genes, the anatomy of the brain, and the effects of prenatal sex hormones on subsequent behaviors.

In recent studies of gay men who had identical twin brothers, "approximately 50 percent" of the twins also were gay, said Green.[14] Later studies found that the likelihood of both individuals having the same sexual orientation was definitely higher in identical twins than in fraternal twins. In cases where the sexual orientation of identical twins is not the same, said Green, researchers have speculated that the differences might be due to "some dislocations of atoms" that can occur "during the early cell divisions."

"Additionally," said Green, "one can also suggest that because a set of twins is genetically similar or identical, that not all prenatal events are necessarily identical. For example, we know that sets of twins differ in birth weight. We also know, for example, that parents can distinguish twins. So there are other prenatal events that occur that can affect the individual members of a twin pair which could account for differences postnatally."

The upshot of all this, said Green, is that there is a "growing body of scientific knowledge showing that, to some extent, sexual orientation has a genetic basis."

But hormones, too, he said, play a role. There is an inherited condition called Congenital Adrenal Hyperplasia (CAH) in which some female fetuses "overproduce" male-type hormones. Two or three studies, he said, have shown that when this happens, the female infant's genitalia may appear somewhat like a penis at birth. As adults, these women "reveal a higher rate of bisexual or homosexual fantasy" and behaviors. This finding, he said, suggests that the levels of male hormones before birth have some influence on sexual orientation.

Other studies, he testified, have shown a similar effect on the female offspring of women who took DES. (Diethylstilbestrol is a synthetic female hormone given to women who had difficulty carrying a fetus the full nine months. The drug is now off the market for use by

14. J. Michael Bailey and Richard C. Pillard, "A Genetic Study of Male Sexual Orientation," *Archives of General Psychiatry* (vol. 48), December 1991, 1089–96.

pregnant women.) The female offspring of mothers who took DES had a higher rate of bisexual or homosexual fantasy and behavior than did their sisters born when the mothers did not take DES.

And some male fetuses, he said, have a condition that leaves them unable to convert the male hormone testosterone into a form necessary to masculinize their genitalia before birth. One study showed that these male offspring appeared to be female at birth and were raised as girls until puberty, when their bodies began developing male genitalia and a sexual orientation toward women.

All of these studies, he said, provide a "growing body of scientific evidence" that the levels of sex hormones present before birth influence sexual orientation.

Concerning anatomy, Green noted that recent studies had found some differences between the brains of men and those of women. Specifically, the difference was in the nuclei between tissue at the front of the hypothalamus, a part of the brain that regulates sex drive, body temperature, sleep, and appetite. In 1991, said Green, researcher Simon LeVay reported noticing that that part of the hypothalamus in heterosexual men appeared to be larger than in homosexual men. "The significance of that, if it's a valid finding," said Green, "is, again, pointing in the direction that there are indeed anatomic, in this case, central nervous system or brain differences, that are associated with sexual orientation."

The strength of LeVay's findings was tempered by the small number (41 brains) and nature (deceased persons) of his subjects: 16 were from men whom LeVay "presumed" to be "heterosexual," 6 were from "presumed heterosexual" women, 18 were from men who had indicated to a physician that they had had sex with men, and 1 from a man who had indicated he had had sex with both men and women.[15] Of the 35 men, 25 had succumbed to AIDS, which is known to have some impact on the brain. Those 25 included 6 who were "presumed heterosexual" men and all 19 of the men who had indicated they had had sex with men.

As LeVay had done himself, Green carefully laid out the considerable caveats surrounding interpretation of the study. For one, LeVay could only hope that his "heterosexual males" were, indeed, heterosexual. With the men who succumbed to AIDS, LeVay was able to identify

15. Simon LeVay, "A Difference in Hypothalamic Structure between Heterosexual and Homosexual Men," *Science* (vol. 253, no. 15), August 30, 1991, 1034–37.

the gender of their sex partners—indicating with some degree of confidence whether they were heterosexual, homosexual, or bisexual—because information about sex partners was recorded for reporting AIDS-related deaths to the U.S. Centers for Disease Control (later renamed the U.S. Centers for Disease Control and Prevention).

All of the men who had been identified as homosexual or bisexual had died of AIDS-related diseases, and some experts wondered if the differences in the sizes of the hypothalamus might be the result of that infection. But, as Green noted, the brains of the six presumed heterosexual men who died from AIDS and the brains of the homosexual men who died from AIDS were different in the same ways from the brains of the presumed heterosexual men who died from other causes.

Green did not explain that LeVay varied his methods during the research. With 15 brains, he measured the volume of the nuclei from both the left and right sides of the hypothalamus (which, like the brain, is divided into two spheres). With 14 brains, he examined only the right side, and with 12 brains, only the left.

LeVay himself carefully laid out these variables in reporting his conclusions and said the study "suggests that sexual orientation has a biologic" influence, and that sexual orientation may be either a "cause or a consequence" of the size of the nuclei at the front of the hypothalamus. Then again, said LeVay, both sexual orientation and the size of the nuclei might be affected by "some third, unidentified variable."

Although he did not go into detail, Green also testified briefly about other brain anatomy comparisons. A study in the Netherlands found that a portion of the back of the hypothalamus was bigger in homosexual men than in heterosexual men.[16] A study at the University of California at Los Angeles found that a cable of nerve fibers at the top of the hypothalamus was larger in homosexual men than in heterosexual men.[17] A more recent study found

---

16. D. F. Swaab and M. A. Hofman, "An Enlarged Suprachiasmatic Nucleus in Homosexual Men," Netherlands Institute for Brain Research, in Amsterdam. Published by Brain Research, 537, 141–48, in 1990. This study, too, suffered from weaknesses. Only 10 homosexual males who died of AIDS were compared to 6 heterosexual males who died of AIDS, and they were compared to 18 males who died from various causes and whose sexual orientation was unknown.

17. Laura Allen and Roger Gorski, "Sexual Orientation and the Size of the Anterior Commissure in the Human Brain," *Neurobiology*, Proceedings of the National Academy of Science USA (vol. 89), August 1992, 7199–202.

another section of the brain larger in homosexual men than heterosexual men.[18]

Although Green did not address this, none of the published studies at that time had examined the brains of women known to be lesbians.

Nature and Nurture

Green's own research contributions in the area of sexual orientation had
to do with hormones and, separately, behavior. He did not ask Winer to
guide him through a discussion of the study concerning hormone levels
and sexual orientation, which he coauthored with two other researchers,
but he did choose to discuss his own controversial "sissy boy" study.
Perhaps because of its inflammatory terminology—about "sissy boys"
and "extremely effeminate" behaviors—the "sissy boy" study had garnered much more publicity for Green than his earlier coauthored study
on the neuroendocrine influences on sexual orientation.[19]

In discussing the "The Sissy Boy Syndrome,"[20] Green testified that
he had monitored a group of young boys for 12 years. One-half of the
boys were "conventionally essentially masculine," he said, while the
other half exhibited behaviors and preferences that were more typically
associated with girls. He dubbed this latter group "sissy boys" and said
that, over the course of the study, between two-thirds and three-quar-
ters of them eventually "emerged" as "homosexual to bisexual."

Green said his study "demonstrates that one can identify features,
at least in the male in the earliest years of life, that are associated with
later sexual orientation." Green further noted that while many of the
"sissy boys" had been entered into "so-called treatment" during childhood to modify their behaviors, "there was no difference in sexual orientation" in later years between those who did and did not receive such
"treatments."

---

18. A Canadian researcher reported November 16, 1994, at the annual meeting of
the Society for Neuroscience, that one part of the corpus callosum (a fiber which connects
the two hemispheres of the brain) was significantly larger in "gay compared to straight
men." The scientists used Magnetic Resonance Imaging (MRI) to study 21 healthy
males—11 homosexual and 10 heterosexual.

19. Brian A. Gladue, Richard Green, and Ronald E. Hellman, "Neuroendocrine
Response to Estrogen and Sexual Orientation," *Science*, 225 (1984), 1496–99.

20. Richard Green, *The "Sissy Boy Syndrome" and the Development of Homosexuality*.
New Haven, Conn.: Yale University Press, 1987.

Green also said that the "sissy boys" had spent "substantially or significantly less" time with their fathers in the first four to five years of life than had the conventionally masculine group. In many of these cases, he noted, the father had apparently tried to spend time with the son but found that his boy was not interested in the same activities that interested the father. Thus, said Green, the father became "discouraged" and decreased the amount of shared time with that son. But, Green said, "When we add up all the variables . . . we find that . . . less than 50 percent of the variance is accounted for by all of these postnatal experiential socialization events."[21]

Sexual orientation, said Green, is not all nature or all nurture; it is "an interaction between nurture and nature," and he added, "most experts in psychiatry agree that sexual orientation is set early in life."

"Precisely what year or years is in some dispute," said Green, "but in the traditional psychoanalytical views, the Freudian views, it was largely set at the Oedipal phase, in the first five to six years."

Of course, Green was not on the stand just to give his own expert opinion. He was also there to refute the experts that the state of Colorado had engaged to convince the court that homosexuality is a "lifestyle choice." So, on the witness stand, Green also acknowledged that there are a "handful" of people who claim they can change a homosexual orientation to heterosexual. These people are refuted by most professionals, said Green, who believe sexual orientation is "certainly not easily changeable" and that it is not a psychiatric disorder. Green alluded to the fact that in December 1973 the American Psychiatric Association (APA) voted to declassify homosexuality as an illness. Prior to that vote, the APA's official diagnostic manual listed homosexuality as a mental disorder—a "sexual deviation," along with pedophilia, exhibitionism, voyeurism, fetishism, and sadomasochism.

Politics of Science

Although Green's testimony did not stretch back to the beginning of "homosexuality," it is interesting to note that homosexual sex—then

---

21. In January 1995, two other researchers reported findings comparable to Green's "sissy boy" study. Published in "Childhood Sex-Typed Behavior and Sexual Orientation: A Conceptual Analysis and Quantitative Review," in *Developmental Psychology* (vol. 31, no.1, 43–55), Michael Bailey and Kenneth Zucker said that adult homosexual men and women recalled having engaged in more "cross-sex-typed" behaviors as children than did adult heterosexual men and women.

called "intercourse against nature"—first appeared in medical nomenclature in 1800, when Frederik Moltke, president of the Royal Chancery of Denmark, appointed a commission to revise that country's penal code. In doing so, wrote historian Wilheim von Rosen of Copenhagen, Moltke suggested that people who engage in sodomy "ought, in my opinion, be treated as lunatics or sick persons, and together with their acts hidden away in secluded places."[22] In his *Gay/Lesbian Almanac*, historian Jonathan Katz explained that one of the earliest uses of the terms "homosexual" and "heterosexual" in the United States came in May 1892, when Dr. James Kiernan announced he was launching a quest to discover the cause of homosexuality.

But Kinsey's research in the 1950s, by showing that same-sex sexual behavior was fairly common, challenged this concept of homosexuality as an illness whose cause needed discovery. And by the end of that decade, another researcher, Dr. Evelyn Hooker, weighed in with her own discovery—that homosexuals are just as happy and mentally healthy as heterosexuals.

In September 1967, Hooker was appointed to head a Task Force on Homosexuality at the National Institute of Mental Health, and two years later, that Task Force submitted a report. The report recommended that the government "remove legal penalties against acts in private among consenting adults" and make "comprehensive statements from an authoritative source . . . that would dispel myths and help to disseminate what is known" about homosexuality.

The news media gave the Task Force's report only passing notice, and the administration of then-president Richard Nixon took no action to circulate it until 1971, when it printed the document but gave no publicity to its availability. Publicity, however, did come after someone leaked a copy of the report to a gay publication called *One* magazine, which then published it.

By this time, Washington, D.C., gay activist Franklin Kameny and a number of prominent psychiatrists had begun lobbying the APA Board of Trustees to declassify homosexuality. The APA did so on December 15, 1973. In its resolution, the APA said that "it is generally acknowledged that a significant proportion of homosexuals are clearly

---

22. Wilhelm von Rosen, "Sodomy in Early Modern Denmark: A Crime without Victims," in *The Pursuit of Sodomy: Male Homosexuality in Renaissance and Enlightenment Europe*, edited by Kent Gerard and Gert Hekma (Harrington Park Press, New York, 1989), 177–204.

satisfied with their sexual orientation and show no significant signs of psychopathology." Thus, the *Diagnostic and Statistical Manual of Mental Disorders, Second Edition (DSM II)*, the standard diagnostic guide for doctors and clinicians working in psychiatry, established that homosexuality "by itself does not constitute a psychiatric disorder" but "per se is one form of sexual behavior."

And that, testified Green, is where medical science had evolved to: that homosexuals are "no more, no less healthy" than heterosexuals and, responding to some brief summary questions at the end of direct examination, he added that homosexual people make "no better, no worse" parents than heterosexual people.

The testimony about gay people as parents was important groundwork to address one argument the state of Colorado planned to offer for why it needed Amendment 2—that the initiative was necessary to protect children. Green noted that recent studies of the children of lesbian parents found "no differences" in general psychological or sociological adjustment or in the incidence of homosexuality among children of homosexual or heterosexual parents.

Green's testimony contradicted the state's notion that gay people pose some threat to children, and he made clear that he believed Amendment 2 posed a threat to gay people by targeting them for prejudice. The "effects on one's self-image, levels of self-esteem, are negatively impacted and may, in fact, be devastating."

State Has No Witness

Winer used Green not only to begin laying the groundwork for the plaintiffs' contention that sexual orientation should be considered a suspect classification and to attack the state's argument that Amendment 2 would promote the psychological well-being of children, but also to attack the credibility of several psychological experts the state planned to call to the witness stand. One of these experts was Paul Cameron, a psychologist who had gained notoriety for his unorthodox research concerning homosexuality. Cameron had contributed his works to a number of political campaigns seeking to overturn civil rights laws protecting gay people. Many of these campaigns relied on antigay literature that he published, claiming that his reports represented accepted scientific research. An example of this literature is a

1992 pamphlet he produced called "What Causes Homosexual Desire, and Can It Be Changed?" In the pamphlet, Cameron wrote, "No one has found a single heridible [sic] genetic, hormonal or physical difference between heterosexuals and homosexuals—at least none that is replicable." To back up this claim, he then cited in a footnote a book written by the esteemed psychiatrist Judd Marmor in 1980, and another journal article written in 1984.

But most of the important research in this area was done well after 1984 and long before Cameron put together his pamphlet, and a number of researchers in the field took issue with his claims. A group of faculty members at the University of Nebraska filed a complaint against Cameron with the American Psychological Association, saying that his public statements and writings about homosexuality often cited research data taken out of context. Cameron, at the time, was a psychologist with a practice in Lincoln, Nebraska, but he had also made a name for himself through his claims that 40 percent of child molestation is perpetrated by "those who engage in homosexuality."[23] The American Psychological Association announced in one of its journals in late 1984 that it had "dropped" this psychologist from its membership on December 2, 1983, "for a violation of the Preamble to the Ethical Principles of Psychologists." The organization would not comment on the details of the decision at the time, saying that the organization's bylaws prohibited disclosure of specific charges made against any member.[24]

Cameron told one newspaper that he resigned from the American Psychological Association in November 1982 and was not expelled. But the association's administrative officer for ethics, David Mills, said the organization would not have been able to bring proceedings against Cameron unless he had still been a member. Soon after this controversy erupted, Cameron created an Institute for the Investigation of Sexuality in 1984 in Lincoln (he later moved the operation to a suburb of Washington, D.C., calling it the Family Research Institute). By August 1986, the American Sociological Association had "repudiated any claims that

---

23. "What Causes Homosexuality and Can It Be Cured?" Pamphlet published by the Institute for the Scientific Investigation of Sexuality, Lincoln, Nebraska, 1984.

24. Lou Chibbaro Jr., "Anti-Gay Psychologist Expelled for 'Gross' Distortions," *Washington Blade*, October 5, 1984.

Paul Cameron is a sociologist and condemned his misrepresentation of sociological research."[25]

On the witness stand, Green testified that Cameron's "findings" were "at odds to other researchers in the area of homosexuality" and that his articles about homosexuality were not published in journals that require expert scrutiny of articles to insure their scientific integrity. Green criticized Cameron's research methodology as "unusual," saying that Cameron based his generalizations on groups as small as 15 to 20 people and used terminology that is not well-defined.

"I don't believe that is good science at all," he said of Cameron's work. "And, as Dr. Cameron admits, his findings are generally at odds with all other researchers in the field of human sexuality, which I think should give one pause."

Plaintiffs also called Dr. Carole Jenny to the stand. The purpose of her testimony was to rebut Cameron's claims that gay people were disproportionately responsible for instances of sexual abuse against children—claims repeated in CFV campaign literature to promote Amendment 2's passage. Jenny was director of the child advocacy and protection team at the Children's Hospital in Denver. She was also an associate professor of pediatrics at the University of Denver Medical School and was president-elect of the American Academy of Pediatrics' section on child abuse.

Jenny characterized Cameron's claims as insupportable, noting that, in her clinical experience spanning 800 cases between 1992 and 1993 involving sexually abused children in Denver, she had found only three cases in which "people came in and said, 'I think someone who's homosexual has molested my child and I want them HIV tested.'"

Although the state initially indicated that it planned to call Cameron to the stand in the Amendment 2 trial, presumably to bolster its argument concerning the well-being of children, and even though hours of deposition and court time had been spent by plaintiffs to refute his claims, the state, during the course of the trial, decided not to call Cameron to the witness stand, saying simply that it no longer needed his testimony. Ultimately, the state never even submitted an affidavit from Cameron.

Winer also asked Green about another expected expert for the state: Charles W. Socarides, a psychiatrist, psychoanalyst, and clinical

---

25. "Council Acts on Cameron Case," January 1987 issue of *Footnotes*, a newsletter of the American Sociological Association, 4, 6.

professor of psychiatry at Albert Einstein College of Medicine in New York City. His specialty, for nearly 40 years, he said in an affidavit filed with the court during trial, had been "sexual deviations, especially homosexuality." He had written two books on the subject, coedited two books, and cochaired a discussion group called "The Sexual Deviations: Theory and Therapy."

Socarides explained in his affidavit that he considered homosexuality to be a "psychiatric psychopathology" caused by an overbearing mother and an "absent or abdicating" father. In this scenario, argued Socarides, a gay son has no "appropriate masculine" role model and a lesbian daughter is deprived of a "feminine" and "maternal" role model. The children suffer a deep fear of the other sex and "neutralize" this fear through their attraction to a person of the same sex.

In his affidavit, Socarides also claimed that the American Psychiatric Association removed homosexuality from its diagnostic manual in 1973 only as a "direct result of relentless intimidation and pressure from gay rights group activists." But Green presented considerable testimony to illustrate that Socarides's views did not represent those of the mainstream of his professions, psychiatry and psychoanalysis, and the state, ultimately, did not call Socarides to the witness stand for questioning.[26]

State Plays Defense

Although the state, too, sought to answer the question "Who are gay people?" it called no witnesses to the stand to testify about the origin of sexual orientation. Instead, it relied on challenging the testimony of the plaintiffs' experts through cross-examination and trying to use those witnesses for its own advantage. So, when cross-examining Green, Jack Wesoky, senior assistant attorney general for Colorado, sought to undermine the notion that homosexuality is an immutable characteristic by attempting to discredit research done in this arena and by illustrating that, for some people, sexual behavior is a choice.

To establish the former, Wesoky relied on an essay about homosexuality that appeared in an outdated encyclopedia. He presented Green with the essay's description of homosexuality, which appeared

---

26. In an interview with the *Washington Blade* (April 12, 1996), Socarides's openly gay son, Richard, said that, at his urging, his father decided not to take the witness stand in Colorado.

in the 1988 edition of the *Encyclopedia Americana.* The lengthy entry was written by former president of the American Psychiatric Association, Judd Marmor.

Wesoky focused on particular sections of the entry:

> Homosexuality can be characterized as behavior involving sexual relations with a member of the same sex. . . . Some pursue [homosexuality] because of an intense erotic attraction to members of their own sex; others, such as prisoners, may seek homosexual outlets only because of prolonged deprivation of contact with the other sex; still others, with defective moral controls, may engage in it for money or adventure, or a need to please, or out of boredom, curiosity, or rebelliousness. . . .
>
> Many misconceptions concerning homosexuality circulate widely despite the absence of evidence for them. These include beliefs that homosexuals are 'born that way'; that they are biologically or hormonally different from heterosexuals; that they can be recognized on sight; that they represent a unique personality type; and that their sexual patterns are irreversible.
>
> There is no convincing evidence that homosexuality is inheritable. Most studies indicate that it is an adaptive response to certain experiences. Hormonal studies show no differences between most homosexuals and heterosexuals.

Confronted with Marmor's statements that at least some people engage in sex with a person of the same sex "for money or adventure, or a need to please, or out of boredom, curiosity, or rebelliousness," Green cautioned that there is a difference between engaging in a "homosexual act" and having a homosexual *orientation.* Wesoky simply ignored Green's remark.

"In the area of choice of homosexuality," said Wesoky, "you've testified that it's not a choice."

"Yes," said Green.

"That would be true for all homosexuals—[that] it's not a choice?" asked Wesoky.

"I think for the vast majority of homosexuals," said Green.

Wesoky pressed Green to define what percentage of homosexuals constitutes this "vast majority" and eventually got him to speculate that for "at least 80 percent," homosexuality is not a choice.

"Approximately 20 percent, then, of homosexuals engage in that as a matter of choice," posited Wesoky.

"No," said Green. "There might be some element of choice in a small minority," but he estimated that to be the case in "no more than . . . maybe one percent."

Asked if he agreed with an article by Marmor, suggesting that the women's liberation movement may have influenced some women to choose homosexuality, Green said "it's probably" true to some extent.

"So, now we know from your testimony," said Wesoky, "I believe, that some women choose homosexuality."

"We know from that," retorted Green, "that some women may choose homosexual *behaviors,* not necessarily homosexual orientation."

Wesoky then tried to blur the distinction between behavior and orientation by noting that Marmor was writing about something he called "homosexuality."

"I was talking about the word *homosexuality,*" said Wesoky. "You said it generally means sexual orientation, homosexual orientation. But Dr. Marmor, in his article in the encyclopedia, didn't use it in that sense, did he?"

"No, he did not," conceded Green. But, Green said, homosexuality "generally means homosexual orientation," and he speculated that, when Marmor took the witness stand later in the trial, Marmor would agree with him.

In attempting to discredit studies that suggest there is a biological origin for homosexual orientation—particularly LeVay's study of the brain—Wesoky had Green acknowledge that some of the studies have contradicted one another and that their conclusions have sometimes been very tentative. Green agreed that the contradictory results of two studies meant their conclusions were "inconclusive," but he would not dismiss every study.

Since LeVay's studies involved the brains of homosexual men who succumbed to AIDS, Wesoky asked, "couldn't you hypothesize that AIDS" accounted for the difference in the sizes of their hypothalamuses. "I don't think so," said Green, noting that several of LeVay's "presumed heterosexual" men had also died from AIDS and that their brains compared generally with those of the "presumed heterosexual" men who died from other causes.

In a further attempt to discredit LeVay's findings, Wesoky got Green to acknowledge that there had been some evidence that men with late-stage AIDS suffer a reduction in their male sex hormones and that, in a laboratory study involving the brain of the Mongolian gerbil, scientists found that testosterone levels influence the size of the part of the hypothalamus that LeVay attributed to sexual orientation.

"I have heard of that study," said Green. "I think it's a controversial one. I don't think there's a consensus as to the findings of that study."

To undermine the significance of Green's testimony about the DES study that seemed to indicate a biological influence on sexual orientation, Wesoky, apparently presuming that lesbians are more athletically active than heterosexual women, had Green acknowledge that another study had "failed to demonstrate" that the DES hormone could account for "a difference in sports participation."

"And didn't that same study also report that marriage and motherhood rates from DES-exposed women and their unexposed sisters were comparable?" asked Wesoky.

Green said he did not recall.

"And didn't that same study also report that DES-exposed women did not differ from their unexposed sisters in athletic ability and interests, as recognized in hours per week spent in sports, number and types of sports participated in, and high school physical education grades?"

"It may have," said Green, who eventually conceded that one could conclude that the study Wesoky brought up did not support a conclusion that sexual orientation was biologically based.

Wesoky also tried to undermine the conclusions of a number of studies about which Green had testified, including the twin brother study conducted by Michael Bailey and Richard Pillard, which was reported in December 1991. In that study, the researchers found that, of 56 gay men who had identical twin brothers, 52 percent of those twin brothers were also gay or bisexual. That compared with only 11 percent of the 57 gay men who had brothers who had been adopted, and 22 percent of the gay men who had fraternal twin brothers.

Wesoky, noting that Green had testified that about 4 percent of the general male population is homosexual, asked whether the finding that 11 percent of adopted brothers are also gay suggests "an environmental factor in homosexuality."

"That's one possible [explanation]," said Green.

And, on cross-examination, Wesoky got Green to agree that homosexuality is "possibly" a reversible condition.

Wesoky then attacked Green's testimony about the American Psychiatric Association's decision to declassify homosexuality as an illness in 1973. He referred Green to a survey, published in a journal called the *Medical Aspects of Human Sexuality*, conducted by Harold O'Leaf in 1977. The survey purported to show that 69 percent of psychiatrists polled said they consider homosexuality to be a "pathological" condition. Wesoky also asked about a book by Ronald Bahr, *Homosexuality and American Psychiatry: The Politics of Psychiatry*, in which Bahr claimed that the APA declassified homosexuality in reaction to political arm-twisting by gay activists, including what was then the National Gay Task Force.

But Green said it wasn't clear that O'Leaf's survey actually polled psychiatrists and that he had no personal knowledge of any gay political activity surrounding the APA vote.

No Single Cause

Judd Marmor, who took the stand for plaintiffs later that afternoon, did know about the vote. He was vice president of the American Psychiatric Association when the vote was taken. Marmor, a psychiatrist, had practiced psychiatry for 56 years and taught it for 45 years. He was a life fellow and past president of the American Psychiatric Association, a life fellow and past president of the American Academy of Psychoanalysts, and a diplomate of psychiatry and neurology for the American Board of Psychiatry and Neurology. He recently had served as chief of the Department of Psychiatry at the Cedars-Sinai Medical Center in Los Angeles and as a professor of psychiatry at the University of Southern California and at the University of California at Los Angeles. Marmor had, at the time of the trial, written six books and about 300 scientific papers, and he had served as an expert witness in about 15 trials.

Marmor testified that he and most other psychiatrists believe multiple factors determine sexual orientation and that sexual orientation is set by age six. "There is no single cause for it," said Marmor. "And it is a situation in which probably some genetic, some early environmental, and occasionally some socio-causal factors may play a role."

Marmor testified that there is "absolutely no evidence" at all for contentions of Cameron that homosexuality is infectious and that children who come into contact with gay men and lesbians will become gay themselves.

Marmor noted that the American Psychiatric Association declassified homosexuality in 1973, and that the American Psychological Association, the American Medical Association, and the American Bar Association subsequently all took similar stands.

And Marmor recounted for the court that, for one year prior to the APA vote, a subcommittee of the organization's Council on Research reviewed "all of the available scientific evidence" on the matter and heard reports both in favor and opposed to declassifying it.

"After a year of intensive study," said Marmor, the subcommittee "came to the conclusion that homosexual orientation in and of itself did not constitute a mental illness and so recommended to the board of trustees."

Ironically, Marmor noted, the vote on whether to declassify homosexuality was "taken at the insistence" of those who wanted to see homosexuality retained as a mental illness. Marmor said that he and two other candidates for president of the American Psychiatric Association decided to send out a letter to the APA's membership to support the proposal to declassify it. While he acknowledged that the National Gay Task Force "offered to finance that mailing" and that the three "accepted the financing," he added that "the wish to make it and the idea to make it came from the three of us." Marmor said that 58 percent of the 10,000 APA members who cast votes supported the declassification, and 37 percent opposed it.

"What part of the decision did gay [activists] play to undo this?" asked plaintiffs' attorney Winer.

"The only part they played," said Marmor, "was to finance the mailing of the letter which all three of us candidates sent out. We wrote the letter with—they gave us a form letter which we modified and made suitable to our own needs and which was sent out under our three signatures. The decision was not based on the board's decision nor . . . on gay activists' pressure at all." Marmor further noted that the APA "reaffirmed" that decision as recently as March or April 1993, in an official fact-finding report.

Concerning O'Leaf's survey of psychiatrists in 1977, Marmor said O'Leaf's results were never peer-reviewed, as is routine for scholarly work, by a jury of experts in the field and, like Green, Marmor noted there were no "safeguards" taken to ensure that all 2,500 respondents to O'Leaf's survey were, in fact, psychiatrists.

"They were self-appointed psychiatrists," said Marmor, "and, in any case, the number of people involved were only a quarter of the number of people who voted in the APA election."

Toward the close of his direct examination by Winer, Marmor told the court that he believed Amendment 2 "promotes homophobia and it injures the psychological and emotional health and self-images of thousands" of people with homosexual sexual orientations.

On cross-examination, Wesoky approached Marmor with the entry Marmor had written in the 1988 *Encyclopedia Americana* about which he had already questioned Green. His mission was to have Marmor acknowledge that he had written that factors other than biology influence homosexuality. Marmor was clearly ready for the questions and simply reiterated that, over the years and with new evidence, his opinions had changed.

"In that article," said Wesoky, "you said, did you not, concerning homosexuality, that [sociocausal] factors are also involved?"

"May also be involved, or are," said Marmor. "If I were writing it today, I would say 'may,' but they are, in many cases."

When Wesoky asked Marmor to confirm that he had written in 1988 that the incidence of homosexuality tends to increase due to certain cultural factors, Marmor said he did, but that he "wouldn't ascribe to that in its full form" now.

"But you said it in 1988?" asked Wesoky.

"I did, yes," said Marmor. "I think a good scientist should be able to change his mind with new evidence."

Such new evidence had apparently prompted the *Encyclopedia Americana* to revise its entry on homosexuality several times since 1988. The 1993 version, for instance, described homosexuality not as behavior but rather as "the tendency to be sexually and/or romantically attracted to members of one's own sex." And it said that people "can be homosexual for many different reasons, involving a variety of combinations of constitutional [biological] factors, life experiences, or both." That revised entry, however, was not written by Marmor. The last entry Marmor contributed was the one in 1988.

Apparently hoping to mitigate Marmor's contention that he had, since 1988, acquired "new evidence" about homosexuality, Wesoky quickly noted that Marmor seemed to have changed his mind from 1965 when he edited a book called *Sexual Inversion: The Multiple Roots of Homosexuality*.

Wesoky clearly figured that these changes in Marmor's opinion over time might undermine Marmor's credibility.

"So you are always changing your mind?" asked Wesoky.

Marmor had the perfect comeback.

"The more I know, the more I'm going to change my mind," he said. And concerning the meaning of "homosexuality," Marmor added that, in his encyclopedia entry, he wrote "homosexuality" to mean "homosexual behavior, not homosexual orientation."

Trees and Chimpanzees

Perhaps the most critical witness to the plaintiffs' case that sexual orientation was an immutable characteristic was Dean Hamer, a molecular biologist and chief of the Gene Structure and Regulations Section of the Laboratory of Biochemistry at the National Cancer Institute. Hamer also served as editor of two technical journals, sat on the advisory board for the American Cancer Society, and acquired the patents for a hepatitis B vaccine and a growth hormone. He had authored more than 80 scientific articles and edited two books on the structures of genes. Subsequent to the Amendment 2 trial, Hamer also released *The Science of Desire: The Search for the Gay Gene and the Biology of Behavior*, about his work in this field.

Hamer stated that both his research and that of others caused him to believe "that sexual orientation is not chosen."

"We and others have shown that there's a strong biological component and a genetic component to sexual orientation," said Hamer. "Since people don't choose their genes, they couldn't possibly choose their sexual orientation."

Hamer testified that Charles Darwin in his theory of evolution was the first to suggest that sexuality is an inherited characteristic. Although he did not explain this on the witness stand, in his book *The Science of Desire,* Hamer said that Darwin enunciated this theory in his 1871 book *The Descent of Man, and Selection in Relation to Sex.* Most of the book, wrote Hamer, described a process "whereby natural selection favors certain traits that make either males or females more successful in mating and therefore passing on their genes." Darwin, said Hamer, "seemed quite certain that variations in behavior . . . must be at least partly inherited."

Hamer added that Darwin's theory was further supported by the hypothalamus studies of Simon LeVay and of Laura Allen and Roger Gorski, and by the twin studies conducted by Bailey and Pillard.

Hamer explained to the court that his own research had two phases—a "pedigree" study and a "linkage" study.

The pedigree study, said Hamer, mapped out the "family tree" of each of 76 gay men, who volunteered to participate and gave permission for researchers to contact their relatives. (During cross-examination later, he explained that most of these men were recruited through the HIV clinic at the National Institute of Allergies and Infectious Diseases or through "a gay group" in Washington, D.C. He interviewed each of the men to find out if any of their relatives had ever identified themselves as gay, he interviewed a total of 143 relatives to determine whether they self-identified as heterosexual or homosexual, and then he drew up family trees involving "roughly" a thousand relatives.)

"We found significantly elevated rates of homosexual orientation in three and only three classes of male relatives," said Hamer. Those three classes were brothers, maternal uncles, and maternal cousins. With all other relatives, said Hamer, the incidence of "homosexuality" was "just about" the same as that seen in the general population. (He did not indicate, nor was he asked, what that incidence was.)

The first conclusion derived from this finding, said Hamer, was that the higher incidence of homosexuality could be attributed to genes rather than to environment, since the elevated rates occurred in relatives who were brought up in different households, cities, and circumstances. Another observation about the family trees—that most gay relatives tended to be on the mother's side of the family—led Hamer to his second conclusion.

He said that he hypothesized that "there might be a gene" on the X chromosome that had something to do with homosexual orientation.

A chromosome, explained Hamer, is a long piece of DNA that carries the material that determines inherited characteristics. The X chromosome is a piece of DNA that men inherit only from their mothers.

To test his hypothesis, Hamer did a "linkage" study. He took blood samples from the parents and siblings in 40 families in which he had already identified two gay brothers, and he examined the DNA in them. From those blood samples, he could examine the DNA of each family member's chromosomes, and in that DNA, he could examine their genes. Such an examination has become possible only in recent years because of the development of more sophisticated tests to analyze blood samples.

For Hamer, the new technology enabled him to determine "whether or not two gay sons got the same bit of DNA from their mother." In most areas of the X chromosome, said Hamer, the test showed that the two gay brothers shared the same bits of DNA only 50 percent of the time. But it also showed that in one particular region of the X chromosome, two gay brothers had the same DNA a "large majority" of the time.

"Our interpretation of that result," testified Hamer, "was that that region contains a gene or genes that was involved in their sexual orientation." Hamer said the scientists labeled that region of the DNA "Xq28." The X stands for the X chromosome, the q stands for the long arm of the chromosome, and 28 identifies a specific location, or band, on that arm.

"It's a very, very tiny region at the very tip of a big long sausage-shaped chromosome," explained Hamer.

Hamer acknowledged that the study, thus far, has been performed only on families where there are two gay brothers and that his study has only been able to narrow the search down to a "few million base pairs."

"We haven't identified the single gene that's involved," said Hamer.

"Our DNA is like a forest," explained Hamer. "It has about a hundred thousand trees in it. There's one particular thicket that has the sexual orientation tree, but we haven't gotten to the exact tree yet." Hamer said he will eventually be able to locate that "tree."

"How certain are you of your results that you have actually found the place on the X chromosome that is associated at least with male homosexuality?" asked plaintiffs' attorney Winer.

Hamer said his group did two standard statistical analyses of their data. By one analysis, he said, "there's only one out of 10,000 chance that we are wrong by some fluke." By another, even more careful analysis, he said, there was "at least a 99.5 percent chance that we have identified a linkage for sexual orientation."

Under closer questioning, he explained that, of the 40 pairs of gay brothers, only 33 pairs shared "a set of five markers" in the Xq28 region. Seven pairs of brothers did not. But Hamer said he believes those seven pairs are gay "either because of some other gene that's not on the X chromosome" or "for other biological reasons that are not inherited." He echoed Green's testimony that the prenatal hormonal environment might play a role or that "it could be for other reasons that we don't know."

"From your study," asked Winer, "can you conclude that sexual orientation is completely genetic?"

"No," said Hamer, "it is not completely genetic. We can only conclude that in our set of brothers, 64 percent of them are linked to this." Hamer said the studies of twins conducted by Bailey and Pillard indicated a likelihood of about 50 percent that sexual orientation is genetically determined.

"Most human traits are not genetic," said Hamer. Height, for instance, is only 90 percent genetic; about 10 percent of a person's height is determined by such things as "what you eat when you are a young child," he said. He also noted that some traits, like baldness, are "largely" genetic but do not express themselves until later in life.

Wesoky had made a point with Green and Marmor to illustrate that some heralded findings from the past have later proven unreliable, and Winer apparently anticipated he would try to undermine Hamer's findings by making this same point. She gave Hamer the opportunity to explain that earlier studies did not have the benefit of the more sophisticated techniques that his study used, and that he thinks his results will stand the test of time.

On cross-examination, Wesoky initially tried to undermine the solidity of Hamer's conclusions by referring Hamer to an article by William Byne, a well-respected psychiatrist and neurologist. In an article entitled "Human Sexual Orientation: Biological Theories Reappraised,"[27] Byne criticized the studies by LeVay and by Bailey and Pillard and called into question their conclusions that sexual orientation was somehow biological. But that line of questioning quickly fell flat when Hamer testified that he had recently received a letter from Byne in which Byne "said [Byne's] article flat out does not reject the idea that biology is important."

Wesoky shifted to questioning to what extent behavioral traits are genetic.

"Are all behavioral traits genetically influenced?" asked Wesoky.

"No, they are not," replied Hamer.

"How about temperament? Some people are quick-tempered; some are laid back. Is that genetically influenced?"

"Temperament is actually a very large field of psychology. There are about 40 different traits," said Hamer. "Inheritability has been stud-

---

27. William Byne, "Human Sexual Orientation: The Biological Theories Reappraised," *Archives of General Psychiatry*, 50 (March 1993), 228–39.

ied, and some have some influence, and others have very little, if any."

"Talk about sexual orientation behavior," said Wesoky. "How about like the old 'Gentlemen prefer blondes'; is there something inheritable in a preference for blondes as opposed to brunettes?"

Hamer, with a completely deadpan expression, replied, "I have never heard of any research on that subject."

"Is that possible? Isn't it possible that there's some genetic influence on choice of what your sexual object looks like?" asked Wesoky.

"I don't know of any research on that topic," replied Hamer again. "It would seem extremely unlikely to me."

"How about choice of a thin person as opposed to a larger person as a sexual object," continued Wesoky. "Do you think there's something genetic that influences that choice?"

"I know of no research on that topic," replied Hamer. "It would seem unlikely to me."

By this point in the trial, Wesoky was establishing himself as an unpredictable and colorful sort. He often appeared to be struggling with the complexity of the scientific subject matter—mispronouncing terms, asking Hamer about information that his study was not designed to produce, asking questions that revealed he was misinterpreting data himself, and unwittingly opening a trap door on his own line of questioning about Byne. He also liked to stand in the middle of the courtroom with his left hand on his hip and challenge the witness to use him as a guinea pig. The technique, during questioning with Hamer—which sometimes became quite testy—often produced comical results.

"The percent of DNA shared by human beings—in other words, the DNA similarities between human beings—is how much?" asked Wesoky.

"On average," said Hamer, "each human being shares about 99.9 percent of their DNA with each other human being."

"So my DNA is almost exactly like your DNA?"

"Your DNA is, on average, about .1 percent different from my DNA, and it's about one percent different from a chimpanzee's DNA."

"So, all the difference from the two of us is accounted for by .1 percent?"

"All of the inherited differences of DNA are accounted for [in] that .1 percent, and all of the inherited differences between you and a chimpanzee's are accounted for [in that] one percent DNA. The rest," said Hamer, "is identical."

"Knowing you and me," said Wesoky, "because I don't know many chimpanzees—I'm short and you are taller; that's accounted for by .1 percent of the DNA?"

"It would actually require much less than .1 percent of the DNA. It's within that .1 percent, that's right."

Referring to the fact that Hamer had a full head of hair, Wesoky, who was largely bald, continued, "You have hair; as you notice, I don't. That's accounted for by the same .1 percent?"

"Predominantly," said Hamer, "and possibly some difference in our age and other factors."

"My bone structure appears a little bigger in places than your bone structure," said Wesoky. "That's accounted for by the difference?"

"It's probably accounted for," said Hamer, "somewhere in that three million differences that you and I have."

The point served to emphasize just how complex and mysterious is each human being's nature. Under further cross-examination, Hamer explained that the Xq28 region of DNA, where he believes the sexual orientation "tree" lies, also appears to be responsible for at least 20 other traits, including color blindness, severe mental retardation, and diabetes. The Xq28 region could account for about a hundred or so traits, he said, but scientists had identified only 20 at this point.

As much as science had been able to pin down to a microscopic level certain factors that influence how each person appears and behaves in the world, thus far, it had—like scientists studying fossils to reconstruct the dinosaur age—dusted off only what evidence was nearest the surface. In the dusting off, a whole host of new questions seemed to have emerged, ranging from inquiries into the mix of factors that influences any individual's sexual orientation to examinations of why some people are quicker to experience, understand, and accept their sexual orientations than others. For all that science could answer at the time of the trial or, indeed, at any time in the future, it was unlikely that even the most advanced genetic research could ever fully resolve the question of who gay people are.

Chapter 4

A History of Hate

After trying to nail down the elusive—the origin of sexual orientation—attorneys opposing Amendment 2 next set out to hammer in the
obvious—that gay people have long been subject to discrimination.
This would advance two goals. First, the plaintiffs' legal team needed
to demonstrate that the real purpose of the initiative was to allow discrimination against lesbians, gay men, and bisexuals. This would
undermine the credibility of the state's various other explanations for
Amendment 2 and help prove the absence of a legitimate reason for the
amendment. Second, in arguing that laws singling out gay people for
negative treatment deserve "strict scrutiny" by the courts, the team
sought to prove that there was a history of antigay discrimination and
thereby satisfy one of three indicia on which the U.S. Supreme Court
frequently relied to determine whether a classification of a particular
group was suspect. To make this argument, as the plaintiffs' team
planned, scientists had testified that gay people shared an immutable
characteristic; political scientists would explain they were relatively
politically powerless; and historians had to tell the court that, "as a historical matter," lesbians and gay men "have been subjected to discrimination."

In an important sense, there were no "lesbians and gay men" in
much of recorded history. The term *gay* was not clearly established to
refer to a particular subculture until the early 1960s, although it was
reportedly in use in smaller circles much earlier. In 1951, for instance, a
writer named Donald Webster Cory wrote, in *The Homosexual in America*, that the word was gaining a secret popularity to "express the concept of homosexuality without glorification or condemnation."[1] But
Cory also acknowledged even then that he was not entirely sure where
the term came from. Instead, he said that he had been:

---

1. Neil Miller, *Out of the Past: Gay and Lesbian History from 1869 to the Present* (Vin-
tage Books, 1995), 358.

"told by experts that it came from the French, and that in France as early as the sixteenth century the homosexual was called *gaie*";

informed by "psychoanalysts" that their homosexual patients were calling themselves *gay* in the 1920s; and

advised that "certainly by the 1930s it was the most common word in use among homosexuals themselves."

The term *straight,* according to Jonathan Ned Katz in *The Invention of Heterosexuality,* showed up in 1941 in the glossary of a book about "sex variants" and was defined as meaning "not homosexual."[2]

From Heaven to Hell

According to the late historian John Boswell, who was openly gay, civilization did not have separate concepts and terms for "homosexual" and "heterosexual" in ancient Greece and Rome.

"The majority of residents of the ancient world," he wrote in his book *Christianity, Social Tolerance, and Homosexuality,* "were unconscious of any such categories."[3] That is not to say that men did not have sex with men or that women did not have sex with women during that time. Writings from Plato give evidence they did. Although "Platonic love" today generally refers to nonsexual love between a man and a woman, for Plato, it referred to love between men. Love, to Plato, could be either sexual and thus beget children, or heavenly and beget "offspring of the soul."[4] The Greek poet Sappho, of the isle of Lesbos, wrote hundreds of poems, many of them about her passionate love for women.[5]

In the fourteenth and fifteenth centuries, some religious and polit-

---

2. Jonathan Ned Katz, *The Invention of Heterosexuality,* Dutton, 1995, 12.

3. John Boswell's book, *Christianity, Social Tolerance, and Homosexuality: Gay People in Western Europe from the Beginning of the Christian Era to the Fourteenth Century* (University of Chicago Press, 1980), carries a full discussion of his views and research in this area.

4. Marsilio Ficino's *Commentary on Plato's Symposium* (Columbia, Mo., University of Missouri Studies), translation by Sears Reynolds Jayne; Book 6, Chapter 14, 207–8, excerpted in "'Socratic Love' as a Disguise for Same-Sex Love in the Italian Renaissance," by Giovanni Dall'Orto, in *The Pursuit of Sodomy: Male Homosexuality in Renaissance and Enlightenment Europe,* edited by Kent Gerard and Gert Hekma (Harrington Park Press, 1989), 37.

5. Bernadette J. Brooten delivers an in-depth discussion of evidence of sex between women from Sappho and beyond in *Love between Women: Early Christian Responses to Female Homoeroticism* (University of Chicago Press, 1996).

ical officials tried to discourage nonprocreative sex for a purely practical reason—to encourage baby-making. Saint Bernardino of Florence, Italy, is said to have railed against sodomy in 1424 because a plague had dropped that city's population by two-thirds.[6] Those same concerns were apparently at work, too, in the American colonies of the 1600s to mid-1700s.

"In these formative years," wrote Jonathan Ned Katz, "the New England organization of the sexes and their erotic activity was dominated by a reproductive imperative. These fragile, undeveloped agricultural economies were desperate to increase their numbers, and their labor force." Colonists were severely punished for sodomy (which at the time included anal intercourse only), bestiality, adultery, or even masturbation.

"The operative contrast in this society," wrote Katz, "was between fruitfulness and barrenness, not between different-sex and same-sex eroticism." For that reason, he noted, sex between men might be seen as men wasting their "seed," whereas sex between women was "not apparently thought of as wasting it. . . . So these were lesser violations of the procreative order."

The discouragement of nonprocreative sex took a number of forms. Depending on the country and time, a "sodomite" could be burned at the stake, whipped, imprisoned, hanged, or exiled. Research published in the *Journal of Homosexuality* in 1989 indicates that authorities in Florence in the 1400s used strict supervision to curtail sodomy; in Spain, in the 1500s during the Inquisition, the penalty was death by fire; in the Netherlands in the 1600s sodomites were executed by strangulation; in France in the 1700s they were burned at the stake or exiled to foreign colonies, such as Mississippi.

The first legal definition of sodomy, as a "crime against nature" under English law of the sixteenth century, referred only to anal intercourse and did not specify its application to either same-sex or different-sex activities. This vaguely worded proscription was commonly adopted by the existing state governments in the United States in the eighteenth century and later, and state courts interpreted it in a variety of ways. Some ruled that it included both anal and oral sex; some ruled

---

6. Michael J. Rocke, "Sodomites in Fifteenth-Century Tuscany: The Views of Bernardino of Siena," in *The Pursuit of Sodomy: Male Homosexuality in Renaissance and Enlightenment Europe,* edited by Kent Gerard and Gert Hekma (Harrington Park Press, 1989), 7–31.

it applied only to sex between people of the same sex; some ruled it applied only to sex between two men.[7]

As early as the 1700s, however, some social thinkers in France began protesting such harsh treatment for sodomites. According to sociologist Michel Rey, one French intellectual suggested that sodomy, "when there is no violence involved, cannot be part of the criminal law. It does not violate the rights of anyone."

By 1800, a medical doctor, Frederik Moltke, advised his colleagues to treat people who engage in sodomy "as lunatics or sick persons."[8] That approach gained support and, by the 1860s, medical literature had given this sickness a label and, at the same time, began to differentiate between partners of the same sex engaging in sodomy and partners of different sexes engaging in sodomy. Katz said German writer and attorney Karl Heinrich Ulrichs began giving different names to these people in 1862—identifying the man who loved men as the *Uranier*, the woman who loved women as the *Urninde*, and the man who loved women as *Dionaer*. Katz said Ulrichs's terms were the "foreparents of the heterosexual and homosexual."[9] At this point, explained Katz, there was only one sexual orientation—a sexual attraction of one sex for the other sex. So a *Uranier* was considered to be a person having a female's attraction to men but with the "wrong" body—that is, the body of a man.

The first person to coin the terms *homosexual* and *heterosexual*, said Katz, was a Prussian legal activist and writer named Karl Maria Kertbeny, first in a letter to Ulrichs in 1868, and then publicly in 1869. In this letter, said Katz, Kertbeny also invented the terms *monosexual* and *heterogenit* (referring to masturbation and bestiality).

Katz said, in *The Invention of Heterosexuality*, that the earliest use of the terms *homosexual* and *heterosexual* in the United States came in 1892 from Dr. James Kiernan. According to Katz, Kiernan used the terms in an article called "Responsibility in Sexual Perversion," published in the *Chicago Medical Recorder* in May 1892. In that article, Kiernan credited a professor of psychiatry in Austria named Richard von Krafft-Ebing with using the terms *hetero-sexual* and *homo-sexual* in a medical context in 1889.

7. Arthur S. Leonard, *Sexuality and the Law: An Encyclopedia of Major Legal Cases* (New York: Garland Publishing, 1993), 79.

8. Wilhelm von Rosen, "Sodomy in Early Modern Denmark: A Crime without Victims," *The Pursuit of Sodomy*, 193–94.

9. Jonathan Ned Katz, *The Invention*, 51.

Both terms, said Katz, were used to refer to what doctors considered abnormal sex or perversion; the key element to distinguish *heterosexuality* and *homosexuality* for these doctors seemed to be whether sex was engaged in for purposes other than procreation.

To Kiernan, *heterosexual* referred to people who felt sexual attraction to both men and women. Kiernan used *homosexual* to describe people whose "general mental state is that of the opposite sex." Both were considered sick.

But to Krafft-Ebing, a *hetero-sexual* was attracted to a person of the other sex and was normal as long as he or she had at least an implicit desire for reproduction while engaging in sex. This attraction to the other sex, whether conscious or implicit in its desire for reproduction, amounted to a sexual orientation.

"The idea of a given, physiological sexual orientation ('healthy' or 'sick,' 'normal' or 'abnormal')," wrote Katz, became a dominant hypothesis of modern sexual theory.

In contrast to Plato's thoughts of "heavenly" love between men, and sexual love to beget children, Krafft-Ebing, noted Katz, would have it that same-sex love was "judged a lowly emotion" while procreative sex might be "judged heavenly."

The concept of sickness launched a quest to find a cause and cure. Notably, there was no parallel search for a cause and cure for heterosexuality even though, noted historian Katz, doctors in the 1890s also referred to the "heterosexual" as a pervert if he or she engaged in sex for reasons that were not clearly intended for reproduction.

"Medical views" of homosexuality, wrote another openly gay historian, John D'Emilio, in *Sexual Politics, Sexual Communities*, "bore a complex relation to the older perspectives of religion and law. In important ways, they reinforced the cultural matrix that condemned and punished persons who engaged in homosexual activity. Whether seen as a sin, crime, or sickness, homosexuality stigmatized an individual. . . . the language of the moralist permeated the scientific literature."[10]

Sigmund Freud suggested that homosexuality involved a narcissistic search for a love object that symbolized oneself, plus a fear of castration in men or penis envy in women, and an identification with the parent of the other sex that provoked fear of incest. Richard von

---

10. John D'Emilio, *Sexual Politics, Sexual Communities* (University of Chicago Press, 1983), 17.

Krafft-Ebing believed homosexuality was a hereditary disease caused by domination of the wrong brain center. Another researcher suggested that heterosexuals developed out of close, preadolescent friendships with peers of the same sex while homosexuals resulted from the inability to separate lust from intimacy. Even in 1901, "heterosexuality" was defined in *Dorland's Medical Dictionary* as an "abnormal or perverted appetite toward the opposite sex"—the abnormal part being an appetite separate from the desire to procreate, noted Katz.

History on Trial

To make its case that gay people had suffered a long history of discrimination, attorneys for the plaintiffs called on George Chauncey, an assistant professor of history at the University of Chicago. Chauncey taught courses on the history of "the lives of ordinary people" in the United States, including gay people. His specialties were the history of gender and sexuality and gay history. Plaintiffs' attorney Jeanne Winer conducted the direct examination of Chauncey on the witness stand. She asked him to start in the seventeenth century in the United States and give the court an overview of how "homosexual conduct" was treated in the colonies. Chauncey testified that a "handful of people were executed in the seventeenth century for sodomy" and that there were no known records of executions in the eighteenth or nineteenth centuries, "so that's an improvement."

"There are records of severe beatings, whippings, and so forth for people who had been convicted of engaging in sodomy," he said.

Chauncey explained that, in the 1800s, as medical science was fashioning its attitude about homosexuality and a host of other phenomena, scientists frequently sought biological explanations for already established social arrangements.

"For instance," said Chauncey, "many arguments were made by doctors that women would be unable to pursue an education or take on certain kinds of jobs because that would take away their reproductive capacities."

Early thought on homosexuality, he said, regarded homosexuals as people who had "inverted" their gender.

"So someone who looked like a male but was attracted to men wasn't really a male," said Chauncey, "but was some sort of hermaphrodite."

Looking at some of the scientific developments from a historian's perspective, Chauncey explained that, whatever the theory, homosexuality was commonly considered both a rare and troublesome illness, and, as late as the 1950s and 1960s, the "treatments" commonly included everything from frontal lobotomy and electroshock therapy to using nausea-inducing drugs and pain for "aversion therapy."

It wasn't until the famous Kinsey studies of the late 1940s and 1950s that people began to realize that same-sex relations were more common than originally understood. With the Hooker studies of the 1960s, they began to grasp that many people with a homosexual orientation could live open and well-adjusted lives. By 1973, when the American Psychiatric Association declared that homosexuality was not a mental illness, science had done its part to establish same-sex relations as a naturally occurring variance in the human population. The group of people who experienced this variance, however, had much further to go to establish themselves as a naturally accepted part of society.

Hidden Culture

"What do people mean when they talk about a lesbian and a gay subculture?" plaintiffs' attorney Winer asked Chauncey.

Chauncey said the term referred to a "nexus of social networks, meeting places, community, and institutions, collective culture norms and the like, that categorize people."

Such a subculture had begun developing in a number of American cities in the United States by the end of the nineteenth century, said Chauncey. The gay subculture, he testified, seemed to grow "with the growing size of cities, the growing numbers of single people, large neighborhoods, transient people living outside the family." Most of this subculture was hidden, noted Chauncey.

"Most people took enormous care to keep their participation in the [gay] subculture secret, to make sure that their everyday associates at work, family members, neighbors, and the like, did not know they were gay," explained Chauncey, "yet, there were certain parts of the city where remarkably visible subcultures developed around the turn of the century."

"It's almost as if there were two subcultures, side-by-side," he said.

Chauncey outlined the development of political groups from out of these subcultures. The first, he noted, started in Chicago in 1924 when an American soldier who had been stationed in Germany during World War I decided to begin here what he had seen there: a group to seek equal treatment for people who were homosexual. In Germany, the group had been called the Society for Human Rights, and it published a newspaper called *Friendship and Freedom.*

This, however, was in 1924, and the members of the Chicago group considered themselves, as did society in general, to have "mental and physical abnormalities." Nevertheless, their aim was to combat public prejudice. The Chicago group's first president was Rev. John T. Graves, a minister who preached to small groups of African-Americans. And although Chauncey did not mention this in his testimony, the Chicago-based group even got a legal charter from the state of Illinois.[11]

In addition to Graves, there were six other names attached to the charter application, all men. One of those men, Henry Gerber, provided the details of the group's fate in a letter he wrote in 1962 to a gay magazine. In that letter, Gerber explained that the society's work came to an abrupt halt after less than a month when its members were arrested for mailing the group's newsletter through the mail. Authorities said the newsletter—whose content Gerber described as strictly political—was obscene. Although the charges against the members were ultimately dismissed, Gerber lost his job as a postal worker and the group quickly disbanded. Chauncey noted in his testimony that no copies of the Chicago *Friendship and Freedom* newsletter survived.

No other organizations emerged until after World War II. Then, after World War II, said Chauncey, two types of groups developed. First, there was a group of gay veterans who organized to try to upgrade their discharges from the military. Second, he noted, was the Mattachine Society.

Although Chauncey was not asked to elaborate on the Mattachine Society, the group was important historically as the first enduring gay political group in the United States. It was founded in November 1950 in Los Angeles by Harry Hay, a man who, at the time, was married and had two children. The name "Mattachine" came from the name of a band of unmarried people in medieval France who wore masks while performing protest comedies.

Like their predecessors in Chicago, the members of the Mattachine

---

11. Jonathan Ned Katz, *Gay and Lesbian Almanac* (New York: Harper and Row, 1983).

Society in Los Angeles in 1950 also considered themselves to have "physiological and psychological handicaps." Their purpose was to foster an "ethical homosexual culture . . . paralleling the emerging cultures of our fellow minorities—the Negro, Mexican, and Jewish Peoples." They anticipated chapters springing up around the country, but they also expected their membership would remain anonymous.

As their numbers grew, so did their internal conflicts and worries. One worry was about Hay, who, at the time he founded the group, was also involved with the Communist Party. At this time, Senator Joseph McCarthy and his House Committee on Un-American Activities were vigorously pursuing Communists and "homosexuals." Hay quit his Communist Party activities to protect the gay group, but two Mattachine members were still called before the Committee on Un-American Activities, and many of Mattachine's anonymous members grew uneasy that the group would be associated with Communism. Some feared the Communist Party would attempt to blackmail Mattachine members and use Mattachine to infiltrate the American political system. By April 1952, the worries were great enough that Hay felt pressured to resign from Mattachine.

Of course, there were plenty of other risks to being a member of the Mattachine Society or of the groups that quickly followed it. Chauncey testified that members of these early groups lived with a "tremendous fear" that they would lose their jobs if their employers found out about their affiliation. Beginning in 1953, the Federal Bureau of Investigation "conducted exhaustive and apparently illegal surveillance of the gay rights movement and its leaders," according to journalist Randy Shilts, in an article in the *San Francisco Chronicle*.[12]

FBI agents "made extensive use of informants," wrote Shilts, "tape-recorded meetings, collected lists of members of gay organizations, photographed participants in early homosexual rights marches and investigated advertisers in gay publications." According to Shilts, J. Edgar Hoover, the FBI director at that time, justified these investigations by citing an executive order from President Dwight Eisenhower. That executive order, No. 10450, said that "the interests of the national security require that all persons privileged to be employed in the departments and agencies of the Government shall be reliable, trustworthy, of good conduct and character, and of complete and unswerv-

---

12. Randy Shilts, "How FBI Spied on Gays: 20 Years of Secret Files," *San Francisco Chronicle*, September 21, 1989, A-1.

ing loyalty to the United States."[13] The order identified security risks to include persons with "any criminal, infamous, dishonest, immoral, or notoriously disgraceful conduct, habitual use of intoxicants to excess, drug addiction, or sexual perversion."

It directed the head of every federal department and agency to investigate each of its civilian employees and that each employee's fingerprints be checked with the FBI. Shilts found one FBI memorandum indicating that Hoover turned over the names collected by FBI surveillance to the U.S. Civil Service Commission, which used the information to purge gay people from its employee ranks.

In addition to the risks associated with merely meeting or belonging to a gay organization, the gay groups also faced difficulty in trying to disseminate information to their members through newsletters and other publications. The FBI, for example, implored postal authorities to block the Mattachine Society from mailing its monthly magazine, *One*. The magazine's staff was able to thwart this directive, however, by dropping its 600 mailed subscriptions in several different postal boxes throughout Los Angeles.

In his testimony before the Colorado court, Chauncey recounted a historic battle of *One* magazine in court. That battle began in October 1954, when the Los Angeles postmaster refused to forward copies of the magazine, claiming the publication constituted "filthy" and "obscene" pornography and that mailing it violated federal laws against using postal services for distribution of such material. The magazine sued and lost in the lower federal courts. But in January 1958, the U.S. Supreme Court—without ever hearing oral argument in the case and with no written opinion to explain why—summarily reversed the federal appeals court decision.[14]

Whether their names were on a list or their faces were at a meeting, gay people in these early years in the United States, said Chauncey, constantly faced the fear of arrest and loss of employment if identified as homosexual. And, ironically, he pointed out, Colorado had its own specific history in this regard:

> Mattachine had a national conference every year over the Labor Day weekend, and in 1959, when it was held on the East Coast,

---

13. *Federal Register*, vol. 18, no. 82, April 29, 1953, 2489–92.
14. *One, Inc. v. Olesen*, 355 U.S. 371 (1958).

they decided to have their sixth conference here, in Denver. And it was considered a tremendous breakthrough to get [the meeting] off the coast. . . . it was the first time that they had dared to have a public press conference where they didn't use pseudonyms and [they] allowed the press to come in, and they felt they got reasonably good coverage in the *Denver Post* especially. Three or four weeks later, three of the organizers of that conference had their homes raided by Denver police. One of them was arrested; he later lost his job. The mailing list to the organization [and other] records were seized by the police.

Even beyond the political tug-of-war, other constraints worked against publishing materials for lesbians and gay men. Chauncey discussed the ruckus around publication of the lesbian novel, *The Well of Loneliness*, by Radclyffe Hall. The book, he noted, was published in 1928 and "instantly suppressed in England."

It was, for many women, the first book ever to mention lesbians—albeit as "inverts"—and provided confirmation that there were women loving women in the world. But when a book house tried to publish it in the United States, police in New York seized the copies and the publisher was taken to trial for obscenity.

In film, gay characters were "usually used to ridicule gay people," said Chauncey, and these films, too, were considered obscene. When Hollywood adopted the Production Code for censoring films in 1934, "something like homosexuality could not appear at all." That lasted until 1960, said Chauncey.

Stage plays, too, had their difficulties.

"There were, in the mid-twenties, two or three plays," said Chauncey, that "were either produced on the New York stage or there was an effort to bring them to the New York stage. One [was] a serious French drama, *The Captive*, about a lesbian teen. Another production, by Mae West, was called *The Drag*.

"The police raided *The Captive* after it made money for a while; kept *The Drag* from coming into the city," said Chauncey, adding that, "in response to this controversy, the state legislature passed a law which prohibited any stage from presenting a play in which sex perversion or sex degeneracy, i.e., homosexuality, was represented on threat of . . . losing access to the theatre, having it padlocked for a year. So there was tremendous consequence."

In the 1930s, around the time of the Production Code, a number of jurisdictions adopted laws, in an attempt to garner support for repealing Prohibition, that promised to limit the congregation of unpopular groups around the consumption of alcohol. In New York City, noted Chauncey, the state liquor authority ruled that "for a bar or restaurant or theater or cabaret or any other place that had a liquor license to serve a drink to a single homosexual or to allow homosexuals to gather on the premises made that place disorderly and could lose the license of the place."

"How would they know that they had served a glass of beer to a homosexual?" asked Winer.

"Well, this is precisely the question that many bar owners came back to the state liquor authority with," said Chauncey. "So, a wide range of behaviors were sometimes pointed to: One man trying to pick up another man, men talking about opera, women wearing trousers in a bar indicated it was probably a lesbian. . . . The way men wore their hair, the way women wore their hair. Someone saying, 'I'm a homosexual.' So, a fairly wide range. But it's clear on the basis of my review of all the court literature—reports from the thirties, forties, and fifties— that the point was to imply that they were closing the bar because homosexuals had been allowed to gather there. . . . most bar owners would not challenge it. It was expensive because they always did lose in courts."

License and Law

Police used the disorderly conduct law to prosecute a wide range of activities, testified Chauncey. For instance, in 1923, disorderly conduct laws were used to raid private parties. There were also licensing regulations for bars that required applicants to be fingerprinted.

"So, if they had ever been arrested in any sort of homosexual context—being at a gay bar or whatever," said Chauncey, "they could be kept from having a license" to operate a bar.

Chauncey said he calculated that in New York City more than 50,000 gay men were arrested over the course of 40 years. Of the 70 gay men he interviewed while researching his doctoral dissertation, "half of them had been arrested at some point in their lives [on] a homosexual charge, which is just a stunning figure."

While records about these types of arrests are fairly common, said

Chauncey, there are very few records demonstrating violence against gay men and lesbians in the early twentieth century.

"Records weren't kept" about incidents of violence against gay people, said Chauncey. "We know it was a problem, but it's hard to say."

The history of discrimination against gay people in the military can be tracked historically to World War I, said Chauncey, when a servicemember could be court-martialed for engaging in sodomy. But a simple declaration of one's homosexuality was not a problem until World War II, when the military sought to exclude people self-identified as homosexual. "Psychiatrists were brought in as the experts," said Chauncey, "who would confirm a diagnosis, but [a diagnosis of homosexuality] initially depended on self-declaration. . . . And they also decided to give homosexuals an undesirable discharge."[15]

Following World War II, said Chauncey, there was again a dramatic increase in the number of gay-related arrests in cities around the country. "In the late forties, more than 3,000 men were arrested in a single year in New York City alone," Chauncey testified. "In Philadelphia, they arrested more than 200 a month. In southern California, they established special police squads to deal with homosexuals. And in Boise, Idaho, an investigation began . . . after there was a charge—a man charged with having sex with three teenagers—that led the police to interrogate 1,400 residents of Boise, forcing gay people to name names of friends. Literally, swarms of people fled the city and left their jobs and belongings behind."

The escalation in arrests after World War II, explained Chauncey, was "linked to other kinds of hostility" against homosexuals, most notoriously the hearings orchestrated by McCarthy and the House Committee on Un-American Activities.

"He supposedly had the names of [gay] men," said Chauncey. "In

---

15. Although psychiatrists are no longer brought in to confirm a self-declaration of homosexuality, this policy of excluding openly gay servicemembers remains essentially intact today, through a law signed by President Clinton after passing with overwhelming support from Congress in July 1993, just prior to the Amendment 2 trial. Under the 1993 law, servicemembers who identify themselves as being homosexual are presumed to engage in a wide range of prohibited sexual conduct the military identified with homosexuality. Unless the gay servicemember can somehow prove that he or she will never engage in such conduct, he or she is discharged. By contrast, a servicemember who indicates he or she is heterosexual is not presumed to engage in the prohibited conduct related to sex and is not made to prove that he or she will never engage in such conduct.

fact, he put so much pressure on that issue that a special subcommittee was established which published a report in December of 1950 called 'On the Employment of Homosexuals and Other Sex Perverts in Government,' which traced the number of people that had been discharged [and] argued there needed to be stricter regulations on homosexuals. The number of people who had been discharged averaged about five a month before this ban; it leapt to 60 a month after that."

While Joseph McCarthy's campaign to smoke out homosexuals and Communists was the most notorious of its time, as Chauncey testified, there was another campaign which he was not asked to chronicle. That campaign was launched in February 1950 by two other senators after a State Department official revealed that the department had "allowed" 91 employees to resign "for personal reasons" and that the majority of those had been homosexuals. Senator Lister Hill of Alabama and Kenneth Wherry of Nebraska embarked on their own inquiry into how many "sex perverts" were working for the federal government. Many of the documents surrounding their investigation were ordered sequestered in the National Archives until the year 2000. But both senators released their own separate reports about their investigation. Senator Wherry urged the Senate to take action.

"The obligation upon society to eradicate this menace and to lift the minds of moral perverts from the extreme depth of depravity to which they have sunk is recognized," wrote Wherry. "But while this wholesome and necessary process is fostered, there should be expeditious action to ensure that the departments and agencies of our government are cleansed of moral perverts, especially to guard and protect security secrets upon which the life of our beloved country may depend."

Senator Hill also felt society had to do something about homosexuals. But he thought the Senate should pass legislation to provide for the medical treatment and rehabilitation of gay people.

The Senate did do something. On May 19, 1950, it passed Resolution No. 280, authorizing another investigation. This one was to look into the employment of homosexuals by the federal government. Hearings, again mostly behind closed doors, began in mid-June under the supervision of Senator Clyde Hoey of North Carolina. In December, the Hoey Commission issued a report saying that 4,954 homosexuals had been discovered: 4,380 in the military and 574 in federal civilian jobs. In writing about this investigation, D'Emilio noted that 192 homosexuals were dismissed from their federal jobs from 1947 through April 1, 1950. The bulk of the 574 in civilian jobs (382) were dismissed in the next seven months alone. In addition, 1,700 job applicants were rejected between 1947 and August 1950 because of "sexual perversion." But D'Emilio said the actual numbers were likely much greater because many departments allowed such employees to resign rather than be fired.

"In 1951," noted D'Emilio, "the State Department fired only 2 employees based on evidence of homosexual conduct. But, during the same period, 117 other State Department employees resigned rather than face a full investigation on allegations of homosexuality."

The commission concluded that there were two reasons to prohibit homosexuals from working for the government: "First, they are generally unsuitable, and second, they constitute security risks." (Thirty-five years later, in 1985, another congressional investigation would come to the exact opposite conclusion of Hoey's Commission.)[16] The conclusions were readily accepted. In 1953, newly elected president Dwight Eisenhower took office and within three months signed Executive Order No. 10450, which had the effect of firing gay people from federal employment.

In an article about the federal government's official policies toward gay people, D'Emilio noted that the Eisenhower order replaced one that originated with President Harry S. Truman in March 1947. Truman's Executive Order No. 9835 authorized investigations of government employees to make sure the employees had "complete and unswerving loyalty" to the United States and that they were not members of "subversive" organizations. In August 1950, said D'Emilio, Congress expanded on Truman's "loyalty" requirement, allowing for the dismissal of employees whose "behavior, moral character, or personal associations made them appear a danger to national security."[17] The Eisenhower order also applied to private companies that had contracts with the federal government.

Chauncey testified about the Eisenhower order, noting that, at the

16. "Preliminary Joint Staff Study of the Protection of National Secrets" was prepared by the House Subcommittee on Civil and Constitutional Rights and the House Subcommittee on Post Office and Civil Service. It was released in October 1985. See "Little-Noticed Report," by Lou Chibbaro Jr., *Washington Blade*, August 1, 1986, 8.

17. John D'Emilio, "The Evolution and Impact of Federal Antihomosexual Policies during the 1950s," March 1983.

time of the order, about a fifth of the work force was employed by private companies that had federal contracts.

"Because of the federal ban on homosexual employment, any number of companies which might have chosen to behave differently were required to fire their homosexual employees," Chauncey testified. "And I think much more generally that the number of federal officials, state, and local officials, who spoke against homosexuality, who warned about the dangers of homosexuality and the like, tended to demonize homosexuals to increase public antipathy toward them."

Out of this general trend of "demonizing" gay people, there developed, said Chauncey, a "general association" of gay people with child molestation.

"In the course of a few months," he testified, "more than 20 states passed laws which . . . allowed courts to order a psychiatric examination of someone convicted of an offense or simply suspected in some states of being a sex deviant which could lead them to be incarcerated indefinitely in psychopath hospitals until their homosexuality had been cured."

The FBI began "cooperating" in this effort, said Chauncey, "to try to get names" of employees in federal jobs.

"Once the gay organizations were established," he noted, "their meetings were sometimes ended by plainclothes investigators. . . ."

"Were they looking for communists or homosexuals?" asked Winer.

"They were looking for homosexuals here," said Chauncey.

Chauncey testified that although "most lesbians and gay men did take very special care to remain very secretive" about their being homosexual, they were vulnerable nearly everywhere.

"They were still in a situation of possibly going to a gay bar once and having it raided. They were in the situation of possibly going to a private party in a private apartment and having it raided and being taken to the police station. They were in the situation of having people lying for them. There was—people hid, but it was sometimes difficult to hide during this period," said Chauncey.

"So if they just stayed home and kept their door shut and didn't do anything, they might be okay?" asked Winer.

"If they just stayed home and didn't read anything related to gays and didn't do anything and never said I'm a homosexual, [they] probably would survive," said Chauncey. "Yes."

A Turning Point

Chauncey noted that this institutionalized hostility toward gay people continued and, in some places, escalated in the 1960s. "In the context of growing civil rights movements for blacks, women, and the like" in the mid-1960s, he stated, "more successful efforts were made to try to curtail some of that police harassment of the gay world. And as courts became more scrupulous about the protection of due process, equal protection, and the like, some of the legislation governing gay bars in some states was eliminated."

According to Chauncey, some laws hostile to gay men and lesbians—like those prohibiting the sale of alcoholic beverages to homosexuals—were slow to die. In fact, some of the laws that emerged in the 1930s as a way of gaining support for the repeal of Prohibition only recently have been repealed. For instance, a Virginia law that promised to keep "undesirables" out of the bars—including homosexuals, pimps, panderers, drunks, and "B-girls"—noted Chauncey, was in place until 1991 when a federal judge declared it unconstitutional.

Even when laws did not target gay people explicitly, police would enforce some general laws specifically against gay people—laws concerned with disorderly conduct, public indecency, and censorship—and that, too, was slow to change.

In Denver, said Chauncey, police used public indecency laws to harass lesbians and gay men.

"Here in Denver," he said, "in 1974, the Colorado Gay Alliance signed an agreement with the police department of Denver in settlement of a suit that they filed in '73, charging a pattern of harassment and of selective discriminatory enforcement of a public indecency [law]. In the settlement agreement, the police department said it would stop going through gay bars and arresting two people simply over holding hands or arrest people for stealing a kiss."

But, instead, those arrests doubled within a year of the settlement, he said. In addition, police stood outside the city's most popular gay bar and gave out jaywalking tickets to "everyone who left the bar."

It was this sort of police harassment that triggered a turning point in American gay social history in June 1969 when patrons of a gay bar in New York City's Greenwich Village, known as the Stonewall Inn, erupted into riots during a police raid. Police documents indicate that undercover officers entered the bar on the evening of June 27, 1969, and determined that it was operating without a license. But gay activists believed police were enforcing the license law selectively against gay bars. According to gay people who frequented the Stonewall and other bars at the time, the Mafia operated many gay bars and paid off police to leave them alone. One of the Stonewall's two bouncers recalled that the owners paid police $1,200 a month in payoffs to avoid being raided.[18]

On June 27, however, there was apparently no payoff, and the undercover team called headquarters for additional officers to help make arrests. According to eyewitness accounts, the raid was proceeding in a routine, almost festive, manner around midnight. Having sequestered the patrons inside, the police had begun releasing them one by one. *Village Voice* reporters Howard Smith and Lucian Truscott IV gave this account:

> As the patrons trapped inside were released one by one, a crowd started to gather on the street. It was initially a festive gathering, composed mostly of Stonewall boys who were waiting around for friends still inside or to see what was going to happen. Cheers would go up as favorites would emerge from the door, strike a pose, and swish by the detective with a "Hello, there, fella." . . . Suddenly the paddywagon arrived and the mood of the crowd changed. . . .
>
> Three of the more blatant queens—in full drag—were loaded inside [the police wagon] along with the bartender and doorman, to a chorus of catcalls and boos from the crowd. A cry went up to push the paddywagon over, but it drove away before anything could happen. With its exit, the action waned momentarily. The next person to come out was a dyke and she put up a struggle from car door to car again. It was at that moment that the scene became explosive. . . . Beer cans and bottles were heaved at the windows, and a rain of coins descended on the cops. At the height of the action, a bearded figure was plucked from the crowd and dragged inside. . . .

18. Lisa M. Keen, "The Stonewall Rebellion: For the First Time, Gays Fought Back," *Washington Blade*, June 9, 1989, Pride Guide, 7. Bouncer Ed Murphy wrote about his account of working at the Stonewall in the June 1989 issue of the New York SAGE newsletter as part of the History Project of Senior Action in a Gay Environment shortly before his death.

Almost by signal the crowd erupted into cobblestone and bottle heaving. . . . The trashcan I was standing on was nearly yanked out from under me as a kid tried to grab it for use in the window smashing melee. From nowhere came an uprooted parking meter—used as a battering ram on the Stonewall door. I heard several cries of "Let's get some gas," but the blaze of flame which soon appeared in the window of the Stonewall was still a shock.[19]

At that moment, additional police reinforcements arrived to regain control over the scene and rescue the many police officers who were still inside the bar itself.

As Chauncey suggested, the Stonewall riot that night and the riots that ensued in the days following it became a catalyst for gay people to fight back against abuse from police and other authorities. But the riots did not end police raids in New York City, as police records show. Just months after the Stonewall rebellion, police arrested and herded 167 patrons of another gay bar into the local police precinct. One of the patrons, a gay man who had immigrated from Venezuela, was so distraught over the likelihood that his arrest would result in his deportation, that he leaped from a second-floor window of the police station. His body was found impaled on a wrought-iron fence post below. He survived, but his plight and the continuing raids fueled more protests and more gay political organizing.

"It was a time when people were rioting all over the country," noted Chauncey.

Even though a gay political movement had been organized and operating since the beginning of the Mattachine Society in the 1950s, those riots at Stonewall, said Chauncey, are frequently referred to as the "beginning of the militant gay movement." Before the Stonewall rebellion, there had been only a dozen and a half gay groups around the country; within three months of the riot, there were, according to *Newsweek* magazine, at least 50 more.

Chauncey added that the Mattachine Society "pretty much disappeared" in the 1970s, when a "new generation of gay groups took shape." At the same time, a handful of gay publications from the existing groups were suddenly joined by a string of regional newspapers for the gay community. Coverage in the mainstream media jumped, too. In

---

19. Howard Smith, "Full Moon Over Stonewall," and Lucian Truscott IV, "Gay Power Comes to Sheridan Square," *Village Voice*, July 3, 1969, 1.

the 20 years before Stonewall, there were only 10 magazine articles written about homosexuality in the general press; in the 18 months after Stonewall, there were 18. Only about 100 books had been written on the topic from 1901 until 1968, but within five years after Stonewall that number doubled.

Life for gay people in the United States did improve after the Stonewall riots, said Chauncey. One reason for the improvement, he said, had been "a kind of polarization in American society on gay issues so that there are a growing number of cities, college towns, and the like, where people feel much safer than they did 25 years ago." More people feel safe identifying as gay publicly, he said, because there are fewer sanctions against them now. There were also a growing number of laws to prohibit discrimination against them where, before Stonewall, there had been none.

A Second Wind

But the plaintiffs' attorneys had to do more than demonstrate a history of discrimination against gay people; they had to prove that such discrimination was still a significant threat. To this end, Chauncey testified that many states continued up to the present to criminalize consensual sexual activity between two adults of the same sex. (At the time of the trial, at least 22 states still had enforceable sodomy laws on the books.) Studies had also shown "a fairly dramatic increase" in violent attacks against gay men and lesbians over time. That violent backlash "became really visible" in 1977, noted Chauncey, when a former Miss America runner-up, Anita Bryant, launched a highly public and hostile political campaign to repeal the Dade County, Florida, ordinance that prohibited discrimination based on sexual orientation. It was one of about a dozen such laws passed by city governments in the years following Stonewall.

Bryant's campaign, just eight years after Stonewall, became a second major turning point in the gay civil rights movement. Within three months of the law's passage, her "Save the Children" campaign had gathered enough signatures to put a repeal measure before the voters. Bryant argued that gay people wanted the new law to gain jobs as teachers and "recruit" children into the "gay life-style." She said homosexuality was a sin and that "the Lord" called on her to fight this law. Her high profile as the commercial spokesperson for Florida's orange juice industry gave the campaign quick national visibility, and on June

7, 1977, Dade County voters repealed the law. When Bryant took her campaign to other cities where such laws had been passed, the voters in each city repealed the laws.

Gay people fought back by staging protests at her various public appearances and calling for a national boycott on Florida orange juice. The attention soon made Bryant the brunt of many jokes and, within a year, her repeal efforts began to fail at the ballot box, as did a highly visible initiative to ban gay people from being teachers in California. But the ballot battles did not go away. Over the next 14 years, 25 more ballot measure campaigns were waged against various local laws prohibiting discrimination based on sexual orientation and two-thirds of those repeal measures passed.

Then, in November 1992, a new antigay initiative effort raised the stakes. Instead of seeking only to repeal an existing law, the measures—including the Colorado Amendment 2 initiative—sought also to prevent any future laws from prohibiting discrimination against gay citizens.

Chauncey said he thought voters approved Colorado's ballot measure for two reasons: one, as a general backlash against the gay civil rights movement's limited successes; and, two, because proponents of the initiatives were successful in convincing the public that the gay civil rights movement was seeking "special rights."

"A campaign which most people would think of as being protecting [gay people] from discrimination . . . is characterized as a campaign . . . for special rights—that [gay people]," said Chauncey, "are going to be able to do something that other people aren't allowed to do."

National Backlash

Chauncey was also asked to testify about the recent gay civil rights struggle on the national level—a struggle that, like Amendment 2, harkened back to the November 1992 ballot. While running for president during 1992, Arkansas governor Bill Clinton made public statements indicating that he considered the ban against gay people in the military to be discriminatory. Shortly after being elected, he was asked by reporters whether he intended to follow through on a campaign promise to gay voters that he would end the ban.

"Yes, I want to," said Clinton. "My position is that we need everybody in America that has got a contribution to make, that's willing to obey the law and work hard and play by the rules. That's the way I feel." The *New York Times* reported that Clinton added that he would consult with armed services chiefs to determine the timing and the best way to go about repealing the ban that originated 50 years earlier out of a now-abandoned belief that homosexuality was a mental disorder.

But even before Clinton was sworn in, right-wing groups began organizing to oppose any change in the policy. In January 1993, Operation Rescue organized demonstrations in cities throughout the country to protest the idea. Former Moral Majority leader Jerry Falwell broadcast a nationwide television program against the inclusion of gay people in the military on Sunday, January 17—just three days before president-elect Bill Clinton took office.

When Clinton finally made his first official move on the matter, on January 29, 1993, he directed Secretary of Defense Les Aspin to consult with military and congressional leaders about it. But the military and key members of Congress had already indicated publicly that they would fight any attempt to repeal the ban, and the national fight over whether gay people should be permitted to serve in the military was on.

Ultimately, Clinton never issued an executive order. Aspin issued a directive that gay men and lesbians could stay in the military so long as they kept their sexual orientation secret and remained celibate both on and off duty. By July, Clinton was talking compromise and endorsed an even more restrictive version of this "new" policy fashioned by U.S. senator Sam Nunn, a Democrat from Georgia. Under the new policy, any acknowledgment of being gay was sufficient grounds for discharge based on the "presumption" that a gay servicemember had a "propensity" to violate the military law's prohibition on "homosexual conduct." The only way such a servicemember could stay in the military would be to rebut that presumption. Heterosexual servicemembers, however, did not have to rebut any presumption that they might engage in sodomy.

In September, Congress passed the Nunn policy and Clinton signed the measure into law.

Attorneys opposing Amendment 2 sought to use the debate over gay people in the military as an example of the widespread discrimination against gay men and lesbians in the United States. Plaintiffs' attorney Winer asked Chauncey, "As a historian, how do you view the recent decision by the Clinton administration not to overturn the ban on gays in the military?" Could it be, she asked, similar to the backlash campaign by Anita Bryant against gay civil rights protections?

"It is," said Chauncey. "I actually think I would say that [Clinton] made two miscalculations which are quite telling. First of all, he did not begin to grasp the depth of antigay hostility in American society. It's very difficult for people who aren't gay . . . to grasp it, just as it's very difficult for people who aren't black to grasp the everyday indignities that black people face in society. So, I think it's clear in the way that he talked about it in his campaign and his assurance about it right after his election and after the inauguration, he had no idea he would get the response he did. And secondly, I think he thought that the gay political movement was more powerful and more effective than it proved to be in that case, where it was clearly . . . outgunned, outmaneuvered by the opposition."

That was not the first time gay people had lost a battle against discrimination at the national level. Even after the witch-hunts for gay people in federal employment in the 1950s, the federal government had made gay people the object of official exclusion. Between 1977 and 1981, Congress passed several measures to prohibit the federal Legal Services Corporation from taking on any cases alleging antigay discrimination. When the District of Columbia government repealed its sodomy law in 1981, Congress—which has control over the D.C. government—overturned that action and reinstated the law. And on the day after lesbians and gay men took part in a mammoth national march on Washington in 1987 to demonstrate their expectation of equal rights, the Senate, on a 94 to 2 vote, approved an amendment introduced by Senator Jesse Helms, a Republican from North Carolina, to prohibit the use of federal funds to support any educational effort—even AIDS prevention—that would appear to "encourage, or promote . . . sexual activities outside of a sexually monogamous marriage." But, no state, of course, allowed a same-sex couple to obtain a marriage license.

Attorneys challenging Amendment 2 also sought to show how the historical stigma against gay people was costing lives currently. They brought to the stand Marcus Conant, an internationally known expert in treating AIDS and a physician with the largest private AIDS practice in San Francisco. Conant testified that prejudice against gay people had made some physicians "unwilling" to care for people with AIDS. Because people with AIDS were often perceived to be gay, said Conant, prejudice against gay people had also made some people "hesitant to come forward and be tested because of fear of discrimination which can result in loss of [their] friends, loss of [their] home, and more importantly, loss of [their] job to which is tied health care insurance."

"If people are afraid to come in and be tested," said Conant, "they don't find out they are infected, they engage in denial which is well documented in the National Commission on AIDS report, and because of that denial they may have unsafe sex, they may transmit the disease."

Reasons and Relativity

While the plaintiffs had certainly made a case that there was a long history of discrimination against gay men and lesbians and that that discrimination continued, their job was not yet over. The state and its witnesses would make two arguments to undermine them on this point: First, that the history of discrimination against gay people had never been as bad as the history of discrimination against other minorities for whom antidiscrimination laws were in effect. And second, that there were good reasons for state law to discriminate against gay people.

The latter argument was the most crucial to the state's case. Ordinarily, a government must have at least a conceivably rational reason for any law or policy that singles out a group of people for negative treatment. But because the Colorado Supreme Court, in its first ruling, upholding the lower court's preliminary injunction of Amendment 2, held that the initiative appeared to infringe upon the fundamental constitutional right of gay people to participate equally in the political process, the state would have to come up with a "compelling" reason for the measure's discriminatory treatment of gay people.

The plaintiffs' attorneys knew that the state's witnesses, who would be called to the witness stand later in the trial, would argue that discrimination against gay people currently was not as bad as that against other minorities or as bad as it had been for gay people in the past. Wilford G. Perkins, a car dealer from Colorado Springs, Colorado, who served as chair of Colorado for Family Values, would argue that discrimination against gay people did not require legal protections because there was no evidence that gay people had been economically or educationally disadvantaged by discrimination. If someone verbally or physically assaults a person because he or she is gay, or destroys that person's property, other laws, Perkins would argue, are already in place to prosecute such criminal activities. But laws prohibiting sexual orientation discrimination, Perkins and other state witnesses would argue, create a "special right." And the plaintiffs' attorneys expected that testimony of state witness Ignacio Rodriguez, a former member of the Colorado Civil Rights Commission, would echo the idea that, unlike Mexican-Americans, gay people did not see in restaurants humiliating signs saying, 'No dogs or Mexicans allowed' and did not have their employment prospects limited because of their sexual orientation.

In anticipation of these arguments, plaintiffs' attorney Winer asked Chauncey, when he was on the witness stand, to comment on such comparisons.

"I don't think it's a contest," said Chauncey. "The various groups which have been marginalized in this country have been marginalized in different kinds of ways."

"Blacks have obviously suffered an extraordinary burden, having been brought here as slaves and [suffered attacks] that kept them subordinate for a number of years. And that attack doesn't lessen a claim that Jews have been discriminated against [or] women have been discriminated against. . . . There was enough discrimination to go around."

Chauncey also testified later that most historians agree that the black civil rights movement of the 1950s and 1960s enabled a gay civil rights movement to emerge. The success of the black civil rights movement in securing laws to prohibit discrimination based on race, he said, made it possible for the gay civil rights movement to consider advocating for similar laws to prohibit discrimination based on sexual orientation.

"I think probably the most useful historical comparison," said Chauncey, "might be between the size of the gay political movement now and the black political movement in the forties and fifties. It's very clear that there was a very powerful system in place subordinating blacks in American society in the forties and fifties. And yet, as a social historian talking about blacks and/or groups, I would want to look at the ways that they did have some political power. And in some ways, they were in a position that the gay movement is" in now.

There were other comparisons, said Chauncey. Moral values and religious values were raised as justifications for discriminating against blacks. To support segregation, said Chauncey, some claimed "God had intended the segregation of the races."

"It seems today obvious that blacks and whites should be able to marry," said Chauncey. "And in the forties and fifties, it was blasphemous, almost, to think that blacks and whites should be able to marry—that this was against God's plan."

Status–Conduct

But while Chauncey had chosen the notorious laws barring interracial marriage to illustrate his point that laws sometimes have no basis other than expression of bigotry, one of the state's attorneys, Gregg Kay, had another point in mind. During his cross-examination of Chauncey, Kay sought to illustrate that, throughout history, laws according disparate treatment to homosexuals did so because of the "conduct" those people engaged in, "not on their status" as gay people.

"All the records we have from the eighteenth and nineteenth centuries would suggest that, yes," said Chauncey.

Even the laws that were not gay-specific, noted Kay, "criminalized someone's conduct, didn't they—the law itself?"

Chauncey could apparently see what Kay was attempting to do—that is, Kay wanted to suggest that laws treating gay people differently than other groups were justifiable because they were aimed at something that gay people did, not just at who they were. Chauncey's responses struggled against Kay's motives:

> *Chauncey:* Well, there are two stages of it really. One would be [the] disorderly conduct law itself which criminalized a kind of behavior. But if we look at the enforcement of it, it's clear that they were arresting people. . . .
>
> *Kay:* I understand you want to separate the law from the enforcement, but the law itself dealt with conduct, didn't it?
>
> *Chauncey:* It . . . depends on the context in which you are discussing. For instance, the liquor authority prohibited premises from . . . becoming a disorderly premises, and they said that the simple presence of a lesbian or gay man at one of those premises constituted disorder.
>
> *Kay:* The law, the written, published law, said if a lesbian or gay man is found at a bar, its license shall be revoked?
>
> *Chauncey:* Well, as is generally the case in regulatory agencies . . .

Kay: Did it say that?

Chauncey: You have to look at the regulations themselves and their enforcement. The law itself refers to disorderly conduct and leaves it to the liquor board to define it, which really defined it as simple presence.

Kay: How did the liquor authority define that? How did they know whether somebody in that bar was a lesbian or gay unless it was based upon their conduct?

Chauncey: Well, it depends on what you want to call conduct. Are you calling speech conduct?

Kay: Well, of course.

Chauncey: Are you calling the way someone dresses conduct?

Kay: Of course. They had to do something to get dressed like that.

Kay was apparently referring to the popularity among some gay men of dressing up in women's clothing as another form of conduct. And, as Chauncey explained, gay people often used "some interesting legal maneuvers" to avoid police raids on their more large and elaborate gatherings where such attire was especially popular. Large "drag balls" held in Harlem during the 1920s and 1930s, he said, registered as "masquerade balls."

In trying to illustrate that many other groups had been treated more harshly than gay people by the legal system, health officials, and society, Kay also attempted to use Chauncey's time on the witness stand to press the state's points that discrimination against gay people today is not as bad as it used to be and not as bad as it has been for other minorities. He noted that some harsh treatments for homosexuality that were popular in the 1950s—such as electroshock therapy and lobotomies—were also used to treat other groups of people in the past and are no longer automatically prescribed today.

"They don't treat the mentally retarded today the way they did in the eighteenth and nineteenth centuries, do they?" asked Kay.

"That's correct," said Chauncey.

He also got Chauncey to acknowledge that, while the Hollywood Production Code had censored gay people from existing on the screen, it censored "a lot more than just homosexual images."

But again, Chauncey apparently could see Kay's strategy and answered very carefully, emphasizing that the Production Code prohibited "*any* homosexual images or characters" but only certain heterosexual ones:

Kay: They were trying to prevent a lot of heterosexual images from being in the films, too, didn't they?

Chauncey: They tried to prevent selected heterosexual images from being in the films.

Kay: Well, they were trying to keep nudity out of the films, weren't they? It didn't matter whether it was heterosexuals or homosexuals?

Chauncey: Yes, that's correct.

To show that society no longer discriminated against gay men and lesbians in many arenas in which it did in the past, Kay moved on to the theater. Again, Chauncey couched his answers carefully:

Kay: Now, you talked about the theater in New York and how that was repressed. They raided the show *The Captive* and others. That's not the case today, is it? In fact, didn't *Angels in America* win a Tony last year? Wasn't that a homosexual theme play?

Chauncey: Well, I guess the way I characterize a censorship campaign in general is that, in the thirties, you had a mass-based censorship unit that threatened boycotts of the studios. The studios capitulated and established an elaborate censorship code. Those codes have discontinued, but you still have mass-based censorship units that regularly threatened advertisers on network shows if they advertised with a gay character represented. We see more of these images today than then, certainly. Just a couple of years ago, *Thirty Something* [a television series] lost a million dollars when it broadcast a scene 30 seconds long with two men in bed together.

Kay: Lots of shows lost a lot of money without homosexual images in it, haven't they?

Chauncey: I'm not arguing that homosexuality is the only thing that's being targeted; but, that doesn't mean that it isn't being targeted.

In other lines of questioning, Kay brought out on the record that, with the exception of the military and some security agencies, the federal government no longer discriminates against gay people in employment; that gay publications are no longer banned from publishing or using the postal system; that liquor boards are no longer shutting down gay bars for catering to gay clientele; and that Hollywood no longer enforces a censorship code to prohibit the appearance of gay characters.

Kay also tried to discredit much of Chauncey's testimony by suggesting that Chauncey had no real authority or documentation to back up his views. Regarding the reports of violence against gay people, Kay said, "That's just all anecdotal evidence, isn't it? You don't have any hard crime statistics on the incidence of homosexual assaults as opposed to assaults against anybody else in the forties and fifties, do you?"

Chauncey said the presumption of Kay's question "sounds dismissive" and noted that historians are often left with such evidence and have to rely on analyzing such information "as best we can."

But, countered Kay, Chauncey's testimony that 50,000 gay men may have been arrested in New York during a certain period of time is not very informative because "we don't know whether that's a hundred percent of the gay male population of New York or whether that's one percent of the gay male population of New York."

Kay's final line of questioning aimed at making his point, in a stark fashion, that discrimination against gay people simply does not compare to discrimination against black people:

> *Kay:* Now, you equated black civil rights in the forties and fifties to gay civil rights today. But gays don't have the same history of discrimination as blacks, do they?
> *Chauncey:* Well, I never equated them. I talked about some relationship between them and some comparable measures. And what is your question about history of discrimination?
> *Kay:* Gays don't have the same history of discrimination as blacks in this country, do they? Gays were never enslaved in this country, were they?
> *Chauncey:* That's true.
> *Kay:* Gays were never prevented from voting in this country, were they?
> *Chauncey:* I'm not aware of gays having been prohibited from voting in this country. Again, obviously, each group has been subject to its own particular history of discrimination.

But attorneys opposing Amendment 2 did not make any concessions in their effort to illustrate a long, significant history of discrimination against gay people. They called Joe Hicks, executive director of the Southern Christian Leadership Conference's Los Angeles chapter, to the stand as a rebuttal witness just prior to the close of the trial. He was a 25-year veteran of the black civil rights movement.

Hicks said he did not believe that extending antidiscrimination protection to gay people would "diminish in any way" the rights of or respect for African-Americans or other minorities. He recalled arguments made by fundamentalists that enforcing protections for African-Americans would require adding staff and financial resources for government enforcement agencies.

Hicks said he felt Amendment 2 "sets a very bad precedent" because it allows "civil and human rights to be put to a popular vote."

"I think had that vote been put to the population around civil rights in the fifties and sixties," said Hicks, "black folks would have lost."

Between the testimony and the affidavits, Judge Bayless received a fairly complete historical tour. But it was not self-evident how much knowledge about the penalties for sexual acts during colonial times, censorship of gay-related themes during the early and mid-1900s, or even raids on bars in the 1960s could reveal about whether Amendment 2 was another point in the history of antigay bias or whether it reflected, as its defenders urged, concerns about "special rights" but not disapproval of gay people as such.

Chapter 5

The Politics of Law

As much as the scientific research and the history of discrimination seemed to dominate the trial, the politics behind the vote for Amendment 2 were at the heart of the legal questions in the case. The measure was, after all, the by-product of what religious right leaders had labeled a national "cultural war" over whose "family values" would be preeminent in society. Reflecting this "warlike" atmosphere, the literature promoting Amendment 2, distributed to voters by Colorado for Family Values, portended the "takeover" of government by "militant homosexuals" intent on foisting a "life-style" upon children. The rhetoric proclaimed that gay activists were using public funds and influence to advance a "gay agenda" on the population at large, and that gay people were diseased, dangerous child molesters undeserving of public respect.

These themes had been sounded for some time, typically by those closely affiliated with the religious right, as conservative leaders brought their scathing antigay messages out from private meetings and religious gatherings to the most public of forums. Presidential candidate Patrick Buchanan was among those leading the cry against gay men and lesbians. Speaking at the 1992 Republican National Convention to a crowd waving signs announcing "Family Rights Forever, 'Gay' Rights Never," he attacked the Democratic party's candidates as "the most prolesbian and progay ticket in history." But it was not just Buchanan whose message had taken hold in the Republican party. Leaders of major religious right organizations with large membership and funding bases, including the Reverend Lou Sheldon of the Traditional Values Coalition in California and Dr. James Dobson of Focus on the Family in Colorado, began to make clear their ambitions to shape state and federal policy-making in a conservative, and antigay, direction. Ironically, at the same time, other religious organizations were becoming more accepting of their lesbian and gay members, even organizing special programs to address gay issues and actively supporting sexual orientation antidiscrimination laws.

Determined to show a new, serious, and influential face of the religious right after a series of embarrassing scandals, longtime religious right leaders, like Sheldon and Dobson, along with a younger generation of religious right leaders—including Ralph Reed, director of the Christian Coalition, one of the nation's largest and most powerful conservative Christian political groups—worked closely with Republican leaders in an effort to assure that the 1992 elections would reflect their interests. In addition to working within the Republican party, their organizations produced voter guides and other materials that focused attention on, among other things, plans to limit the rights of lesbians and gay men. Declaring that "family values" had been suffering a severe decline and that increasing recognition of the rights of lesbians and gay men was in part to blame, Buchanan, Sheldon, Dobson, and their compatriots announced that a "cultural war" had erupted. For civilization to continue along a positive course, they concluded, the rights of gay people had to be restricted.

Interestingly, these organizational heads, along with Reverend Pat Robertson, who founded the Christian Coalition and numerous other religious right organizations, did not blame any of the decline in family values on the examples set by their own fallen colleagues. Rather, in their literature, radio broadcasts, and public commentary, they focused their blame on gay people, feminists (often called "feminazis"), defenders of reproductive freedom, and "liberals" generally. Campaigns targeting gay people as responsible for society's problems, religious right organizations found, were a particularly easy and effective way to raise money, by tapping into popular dislike of or discomfort with gay people.

Amendment 2 became the subject of one of these campaigns. In addition to being an effective fund-raiser for right-wing religious groups, Amendment 2 became an outlet for those who believed lesbians and gay men had gained too much influence in the political process and for those harboring antigay antagonism. Both of these sentiments remained strong despite the lack of evidence showing that gay people had strong, much less disproportionate, influence over the Colorado legislature. For example, as of 1992, no bill had even been introduced to prohibit sexual orientation discrimination statewide. At the time of Amendment 2's passage, ordinances prohibiting sexual orientation discrimination in employment and other areas had been passed in the Colorado cities of Denver, Boulder, and Aspen either by local city and county councils or through the initiative process. Insurance law, a governor's executive order, and several public universities also prohibited discrimination based upon sexual orientation. This configuration mirrored that in most other states in the early 1990s: No statewide law prohibited sexual orientation discrimination in employment, housing, or public accommodations in Colorado or most states, but those who lived and worked in some major cities or for state government enjoyed limited protections.

Amendment 2's Origins

By positioning Amendment 2 as an initiative requiring voter approval rather than as a bill for the legislature, supporters of the measure hoped to appeal to those who feared gay people were an overly powerful "special interest group." They calculated that, by seeking out voters directly, they had a greater likelihood of success than if they went to elected legislators who they believed were subject to the influence of gay civil rights leaders. Explaining this strategy to the court during the trial of Amendment 2, CFV cofounder Will Perkins testified that "we wanted to use the initiative process instead of trying to go through the legislature [because] we were very aware of the fact of the very strong political influence that the homosexual proponents had. And it's much easier for them to influence a small group of legislators as opposed to having everyone have an opportunity to express their opinion on the issue." As Perkins indicated, the initiative process enables the public to legislate directly and counteract political backroom dealing. However, unlike the legislative process, public ballot contests regarding proposed legislation typically do not involve structured public hearings to examine the proposal's practical consequences but instead are more frequently swayed by emotional rhetoric and sound bites. CFV could reasonably expect that voters going into the booth in Colorado in November 1992 would make their decisions based not on Amendment 2's text but rather on the questions made popular during the campaign, such as whether one is "for or against" homosexuality or whether one opposes "special rights."

The antidiscrimination laws and policies in place were, according to Amendment 2's proponents, the product of aggression by gay militants. CFV leader Tony Marco explained, for example, that, "as a result of Governor Romer's executive order [which prohibited sexual orientation discrimination in state employment], pressure [was] being exerted by the gay militants on the student affairs departments of universities and the University of Colorado . . . to make it mandatory [for] all clubs, whatever their nature on campus, to either accept devout gays in membership or lose all privileges."

It was the success of lesbian and gay advocates in achieving these few laws and policies prohibiting discrimination that, Amendment 2's proponents said, triggered the campaign for Amendment 2. But why did CFV care that Denver, Boulder, and Aspen had sexual orientation antidiscrimination laws? CFV leader Kevin Tebedo explained at trial:

> It wasn't so much that we cared about Denver, Boulder, and Aspen. What really concerned us was when the Colorado State Human Relations Commission had voted four to two, I believe, to introduce legislation. To get that kind of law at a statewide level, it became clear to me at least that what had happened in five other states including at that time Hawaii was a real possibility—to say that in Colorado a small elite number of individuals in the Colorado state legislature would impose a homosexuality law on the entire state. So no matter where you live in the state of Colorado, this law was going to affect you.

Tebedo characterized members of the state legislature, and officials elected by the majority of voters, as an "elite" class intent on imposing its will on Coloradans at large. CFV's leaders also stressed that, in their view, lesbians and gay men had undue influence over these popularly elected representatives. Ignored in these allegations was the fact that voters themselves had chosen these "elite" legislators to represent them and had the option of voting in other candidates in future elections. As the plaintiffs argued, all citizens, including gay citizens, had a constitutional right to lobby their elected legislators as part of the democratic process. Also disregarded by CFV was the history of religious right organizations going directly to these same "elite" legislators, some of whom they had supported, to seek limitations on abortion rights and on recognition of gay couples' relationships, and expansion of the rights of religious schools and other institutions.

CFV leader Tony Marco testified at the Amendment 2 trial that the measure was "necessary because it was obvious that the aggression of gay militants through the legislature was not going to cease." He continued:

The legislature is very vulnerable to all kinds of lobbying and other activity without citizens' direct representation on that activity— lobbying for which I discovered gay militants were very, very well equipped and were very well experienced. And so the only way to insure that this kind of activity would stop would be through passage of [a] constitutional amendment.

With that in mind, Marco said, he called a meeting of citizens from around the state and began the move toward Amendment 2. He and colleagues from CFV contacted a variety of attorneys, including lawyers at the National Legal Foundation, a legal organization founded by Pat Robertson that described itself as "ever ready to defend religious liberty." Those attorneys assisted with drafting the amendment according to guidelines provided by CFV. As Marco explained, "the fundamental principle behind the drafting of the initiative language was, quite simply, to take those factors which we felt that gay militants had themselves said they desired, plus all of the factors that are attendant on achievement of or awarding of protective class status, and simply say no to those."

To reinforce this view, the state called George Mason University Law School professor Joseph Broadus as a witness. Broadus told the court that "essentially what [Amendment 2] does is to say to these local governments that have been so completely reckless in their basic concern for the constitutional items in the areas of privacy and freedom of association, . . . 'If you don't know how to play with your toys, we are going to take them away from you. You are simply not going to be permitted to legislate in this area.'"

This claim that lesbians and gay men had amassed such a high level of political power that a constitutional amendment was necessary to defend against their influence on elected officials persuaded many and played a critical role in Amendment 2's ballot box success. But, ironically, at the same time as Amendment 2's proponents were claiming that gay people had obtained this extraordinary political power, the political clout of lesbians and gay men was being put to an unprecedented test nationally. First, of course, Amendment 2 had passed—devastating Colorado's lesbian and gay communities and shocking the rest of the nation's gay citizenry with the message that Amendment 2–type measures might soon be sweeping the country. Second, and more surprising, the national debate about the rights and the lives of gay people that exploded shortly after the newly elected president, Bill Clinton, was inaugurated revealed that antigay hostility remained deeply entrenched.

Although some took Clinton's campaign promise to lift the ban on military service by lesbians and gay men as a sign that gay people had truly gained meaningful political power, others, including some lesbians and gay men, thought Clinton's effort to end this ban as his first gay-positive step was an extraordinary and damaging political error. If there was an elite in the United States, it was the military—given significant deference by the courts and politicians because of its role in preserving national security. Many gay leaders were concerned that the surge in visibility of gay people around this public debate and the increased access some gay leaders suddenly had to key decision makers was not translating into effective influence or action in any arena, including the military. Much of the antigay rhetoric that dominated the Republican convention and the Amendment 2 campaign was now on the national news, where night after night the public debated the merits of lesbians and gay men serving in the military.

However well-intentioned his initial announcement might have been, Clinton's promise turned into a major "compromise," with lesbians and gay men on the losing end. Clinton signed into law a bill that purported to be an improvement on the old ban but in fact retained virtually the same restrictions as its predecessor—any gay person who wanted to serve in the military would have to hide his or her sexual orientation. The "new" policy, codified by Congress, did not reflect a growing acceptance of gay people in America; instead, the law, dubbed "don't ask, don't tell," became a despised moniker among lesbians and gay men that reflected the federal government's acquiescence to the more powerful voices of those, including many in the religious right, who wanted lesbians and gay men neither to be seen nor heard.

This tremendous national debate, as well as the behind-the-scenes political maneuvering at the state and national level by religious right leaders with antigay agendas, all joined to color the environment as Amendment 2 was headed to trial. To gay people, the new military law along with the proliferation of antigay initiatives like Amendment 2 made clear that the militant aggression was being successfully accomplished not by lesbians and gay men but rather by the religious right.

History Repeats Itself

It all had a familiar ring. Thirty years earlier, groups similar to CFV had organized petition drives and proposed measures to bar government from ever passing laws against race discrimination. Urging that it was time to stop government from according "special rights" to racial minorities, these citizen groups in the 1960s attempted to take power away from what they saw as "militant" civil rights activists who they believed had too much influence over elected officials. By putting the issue of civil rights laws directly to voters through the initiative process, proponents of these measures knew they could capitalize on a frightened and poorly informed public.

And, not surprisingly, the measures that made it to the ballot in the 1960s passed. The first of these to be addressed by the U.S. Supreme Court was an initiative passed by voters in California in 1964. It had amended the state's constitution to prohibit the state from ever interfering with property owners' rights to transfer or *not* to transfer their property as they chose. The amendment at issue in that case, *Reitman v. Mulkey*, did not explicitly single out racial minority groups and block government from prohibiting discrimination against them, as Colorado's Amendment 2 did with respect to lesbians, gay men, and bisexuals. However, in intent and effect, the two were quite similar. Both surfaced during the very time period that laws against discrimination were being enacted, and both aimed to thwart enactment and enforcement of those and similar measures. Further, both claimed to position government in what the amendments' supporters called a "neutral" position with respect to discrimination.

Recognizing that the California amendment in the *Reitman* case was motivated by prejudice against racial minorities, the U.S. Supreme Court declared it unconstitutional. A closely divided court ruled that

> the right to discriminate, including the right to discriminate on racial grounds, was now [with the California amendment] embodied in the State's basic charter, immune from legislative, executive, or judicial regulation at any level of the state government. Those

practicing racial discriminations need no longer rely solely on their personal choice. They could now invoke express constitutional authority, free from censure or interference of any kind from official sources.[1]

Just two years later, in 1969, the Court took a look at another measure that, like Amendment 2, made it more difficult for minority groups to have laws passed in their interest. In that case, *Hunter v. Erickson,* voters in Akron, Ohio, had amended their city charter through the initiative process to require popular approval by referendum for any local laws prohibiting housing discrimination based on race, religion, and ancestry. Any other antidiscrimination laws could take effect following passage by city council. An African-American woman, Nellie Hunter, who was denied housing based on her race, filed a lawsuit challenging the amendment's constitutionality. Hunter had gone to a real estate agent looking to buy a house, but the agent refused to show her a list of houses for sale because the owners refused to sell to "negroes." When Hunter addressed a complaint to the city's Commission on Equal Opportunity in Housing, which had been established to enforce the city's antidiscrimination ordinances, including one prohibiting race discrimination in housing, she was told that the city's fair housing ordinance had been undone by the charter amendment.

The Akron measure was more specific than California's in that it singled out and blocked particular civil rights laws. Like California's, it appeared to apply to both whites and racial minorities by barring the city council from prohibiting housing discrimination against either group absent popular approval. Again, the U.S. Supreme Court invalidated the measure. The Court considered the context of the amendment's introduction, noting that the amendment had been proposed shortly after laws prohibiting racial discrimination in housing had been enacted at the local, state, and federal levels, and that the measure's true impact fell on those in the minority group.[2]

These and other voter initiatives to block passage of laws prohibiting discrimination based on race, like the more recent spate of antigay measures, reflect the popular backlash that typically follows civil rights advances. In seeking voter support, initiative promoters often succeed

1. *Reitman v. Mulkey,* 387 U.S. 369, 381 (1967).
2. *Hunter v. Erickson,* 393 U.S. 385 (1969).

by appealing to fears and misunderstandings about civil rights laws in the general public. Unlike elected officials, who presumably have a basic understanding of the purpose and limitations of the laws they pass, the general public, faced with voting directly on an initiative, is often dependent upon hyperbolic media campaigns to understand such laws. These media campaigns often cater to prejudice and rarely provide full and accurate information about the issue up for vote.

In defending Amendment 2 in court, the state made numerous comparisons between gay people and racial minorities, too. The state's point, however, was that lesbians and gay men were politically powerful compared to racial minorities because, in contrast to other groups such as African-Americans, gay people were never enslaved or denied the right to vote. Ironically, though, the very same initiative tactic used in an attempt to deprive African-Americans of civil rights in the 1960s was, in the 1990s, simply being retooled for use against lesbians and gay men.

Measuring Power

Were Amendment 2's sponsors correct in their claim that lesbians and gay men had taken control of Colorado's local and state governments? Was there a "gay agenda" that elected officials were putting into effect at the behest of their lesbian and gay constituents?

In presenting testimony at trial, the plaintiffs' legal team addressed these inquiries to prove their legal claims that Amendment 2 violated a fundamental right, made a suspect classification, and lacked a rational basis for singling out lesbians, gay men, and bisexuals. The issue of how to define political power and measure how much power gay people have took on an especially significant role as the plaintiffs' team sought to show that Amendment 2 aimed to squelch gay people's political influence and that Amendment 2 made a suspect classification because, within the mainstream political process, gay people were relatively powerless.

Courts are not often in the business of applying broad social science concepts—such as "political power"—to legal tests and categories. Questions such as "Who comprises the group of lesbians and gay men?" and "How is that group's political power measured?" are not typical fare for the judiciary. Nonetheless, many people, including judges, hold the view that gay people are a disproportionately powerful group in American society, based primarily on the increased visibility of lesbians and gay men in the media. Thus, it was critical for the plaintiffs to gauge the political clout of gay people in a factual and deliberate fashion at trial. In the public campaign for Amendment 2's passage, issues of gay political power had relatively little fact-based examination. Citing statistics purporting to show that gay people were wealthier and better educated than most other Americans, proponents of Amendment 2 sought to reinforce popular notions that gay people, as compared to other minorities, did not need protection against discrimination.

The legal team opposing Amendment 2 saw the trial in October 1993 as an opportunity to correct this provocative misinformation and to help establish sexual orientation as a suspect classification and obtain heightened judicial scrutiny for antigay discrimination by showing that gay people are relatively politically powerless. The team chose as its expert witness in this area someone viewed by his colleagues to be among the leading political scientists to apply political power theory to lesbians and gay men. Kenneth Sherrill, a political science professor at New York's Hunter College who was openly gay, had studied the relationship between political participation and democracy, focusing particularly on questions of "tolerance and intolerance, and [on] questions of how individual citizens and groups of citizens can be effective." His testimony was not specifically law-related but was much more familiar to many in the room than the discussions of chromosome markers and complex genetic studies that had occupied the previous days and that morning of trial.

Guided by the plaintiffs' trial attorney Jeanne Winer, Sherrill defined political science as "the study of power," or, "who gets what, when, and how it's decided." He provided the court with a brief political science primer, explaining that the United States is a pluralist democracy—which means "that the American system not only is representative but [also] protects the rights of a wide range of citizens—most notably the right to compete on an even playing field." Such a system avoids tyranny of the majority, which Sherrill defined as "anything the majority might do which would deprive the minority of its natural rights." Sherrill explained that this pluralist theory was set forth in the Federalist Papers, the set of published arguments advocating adoption of the proposed American Constitution. The genius of the American democratic system, said Sherrill, is its checks and balances on power—

a separation of powers in different government branches, an independent judiciary, and multiple points of access to the political process. These safeguards ensure that all groups have a "fair chance not only to have [their] opinions heard but also to prevent action which would deprive them of their rights."

Sherrill suggested that one way of measuring any given group's political power is to "look at the net balance of victories and defeats" the group has experienced. But, he said,

> You . . . couldn't merely count the victories and defeats, because your group might achieve a substantial number of victories on matters of relatively low priority or importance and fail massively on an issue of great importance. So . . . you have to get a balanced picture.
>
> *Winer:* What about if some individuals who are members of a particular group are powerful, does that mean that the group itself is necessarily powerful?
>
> *Sherrill:* No. No.
>
> *Winer:* For instance, some of the state's witnesses mentioned the fact, in their affidavits, that there are openly gay people in elected office. Does that mean that gays are powerful?
>
> *Sherrill:* No, it doesn't. And if one looked at the number of openly gay people in elected office in the United States, one would find that it is, I believe, in the range of one-tenth of one percent of all people in all elected offices in this country.

Power Resources

Sherrill testified that "the best way for a pluralist system to function would be for all groups to have fair and equitable access to power resources," which are the resources "a group might use to advance a political goal to try to achieve a political end." Some of these, he said, are "scarce resources" that are, by definition, not available to everyone, such as wealth and fame. Other resources are in boundless supply, such as trust, respect, and affection. Safety, too, is an important power resource, as Sherrill testified: "Obviously, being able to go about your life without fear of violence is a major component of being an effective person in the political world."

Less tangible "resources," like having allies and access to people in power, are also "absolutely critical" because pluralist democracy requires coalition building to achieve success. That, Sherrill continued, "mean[s] that people must be willing to enter into coalition with you." Also, shared identity is a power resource, Sherrill explained, because it is a prerequisite to group formation—"people must think of themselves as members of the group." Continuing, Sherrill explained:

> Not only must people think of themselves as members of the group, but often [that membership] must be [their] prime identity because we are, in fact, members of many groups which will overlap. This again is critical to pluralist democracy. We say, "Not only am I a union member, I am also a," fill in the blank with any other group—"I am a man," "I am a woman," or whatever. . . . People have overlapping memberships, and you have to say which membership matters to you the most. So it's not only identity, but it's also a question of prime identity.

In reviewing all of the various power resources, from group size, to access, to money, Sherrill explained that "you have to look at them on balance" to assess a group's power. "In many ways," he testified, "you have to ask the question, 'Does a group have access to a sufficient number of them and know how to use them sufficiently. . . ?'" Further, certain resources, such as shared identity, are "absolutely fundamental prerequisites. It would be very hard to conceive of any group being able to take effective political action," he said, "if it did not have a substantial amount of shared identity. On the other hand, you don't have to have a lot of money."

Before examining these specific power resources in the lives of lesbians and gay men, Sherrill offered illustrations of how gay people lacked political power. He first pointed to a legislative amendment proposed by the North Carolina Republican senator, Jesse Helms, that sought to block federal funds for organizations that addressed homosexuality in a positive light, including funding for the production and distribution of AIDS-related materials aimed to educate gay men about how to avoid contracting HIV. Congress passed the Helms amendment in 1987 even though its potential consequence was the further spread of HIV among gay men. And Congress did so despite the fact that gay men and lesbians used all of their political resources to oppose the amendment. It was, said Sherrill, a stark example of how little political power gay people had.

> The failure on . . . what was basically a life and death issue, and which . . . the Congress of the United States was deciding to with-hold life-saving information from people, is the most devastating loss that a group of citizens has had in the Congress of the United States in modern times.

Another measure of the political power of lesbians and gay men, said Sherrill, was the congressional debate in 1993 about "gays in the military." Even with the early support of the president of the United States, gay people could not overcome the powerful opposition in Congress to permitting openly gay and lesbian Americans to serve in the military. Winer asked Sherrill about the state's assertion that the national debate showed that gay people had considerable political power.

> *Winer:* . . . Sir, some of the state's witnesses are also claiming that the recent struggle for equality in the military, even though gays lost, . . . actually proves that they are powerful. Could you discuss how that could be?
> *Sherrill:* I think that [claim is] mind-boggling.

Sherrill did not examine whether the fact that the president made a campaign promise to support equal treatment of gay people reflected gay political power. Instead, he pointed out that the president originally supported rescission of the ban and that independent respected research studies had shown that being gay was not incompatible with military service. Nonetheless, the ban was codified into law based, in large part, on arguments that unit cohesion would suffer because non-gay soldiers would be uncomfortable living and working with gay soldiers. This, according to Sherrill, amounted to elected officials giving in to bigotry.

The next phase of Sherrill's testimony focused on assessing the quantity and quality of power resources available to lesbians and gay men and how these resources shaped the battle against Amendment 2. Winer posed an important question about the link between political

power and the substantial financial resources Colorado's gay community marshaled to fight the amendment, touching for the first of several
times on the issue of wealth among gay men and lesbians.

> *Winer:* There was a very recent struggle which occurred here in
> Colorado, and, according to the state's witnesses, various coali-
> tions to oppose Amendment 2 supposedly outspent Colorado
> for Family Values and persuaded 46 percent of Coloradans who
> voted to vote against Amendment 2. Doesn't that prove that
> gays and lesbians are quite powerful?
>
> *Sherrill:* No. . . . The first point is that, when what is on the ballot is
> the power of the government to protect a group of people
> against discrimination and that group loses, that group is pow-
> erless, period.
>
> Secondly, the fact that you can raise a good deal of money
> does not mean that you know how to spend it. . . . If you expect
> to win, you don't have to raise that much money. If you expect
> that you are going to have a hard time, you are going to raise a
> lot more. . . . The intensity of the opposition, the numbers of the
> opposition, the intensity of feeling on the part of the other side
> and the possibility that . . . people relatively new to the political
> process are not that experienced and consequently not that skill-
> ful in the use of political money also comes into play.

Stepping back to an even more fundamental question, Sherrill discussed how the size of the gay population affects the group's political
power. The state was arguing that, with only about 10 percent of the
population identifying as lesbian or gay, the campaign against Amendment 2 convinced 46 percent of voters to reject the initiative, suggesting
that gay people in Colorado had clout beyond their numbers. Sherrill,
however, said that being 10 percent or less of the population means that
"you are going to have a very hard time entering into any coalitions.
And you have to attract a large number of allies. And it's not going to
be easy to build up credits because what you can add to a coalition for
somebody else isn't going to be that much." Citing Congress's negative
treatment of gay people in the military and its refusal to pass a federal
law banning sexual orientation discrimination, he noted that lesbians
and gay men do not have many allies at the federal level. Even in Colorado, he noted, antigay hostility had escalated to such a high level that

the president of the University of Colorado was forced to wear a bulletproof vest while addressing a gathering of lesbians and gay men because of threats on his life for addressing what had been termed a "fag rally" by one opponent.

"It seems to me," Sherrill testified, "if the president of a university has to wear a bulletproof vest to speak, that the risks of becoming an ally are rather vast."

Fears of being associated with an unpopular cause exacerbate the difficulties of gaining allies and of even mustering support of the group itself. Sherrill testified about the "spiral of silence," a political theory that holds that people generally know when their views are unpopular and that they often fear retaliation or social isolation for expression of those views. The author of this "spiral of silence" theory, Elisabeth Noelle-Neumann, conducted studies in which she asked people whether they would fear having their tires slashed if their car sported a bumper sticker supporting an unpopular cause. Many respondents said that not only would they be afraid, but also they would be unlikely to put the sticker on their cars. Consequently, support for unpopular views is often much more than what appears on the streets or is heard in public discussion, Sherrill said.[3]

This spiral of silence has two important effects, Sherrill testified: "It discourages people from articulating unpopular viewpoints," and "it multiplies the apparent power of dominant groups in society." Regarding the political power of lesbians and gay men, he said, the spiral of silence diminishes two resources—group numbers and allies. It "discourage[s] people from indicating to others that they are gay or lesbian," and "discourage[s] people whether or not they are gay or lesbian from articulating views in support of gay rights," he explained.

Because popular culture images and public discourse about gay people reflect this silencing effect, they are a valuable indicator of a group's social status and, therefore, its political power. Sherrill noted that, in the media, "gay people do tend to be totally invisible." This is significant, he explained, because gay people "do not grow up in gay homes. So that much of what they learn about their identity must come from media representations of gay people."

Where gay issues are addressed publicly, expressions of hostility

---

3. Elisabeth Noelle-Neumann, *The Spiral of Silence* (University of Chicago Press, 1984), 6–7.

tend to dominate the popular discourse, Sherrill testified. Vulgar epithets are common. Even allies often feel that they must avoid appearances of affection toward gay people. As an example, Sherrill pointed to the remarks of "presumably well-enlightened" U.S. senator Bill Bradley, a Democrat from New Jersey, during debate over inclusion of sexual orientation as a category for collection of statistics in the Federal Hate Crimes Statistics Act.[4] Sherrill noted that Bradley said, "I don't want anybody to think I'm voting for this because I approve of this." Sherrill noted, "One couldn't imagine . . . saying 'I don't want anybody to think that I approve of different religions or different races or anything else of that sort.'" The bill under consideration called only for *counting* hate crimes against gay people, and yet, said Sherrill, "people like Bill Bradley had to get up and apologize for voting to collect this information. This sends a strong message as to what's acceptable and what's not acceptable." In sum, Sherrill opined, the spiral of silence "has a chilling effect of unbelievable dimension" on the political power of gays and lesbians.

Underlying this spiral of silence is a related power resource—popular affection toward a group—which Sherrill explained is measured best by the warmth of feelings a person has to other groups. Since 1964, the National Election Studies conducted by the Center for Political Studies at the University of Michigan used a technique known as the "feeling thermometer." Respondents are told to imagine a thermometer which records the warmth or coldness they feel toward various groups of people. Respondents are told that the thermometer records the nicest, warmest possible feelings toward a group at 100 degrees and the most hostile, or coldest, at zero. Feelings that are neither warm nor cold register at 50 degrees. Since 1984, the feeling thermometer has gauged respondents' feelings about "homosexuals." And since that year, Sherrill testified, gay people have been consistently identified as the object of the coldest feelings of any group in the American population. The only group ever posting a lower average feeling was "illegal aliens" in 1992, but even then, 24 percent of those surveyed placed their feelings toward gay people at zero degrees—the coldest possible extreme, outnumbering those holding "illegal aliens" in such very low esteem.

---

4. Federal Hate Crimes Statistics Act, Pub. Law. No. 101-274, 104 Stat. 140 (1990) (codified at 28 U.S.C. §538).

Sherrill explained that the power resource of safety, which is related to the popularity of a given group, also substantially affects the ability of lesbians and gay men to organize.

If you know that you are risking your well-being, your life, [and] limb, or if you have good reason to fear it, you are not likely to do something which puts you in a position to have that occur. That is, if you have good reason to believe that you are going to be the object of violence because you state something about yourself as a person or because you advance a political claim, many people will find it prudent not to say those things.

Sherrill then reviewed statistics showing the high levels of violent crime against gay people. Relying on a Denver Police Department study, Sherrill told the court that half of all hate crimes recorded in Denver were committed against gay people, up from 30 percent the year before. "For a small group in the population to be targeted [with] a third or half of the hate crimes in the town of Denver is extraordinary," he stated.

Winer next asked whether the lack of safety of lesbians and gay men is a source or consequence of powerlessness. "Both," Sherrill replied. "It's reinforcing—it is a source of powerlessness, but the more it happens, the more powerless [a group] becomes."

Another integral part of pro–Amendment 2 argument made during the campaign and at trial rested on suggestions that gay people are wealthier than the average American. CFV literature was riddled with statistics selectively chosen to show that gay men had more money, more "frequent flier" miles accumulated through air travel, and better education than most others in the population. This "information" was used to buttress the arguments of Amendment 2's defenders that laws prohibiting discrimination against gay people were unnecessary. But, in reality, the statistics were mixed, and at trial, both sides debated this hotly contested point.

Sherrill was the first expert at trial to address the issue. He testified about a range of studies. One, based on data accumulated in the General Social Survey by the National Opinion Resource Center at the University of Chicago and analyzed by University of Maryland associate professor of economics M. V. Lee Badgett, showed that gay men earn approximately 20 percent less on average than heterosexual men and that lesbians earn about the same as or less than heterosexual women.[5] These findings, Sherrill asserted, "indicate that, as a group in society, gay people are economically disadvantaged."

Winer next asked Sherrill about campaign contributions to gay political action committees (PACs). The state was expected to use the success of one gay PAC to suggest that gay people are disproportionately wealthy. Sherrill noted several flaws with the argument.

> The first is purely as a logical matter, that you generally do not know the sexual orientation of a person who makes a campaign contribution [to any PAC]. . . .
>
> The second is that the dominant view in political science is that wealth is probably overestimated in the lay public as a political resource. It's one of those things that you use when you don't have anything else and has relatively brief effects. . . .
>
> The third problem is that in order to demonstrate that there is a connection between campaign contributions . . . , wealth, and political outcome, you have to look at whether or not public policies are in some meaningful fashion affected by the contributions and whether or not one can establish empirically a link between receiving a contribution and behavior in office.

Sherrill testified that overwhelming evidence indicates that campaign contributions have no effect on the political process. He offered two explanations: First, elected officials receive campaign contributions from all kinds of PACs so that, often, groups on different sides of an issue will contribute to the same candidate. Second, by law, the size of PAC contributions are limited and each PAC's contribution to any candidate constitutes only a tiny percentage of the cost of any campaign.

Winer asked specifically about the Human Rights Campaign Fund (HRCF), a PAC dedicated to supporting federal candidates who support equal rights for gay people.[6] In the 1989/90 election cycle, Sherrill reported, HRCF was listed among the top 50 PACs by the Federal Election Commission, which monitors such groups. But Sherrill told the

5. M. V. Lee Badgett, "The Wage Effects of Sexual Orientation Discrimination," *Industrial and Labor Relations Review* (48, no. 4), July 1995, 726–39.

6. In 1995, the Human Rights Campaign Fund changed its name to the Human Rights Campaign and remained high on the list of the top 50 political action committees, according to the FEC.

court that there is no way to know the sexual orientation of the PAC's contributors and, therefore, the HRCF data provided no basis for reaching conclusions about the wealth of gay people.

Sherrill next addressed the state's claim that lesbians and gay men average around $55,000 in annual income, that they are more likely to be college-educated than other Americans, that they travel overseas more, and that they are more likely to be in managerial positions. Sherrill said that the studies relied on by the state as support for these contentions were market research surveys done by the research firms of Simmons Market Research Bureau and Overlooked Opinions. The surveys, he noted, are designed to appeal to and convince potential advertisers that they can reach an affluent market by buying space in gay and lesbian publications. Respondents to such surveys, Sherrill stated, tend to be people wealthy enough to subscribe to the publications surveyed, rather than gay people in general. Sherrill made clear that such market survey samples do not represent the entire gay and lesbian population.

> *Sherrill:* . . . I don't believe that anyone would—and certainly not anyone who had any competence or expertise in the area of survey research would—suggest that this was a sample of a gay or lesbian population.
>
> *Winer:* Would a reputable social scientist rely on this type of data at all?
>
> *Sherrill:* Certainly not as evidence of the characteristics of lesbians and gay men in the United States. They may be representative of those people who read those magazines and newspapers and, even there, it's questionable because it was a mail-back questionnaire, and that builds in bias in the direction of upper status and upper income and higher levels of motivation.
>
> If one were to think for a moment about the difference between people who see a questionnaire in a magazine and throw it out and people who see a questionnaire in a magazine and fill it out and mail it back, there are large . . . motivational factors [that] are highly associated with income and education.

Sherrill said it is very difficult to find a representative sample of lesbians and gay men through such surveys, "given everything we've said thus far about the reasons why lesbians and gay men feel the need to conceal their identity."

On cross-examination, state's attorney Gregg Kay grilled Sherrill about a *USA Today* article analyzing United States Census data that seemed to parallel that in the Simmons and Overlooked Opinions market research studies. The data showed relatively high incomes in same-sex households. Sherrill offered similar caveats and, in a short redirect examination, Winer asked Sherrill what specific flaws he found with the *USA Today* article's analysis of data on households where same-sex "partners" identified themselves as such. Sherrill noted that at least three-fourths of people in the United States live in parts of the country where there is no protection against sexual orientation discrimination in housing or credit. Consequently, he said, it is typically only people with "substantial wealth" who feel they can afford to identify themselves as gay and as living with a partner in a census survey.

On a later trial day, another of the plaintiffs' witnesses, civil rights expert Burke Marshall, also addressed the contention that gay people are, on average, not an impoverished group and consequently undeserving of antidiscrimination protections. He responded to questions from his attorney, Kathryn Emmett.

> *Emmett:* Let me ask you this: Is it somehow thought in the community of those involved with antidiscrimination legislation that because a group may be perceived to be or may in fact, arguendo, be more affluent, relatively more affluent, or well-educated, that for some reason protection should not be adopted for such a group?
> *Marshall:* No. That's not the history of this [practice of enacting antidiscrimination legislation], and that's not the purpose of it. As I say, it doesn't have to do with wealth or affluence. The discrimination can go against the wealthy as well as against the poor. If you're not accepted because you're a Jew, or if you're not accepted because of your perceived sexual orientation, that lack of acceptance, the discrimination involved in it, in private life, in public life, and in economic life, has nothing to do with whether or not you're wealthy, and I don't think that you could possibly, taking a survey on the kinds of groups that are protected by this kind of legislation, say it has to do with their wealth or lack of wealth.

In addition to wealth, group cohesion is another important power resource, the last addressed by Sherrill. Consistent with the definition of power that asks whether one group can get others to do what it wants them to do, it is imperative, said Sherrill, that the group decide what it wants others to do. "And that means having discussions, forming community, . . . getting people to self-identify and to identify with the group," he stated. Self-identification is particularly difficult for lesbians and gay men, he explained:

> Gay people are uniquely disadvantaged in American politics and, I would argue, virtually in world politics, in that gay people are randomly distributed at birth. Gay people are born into a diaspora. Gay people are not raised, for the most part, by gay parents. They don't have role models. The entire childhood socialization process does not bring them into a gay culture or a gay community from which they can form the ability to take collective political action or even to engage in the kind of discussion that would enable the average gay or lesbian in the street to participate in the formation of a list of problems the government would need to deal with them.

Even where gay people do agree on a goal, however, such as the defeat of Amendment 2, Sherrill said that the other factors he had identified interfere with their ability to achieve those aims. He noted that, for example, even though equal rights for gay people is a goal of many gay activists, relatively few jurisdictions in the United States have enacted laws prohibiting sexual orientation discrimination. At the time of the trial, only eight states[7] and approximately 125 municipalities had such laws.

Ultimately, Sherrill concluded, in light of the limited power resources available to lesbians and gay men as well as the extreme hostility with which gay people are commonly viewed, gay people do not possess much political power at all within American society.

Enter the Defense

Four days later, on Monday, October 18, Clemson University political science professor James David Woodard took the witness stand to serve as the state's chief rebuttal to Sherrill. Although the court agreed

---

7. The eight states that had laws prohibiting sexual orientation discrimination on a statewide basis at the time of the Amendment 2 trial included California, Connecticut, Hawaii, Massachusetts, Minnesota, New Jersey, Vermont, and Wisconsin.

to designate Woodard as an expert in the area of political science in general, and in the area of the political power of gays, lesbians, and bisexuals in particular, Woodard conceded on cross-examination that he had never published any articles or books addressing lesbians and gay men in the political process (his two books were *The Burden of Busing* [1985] and *American Conservatism from Burke to Bush* [1991]), and that he had never, until that day, given any presentations about gay and lesbian people in the political arena.

Woodard began his testimony on direct examination by agreeing with Sherrill's basic theory of political power. However, he identified two additional sources of power that he maintained should be added to the calculus: "intensity preference," which, he said, reflects how strongly people feel about an issue; and protests, which he said can "win a lot of awards from decision makers." He also testified that lesbians and gay men comprise closer to 1 percent than 10 percent of the population.

Woodard said he believed the "spiral of silence" theory had been largely discounted by two political scientists in a recent journal, who showed that liberals in a politically conservative county felt comfortable discussing their views among their peers. He agreed with Sherrill that the "feeling thermometer" is a popular tool among social scientists and that lesbians and gay men were among the least "warm" on the thermometer. Although he recognized that only one-third of Americans believe that gay people should be school teachers for young children, he went on to testify that the Gallup Poll since the 1970s has shown that the majority of Americans believe that gay men and lesbians can serve well as salespeople and physicians. He noted, too, that over a third of Americans said they were willing to vote for a man or woman they believed to be gay. "My point," he summarized, "is that [the data] do show gays and lesbians may be held in lower esteem by some questions; when asked other questions, for instance, occupational questions, they are not held nearly as low in esteem. There's a wide variety of feelings about them."

In response to a question from Kay about antigay violence, Woodard responded that he did not "have real strong feelings about the safety issue. It's really not my field. . . ."

Turning to media coverage of gay people, Woodard appeared to be much more comfortable with the theories and research in the field, making evident this was an area closer to his expertise and interest. Explaining the power of television, he testified:

> We get most of our information about politics from television, so visual images are very important as to how we perceive various groups. And getting on television is one way of saying and showing that you have political power. It's one way of raising your agenda. It's one way of raising your visibility in society. So television appearances do count. People tend to remember visual images quite a while even though they can't fill in maybe the content of what was said. . . .

Woodard then discussed his study of print media coverage of lesbians and gay men—a study that he had done by comparing the number of articles available in the Readers Guide to Periodical Literature data base related to gay people, women, and racial minorities. He said he found that gay people receive a large amount of print media attention, in news and feature stories combined—less than women but more than "minorities." Woodard acknowledged, however, that he had not performed a content analysis of the coverage and thus did not know whether the coverage he counted had been favorable or hostile. Nonetheless, the sheer number of articles, he contended, meant that "the gay lifestyle [had become] an accepted part of the mass media culture."

Shifting his attention to sexual orientation antidiscrimination laws, Kay asked how laws and policies could have been passed in more than 100 jurisdictions if gay people numbered only 1 to 10 percent of the population. Here, Woodard stated that gay people have the power of "intensity":

> They are very intense about their goals. . . . As I understand, gay, lesbian, and bisexual people . . . feel very strongly about their sexuality, given the AIDS crisis and other things [that] force them to a very high visible political profile, so they are quite active. I wouldn't use the word "militant" but I would use the word "intense" [to describe] how they feel, and to draw on [one scholar's study of] intensity preference, the extreme positions like boycotts and public demonstrations and other things forced decision

makers to try to give them rewards rather than put up with sort of intense, highly visible protests that will come if they do not. So, for that reason, many times they are very successful disproportionate to the size they are because of the intensity and how really [hard] they work at their issue.

Woodard cited the Americans with Disabilities Act to exemplify gay political power because the act "had something in it about discrimination against those who were HIV positive." While admitting he had not studied the ADA's passage, he testified nonetheless that the act "is evidence [of] a reward won before Congress because of the lobbying efforts of gays and lesbians." Gay and disability rights activists, on the other hand, believe that a confluence of factors, including lobbying efforts spearheaded by many nongay groups, secured the passage of the ADA and coverage of HIV within it.

Turning to examine the wealth of lesbians and gay men, Woodard told the court that, from "most reliable resources," he had found that gay people have incomes "on average or median of over $50,000 a year and, as a result, compared to the normal or the average income, their income is quite high." They have larger amounts of discretionary income than most Americans, he added. Woodard said that the Simmons market research study of readers of the *Advocate*, a glossy national magazine read primarily by gay men, formed the basis of his opinions. He acknowledged that the survey "may not be a good indication of homosexuals everywhere, but it's an indication of *Advocate* readers, and we [political scientists] do these kinds of surveys all the time." He asserted that the information could be used as an indirect indicator of gay people's income generally.

Woodard said that market research statistics from Overlooked Opinions and the report by *USA Today* analyzing U.S. Census households with same-sex partners data confirmed for him that average income in gay male households was well above $50,000 annually. He criticized the Badgett study, on which Sherrill had relied to show household income of gay and lesbian couples to be equal to or less than that of heterosexual couples. According to Woodard, the Badgett study was not reliable because it reported findings that were not statistically significant and had not yet been published in a professional peer-reviewed journal. The findings were not statistically significant,

Woodard said, because the sample size was too small—30 lesbian and bisexual women and 47 gay and bisexual men—to generalize meaningfully to the population at large. The Simmons, Overlooked Opinions, and *USA Today* studies were not perfect, Woodard concluded, but they were "much more accurate [than the Badgett study] because all three of them seem to overlap in giving a view of income."

Woodard testified that the budgets of the six largest national gay and lesbian organizations also provided evidence of gay wealth and political influence. A chart published in the *Washington Blade,* a D.C.-based newspaper, illustrated that the cumulative budgets of the six wealthiest national gay organizations in 1993 totaled $12 million. The state had submitted this chart as part of its evidence, and Woodard said it demonstrated that gay men and lesbians had "growing" power. But, on cross-examination, plaintiffs' attorney Winer startled Woodard and the state's attorneys by pulling out a second chart from the same *Washington Blade* article. The second chart showed that the budgets of the top six religious right organizations amounted to nearly twenty times that of the six gay groups.

While still responding to Kay's direct examination, Woodard focused on the Human Rights Campaign Fund, the gay and lesbian issues PAC discussed earlier by Sherrill, which he noted was in the top 50 of approximately 4,700 political action committees and was one of the fastest growing among the group. Woodard indicated that contributions to HRCF were relatively high, which he testified was a "rough indicator of power" because "one group working in alliance with other groups can have a lot of political power and input." Woodard said that HRCF had backed a relatively large number of winning candidates—21 of 28 in close elections.

He then compared HRCF's success rate to the Conservative Victory Committee's less successful ranking—noting, however, that "I'm not trying to say the two are comparable." On cross-examination, Woodard admitted that his comparison of HRCF to the conservative political group was based on "a shot in the dark" to make a comparison. But he stuck by his view that both gay people and African-Americans are "politically powerful" groups in the United States today and confirmed his view, stated at a deposition several weeks earlier, that "Blacks would have been better off if they would pursue economic resources rather than civil rights protections."

After explaining the operation of coalition-building and informal alliances which are critical to exercising political power, Woodard summed up, offering his opinion of lesbians and gay men in this arena.

Given the economic and the organization intensity of the homosexual community, I think we can say it's a powerful interest group that forms some alliances. Now, I don't know exactly which ones they are working on right now, but I would say that we can see evidence of this in . . . for instance, gays in the military or lots of groups that supported the particular need of gay, bisexual people wanting to get in the military who maybe weren't themselves gay but maybe sympathetic to that agenda or idea—certainly labor groups or something like that.

On cross-examination, Winer focused on unsettling the various assumptions on which Woodard based his conclusions. Regarding Woodard's small estimate of the size of the gay population, Winer forced Woodard to acknowledge that the studies he relied upon were conducted with door-to-door inquiries—a technique Woodard had criticized as a "weak" methodology during his deposition taken shortly before trial. Rather than offer a defense of his estimate, Woodard responded simply, "I think it would be difficult to get people's sexuality in a social science research experiment using any methodology."

On the issue of antigay violence, Woodard admitted he had not heard of studies at several different universities around the country showing high percentages of lesbian and gay students who had been physically assaulted or verbally harassed. And in response to Winer's queries regarding the Simmons and Overlooked Opinions studies, Woodard conceded that "it would be improper to survey from a magazine and say this is the way all homosexuals are."

The next day, the state continued its effort to prove that lesbians and gay men were politically powerful by calling to the witness stand Robert Knight, director of cultural studies for the Family Research Council in Washington, D.C. Describing himself as an "opponent of the gay rights movement," Knight testified that he believed the gay community in the United States "has an inordinate influence on the media." Resting his views on his experience working as a journalist and "as a reader of articles and a viewer of network broadcasts," Knight told the court he believed that journalists "sincerely believe the gay rights issue is a civil rights issue and, since journalists by and large believe in civil rights protections, they don't accord objections to . . . the gay rights agenda as having any legitimacy at all, hence you don't see opposing points of view very often in the major press." Knight testified that daytime television talk shows and other news media programming "all reflect a pro gay bias." In sum, Knight testified, "I feel . . . that there is much more sympathy in the nation's newsrooms for the objectives of the gay rights movement than there is in the general population."

Knight also testified that lesbians and gay men comprised a powerful group. Referring to the platform for the 1993 March on Washington for Lesbian, Gay and Bi Equal Rights and Liberation, he said the gay movement had achieved many of its political aims—including increased AIDS funding, an end to mandatory HIV testing, access to a safe and affordable abortion, recognition of domestic partnerships, and other goals. However, on cross-examination, Knight admitted that many of the goals of the platform either were not achieved or were realized years before the march even took place.

Remaining Questions

Did gay people have access to political power? Were the state's contentions regarding the wealth and influence of lesbians and gay men legitimate? How much should that matter to the court in evaluating government actions that discriminate against gay people?

To measure any group's political power, one has to have a sense of who comprises that group. Yet, as the expert testimony illustrated, defining a group can depend on a whole host of variables. While, from a psychological or scientific vantage point, being gay may relate to a person's inner sense of attraction to others, from a political power perspective, public self-identification is critical. Unless a person participates as openly gay or lesbian in some realm of the political process, the fact that he or she may be gay will have little bearing on the power of gay people as a group. Indeed, access to power resources of all sorts, including safety, wealth, allies, and popular affection, depends on lesbians and gay men finding ways to know each other and to develop a shared identity for political purposes. But, as the trial moved forward, the multifaceted dimensions of gay identity continued to reveal themselves. There was no simple answer to the question of what it means to be lesbian or gay.

Chapter 6

Civil Rights and "Special Rights"

"Stop special class status for homosexuality" proclaimed the banner headline on pro–Amendment 2 literature dropped at front doors of voters around the state by Colorado for Family Values (CFV), just prior to the November 3, 1992, election. "Special rights for homosexuals just isn't fair—especially to disadvantaged minorities in Colorado." Countering that message both before and after Amendment 2's passage, opponents of the initiative sported their own buttons and bumper stickers declaring "equal rights for all" and "civil rights are equal rights."

Raging debates about civil rights—what they are and whether gay people "deserved" them—filled both public and courtroom discussions about Amendment 2. In the undercurrents was the equally important question of whether Amendment 2's attack on the rights of gay people represented a first step in a strategy that would ultimately brand all civil rights laws as "special rights" to be foreclosed by majority vote.

Historical Reflection

Logically, everyone in society should have a vested interest in equal treatment: Every person is, or has the potential to be, part of a minority—by growing older, suffering an injury, getting divorced, or becoming ill. But discrimination against members of various minority groups has been part of U.S. history since the country's earliest days. And, likewise, the debate about the meaning of equality and the rhetorical equation of civil rights with "special rights" has riveted Americans since well before the age of the media sound-bite. From the time of the Dec-

133

laration of Independence through modern times, the tension between equality and individual "freedom to discriminate" has propelled citizens into face-offs with each other and has escalated the competition among various political factions seeking control of government.

The inherent danger of a nation in which the majority's will is capable of overwhelming all others greatly concerned the framers of the U.S. Constitution. James Madison, an author and defender of the proposed governing charter, stressed, in *The Federalist Papers,* the great risk for abuse of majority dominance. Without some restraint of the majority's will, he wrote, the compact among citizens to relinquish individual power to government in exchange for life in a civil society would mean little for those in the minority. Where a common passion is felt by the majority in a democracy without constitutional limitations, Madison argued, "there is nothing to check the inducements to sacrifice the weaker party or an obnoxious individual."[1]

Slowly, the U.S. government began to respond as an institution to this tension between the will of the majority and the rights of a minority. Nearly a century after the Constitution was adopted, amendments to the Constitution to secure basic guarantees of equality laid the groundwork for future civil rights legislation. In 1865, after the Civil War, the Thirteenth Amendment abolished slavery. The Fourteenth Amendment, which guarantees "equal protection of the laws" to all persons, was enacted three years later, in 1868. Even this simple guarantee, however, was approved only after a debate about whether this equal protection guarantee conveyed "special rights." In 1875, to supplement the Fourteenth Amendment's equal protection mandate, Congress enacted legislation to prohibit discrimination in public accommodations, including inns, public conveyances, theaters, and places of public amusement, based on race, color, and previous condition of servitude. But the U.S. Supreme Court, in *The Civil Rights Cases,* invalidated that new protection as an improper exercise of the federal government's power. Justice Joseph P. Bradley wrote that "when a man has emerged from slavery, . . . there must be some stage in the progress of his elevation when he takes the rank of a mere citizen, and ceases to be the special favorite of the laws."[2]

---

1. Number 10, *The Federalist Papers* 81 (New American Library, 1961 ed.).
2. *The Civil Rights Cases,* 109 U.S. 3, 25 (1883).

A Civil Rights Protocol

The historical debates foreshadowed one of the burning questions both in the Amendment 2 trial and before the public generally: When, if ever, should the state be involved in prohibiting discrimination?

Antidiscrimination laws across the country prohibit discrimination based on a wide range of categories. These "protected classifications" frequently include race, gender, religion, national origin, and disability, and often include age, marital status, and status as a war veteran. Beyond those classic groupings, however, great variety exists. The antidiscrimination ordinance of Aspen, Colorado, for example, prohibits discrimination based on more than a dozen classifications, including political affiliation and family responsibility, as well as sexual orientation. In Cincinnati, Ohio, people of Appalachian regional ancestry are explicitly covered under the city's human rights ordinance. And in Washington, D.C., residents are protected from discrimination based on appearance.

What accounts for these variations? Many local and state governments enacted antidiscrimination laws in the 1960s and 1970s when support for the equal rights of gay people was largely underground. The eight states that had enacted laws prohibiting sexual orientation discrimination by the early 1990s—California, Connecticut, Hawaii, Massachusetts, Minnesota, New Jersey, Vermont, and Wisconsin—had done so through amendments to existing civil rights laws.

The success of recent efforts to amend general civil rights laws to cover other characteristics, including sexual orientation, has depended largely on whether the small group of advocates for the amendments can garner sufficient support from a broad-based group of individuals in the community, including from influential community leaders who can mobilize their constituents to lobby for the bill's passage. This, in turn, required the larger group to be convinced that antigay or other forms of discrimination should be condemned by law.

Why was sexual orientation not included—or even considered—as a protected classification in most antidiscrimination laws at the outset? Yale law professor Burke Marshall, an expert witness for the plaintiffs, addressed this question during his deposition for the Amendment 2 trial. (Because Marshall was physically unable to travel to Denver for the trial, his testimony was videotaped in the form of a deposition and was shown during the fourth day of trial.) Certainly, Marshall said, there was little question that lesbians and gay men suffered severe social stigma and discrimination in the 1960s and 1970s at the time many of these general antidiscrimination laws were being passed. Marshall himself had helped draft, lobby for, and then enforce the passage of the Civil Rights Act of 1964 while serving as assistant attorney general in charge of the Civil Rights Division in the U.S. Department of Justice, and he was selected by the plaintiffs as an expert witness to distill lessons from this experience for the court.

> *Gregg Kay:* [In] 1964, when the Civil Rights Act was passed [to prohibit discrimination in employment, public accommodations, and other contexts], the only groups that you protected with that legislation that you helped draft were race, national origin, gender, and in some cases religion?
>
> *Marshall:* That's correct.
>
> *Kay:* In 1964, gays and lesbians were being discriminated against, weren't they?
>
> *Marshall:* That's correct.
>
> *Kay:* But you didn't add them to that list in 1964, did you?
>
> *Marshall:* No. We were not all wise. We're not all-foreseeing.
>
> *Kay:* But everyone knew that gays and lesbians were being discriminated against in 1964. This is not something new that's popped up in our society.
>
> *Marshall:* I would agree that it was not something new that's popped up in society. I would agree that it existed in 1964. The perception of that discrimination did not exist in 1964 in my knowledge.
>
> [. . .]
>
> *Kay:* And everyone knew that the discrimination existed?
>
> *Marshall:* I question whether it was apparent at the time.
>
> *Kay:* Well, the hostility, the social hostility against gays and lesbians in our society has gotten better in the last 30 years, hasn't it?
>
> *Marshall:* The whole problem has become open. In 1964 it was not open. People disguised their sexuality with respect to this in 1964. . . . Therefore, the problem was not as apparent to Con-

gress, wasn't apparent at all to Congress, wasn't apparent to me as an assistant attorney general, wasn't apparent to the president, wasn't apparent to society.

Kay: You knew homosexuals existed in 1964, didn't you?

Marshall: I have no doubt that they did.

Kay: And you knew that they were being discriminated against in 1964, didn't you?

Marshall: I must say, Mr. Kay, in 1964, I didn't think about that. I was in charge of the division . . . that had a very full plate, and the very full plate didn't cover all injustice in the world. It covered principally injustice to black people, and that was what the Voting Rights Act was about. That's what our cases were about.

In short, no rigid rules dictate which characteristics are protected against discrimination and which are not. The composition of legislatures, the general public's awareness and sentiments, coalition politics, and the publicity given to certain types of discrimination all go into the mix of factors that result in passage of a particular antidiscrimination law.

Still, questions at the Amendment 2 trial, and in society generally, focused on the scope and consequences of civil rights protections, whether laws prohibiting sexual orientation discrimination were necessary, and whether a social consensus existed to support their enactment and enforcement. During the trial, the state offered every possible objection to civil rights laws in general and to those specifically prohibiting sexual orientation discrimination, basing its arguments on economics, politics, and morality, as well as on plain dislike of lesbians and gay men.

Civil Rights or *Special Rights*

As a general matter, witnesses for both sides at the Amendment 2 trial shared the same basic view that the goal of civil rights laws is to enforce equal treatment. For example, the plaintiffs' expert witness Marshall used the Civil Rights Act of 1964 to illustrate the purpose of civil rights laws.

Marshall testified that the Civil Rights Act of 1964 "was occasioned by the perception of the Congress, by the people of the United States and, by the people directly affected by it, of the pervasive discrimination . . . in all parts of society." Designed "to eliminate by law discrimination that is otherwise the social norm or the economic norm, or the political norm," the Civil Rights Act prohibited discrimination based on race as well as other characteristics to protect individuals, including African-Americans, who "were perceived at that time as requiring protection by law in order to be able to participate fully in the life of the United States, including its economic life."[3] Marshall reminded the court that "large parts of the country . . . permitted pervasive, endemic discrimination against people" based on factors irrelevant to their job performance. The Civil Rights Act's aim "was to bring that kind of invidious discrimination under the control of law."

Commenting on antidiscrimination laws enacted in Colorado subsequent to the federal act's enactment, one of the state's witnesses, a former member of the Colorado Civil Rights Commission, Ignacio Rodriguez, echoed Marshall's analysis while testifying in defense of Amendment 2. The purpose of civil rights laws, Rodriguez stated, is to "correct past discriminatory practices which grievously injure groups of people" and to promote equality.

Despite this agreement about the general purpose of civil rights legislation, the two sides disagreed strongly over many questions, including whether laws prohibiting discrimination provided "special rights" or preserved equal rights for members of minority groups.

Prior to the November 1992 election, the promoters of Amendment 2 argued forcefully to the public that having legal protection against discrimination is a "special right" that lesbians and gay men do not deserve. CFV's Will Perkins, along with two other citizen-leaders of CFV, spearheaded the adoption of the "No Special Rights" theme used to promote Amendment 2. Perkins testified that, in gathering signatures required to place Amendment 2 on the ballot, the "whole premise of the people that I talked to was that [gay people] have equal rights, and they certainly don't deserve any special rights. And that's why they signed the petition."

Explaining how some rights become "special rights," Perkins testified that

---

3. The legislative history of the Civil Rights Act of 1964 reflects the strong disagreement over its enactment. Just before the act was set to pass, a Southern senator proposed an amendment to have the act forbid discrimination based on sex in addition to the other protected categories, believing that the amendment would doom the act to defeat in Congress. Contrary to his expectations, the act passed as amended, which is why Title VII and the other provisions of the Civil Rights Act prohibit sex discrimination as well as discrimination based on race, color, religion, and national origin.

the special right of protected class status is a special right because everybody doesn't have it in every situation. Now, if everybody has this special right in every situation, then who has a special right? And the answer is nobody. And who loses in that group? The losers are the very people for whom the Civil Rights Act was initiated. People who—groups in society that needed a leg up to get started in education, jobs, employment, through affirmative action.

Former Colorado civil rights commissioner Rodriguez echoed this view, telling the court that, while on the state's Civil Rights Commission, he voted against amending Colorado's civil rights laws to prohibit sexual orientation discrimination. He did so, he said, because of his belief that equal rights protections are a "special right" that gay people do not deserve. "Protected status," Rodriguez testified, "is a bit over and above what the ordinary citizen enjoys. . . ."

CFV cofounder and executive director Kevin Tebedo reinforced this view that civil rights laws provide "special rights" to minority groups only:

It was a concern to me that if we granted sexual orientation and homosexuality protected class status, we would, in fact, nullify all of the civil rights law[s] in the nation. Everybody has a sexual orientation. I could see at no time no distinction that could be made whatsoever for these groups that were truly discriminated against.

Perkins acknowledged that a consulting attorney to CFV advised him "that special rights is not a legal term and should not be used in the wording of the amendment itself," for legal reasons. But for a campaign theme, it was a winner! Of those supporting Amendment 2, 40 percent surveyed in exit polls told one of Colorado's leading pollsters they voted "yes" because gay people "should not have special rights," while only 3 percent said they supported Amendment 2 because "homosexuality is wrong."[4]

Amendment 2's challengers anticipated these views and, through

---

4. Affidavit of Paul Talmey. Although most voters told pollsters they supported the amendment because they opposed "special rights," some organizers of the opposition to Amendment 2 said they believed many pro–Amendment 2 voters disliked or disapproved of gay people but feared being perceived as bigoted and cited the "no special rights" reason to pollsters instead of indicating their true sentiments.

witness testimony, sought to lay the groundwork for a different understanding of the effect of civil rights legislation. Again relying on the ban
on employment discrimination in Title VII of the 1964 Civil Rights Act
as an example, Duke University law professor Jerome Culp emphasized that civil rights provisions do not protect specified groups but
prohibit use of a general classification, such as race or sex, as the basis
for discrimination against *anyone*. Under Title VII, explained Culp,
"white males have a right to bring a claim. Under Title VII, people who
are from a majority religion have a right to bring a claim. The statute is
written so that what's prohibited is the use of a category, and everybody has some part of that category. Everybody has a gender. Everybody has a race. Everybody . . . has a sexual orientation, and therefore
everybody is protected."

In other words, civil rights laws provide no more protection to
those in the minority than to those in the majority. In prohibiting discrimination based on sexual orientation, as Culp explained, the law
protected nongay people as much as gay people. The claim by Amendment 2's supporters that only certain individuals received "special"
protections by virtue of being part of a minority group, Culp said, was
simply inaccurate.

Culp identified sexual orientation antidiscrimination laws as part
of a large-scale civil rights movement that sought to achieve equality
for all people, and he criticized the state's reliance on the "special
rights" argument as a notorious political sleight of hand. Culp, an
African-American man, testified that he

> first encountered the notion of "special rights" when [he] was a
> graduate student in Boston and . . . tried to rent an apartment in
> Charlestown, and that happened to be during the situation of bus-
> ing in Boston and people said that blacks in Boston wanted special
> rights, and part of that result was that people got beat up on the
> streets of Boston because they were black and were in the wrong
> area. . . .

Joseph Hicks, executive director of the Southern Christian Leadership Conference of Greater Los Angeles and executive vice president of
the Martin Luther King Legacy Association, reinforced this point as a
witness for the plaintiffs. His views on civil rights as "special rights"

were provided to the court through this exchange with plaintiffs' trial attorney Gregory Eurich.

> *Eurich:* Mr. Hicks, the campaign slogan or a campaign slogan of Colorado for Family Values in the Amendment 2 campaign was "No Special Rights." Does that phrase mean anything to you as an expert in the civil rights movement in the United States?
>
> *Hicks:* No, it has no meaning to me, and I can't perceive of what it actually means because extending civil rights protections, human rights, to people are not special rights. . . .

Surprisingly, the state never argued that when sexual orientation is added to an antidiscrimination law, gay people are in a different or "special" position relative to others discriminated against for reasons not protected by law. For example, although lawyers or used car dealers might suffer discrimination based on their professions, antidiscrimination laws typically do not forbid profession-based discrimination. Again, however, the plaintiffs could have responded by explaining that the political process must be open on an equal basis for all who need protections to seek them, and that if lawyers or used car dealers wanted to organize to pass protective legislation and could persuade others of the need to do so, such laws could be enacted. Also, the plaintiffs could have reiterated that antidiscrimination laws help to ensure equal opportunity to vulnerable groups in the face of discrimination. That other groups also suffer discrimination, but are not included in existing antidiscrimination laws, does not require a ban on existing protections.

Economic Objections

In addition to their argument that civil rights constituted "special rights," the state's witnesses offered an array of objections tied to the cost to employers and others of complying with these laws. Their central theme was that civil rights laws burden free economic enterprise and are proper only when necessary to give a "leg up" to an economically disadvantaged minority. Not surprisingly, this focus on economic burden to private business has driven a multitude of efforts to dismantle all forms of civil rights laws, including campaigns to repeal and override laws enacted in the 1960s to stop discrimination based on race and other characteristics as well as more recently enacted sexual orientation laws.

George Mason Law School professor Joseph Broadus, in defense of Amendment 2, testified that "every civil rights provision ends up awarding special privileges." Because civil rights laws can affect how property owners use or sell their property—for instance, a homeowner may not refuse to sell his or her house to a prospective buyer based on that person's race, he stated—the laws transfer control of the property from the owner to the protected class. Reflecting this perspective, Broadus described Title VII's prohibition of employment discrimination as "an extraordinary remedy because it makes the government intrude in economic ways in which the government hasn't previously done."

This view, which forms the basis for many employers' opposition to *all* civil rights laws, was reinforced in laypersons' terms by CFV's Perkins. Perkins testified that he fears "gay rights" laws will render him vulnerable to frivolous litigation any time he fires or refuses to hire or promote someone who is gay. Because of this fear, he told the court, a sexual orientation antidiscrimination bill proposed in Colorado Springs was the catalyst for his involvement in the movement opposed to civil rights for gay people. The bill's "potential impact," he said, was "just more red tape and more problems involving this type of complaint." He explained:

> The things that caught my eye were primarily the fact that, as a business person, if one of my employees filed a complaint against me . . . they could make me give them any information I had in my business or home, and then the [human rights] commission was the judge and jury, and frankly, I thought something like that would make a gestapo embarrassed and I saw this as a real potential problem for business and that's what got me involved, why I went to the hearings.

Another CFV coleader, Tony Marco, testified that he believes that laws prohibiting sexual orientation discrimination create a costly tool that employees can use to harass employers and potential employers. In explaining his opposition to the Colorado Springs bill, Marco testified that the proposed ordinance would have "created a little KGB in

Colorado Springs with unlimited power to harass almost every citizen in the state or in the city with an unlimited budget." Marco added that "granting these protections allows an immediate factor of intimidation to enter into the employment practice or the practice of hiring in business."

It is true that those who are most often the victims of discrimination—whether women, older people, or members of racial, ethnic, religious, or other minorities—are most often the ones to bring discrimination lawsuits. And it is true that, as with all lawsuits, some have merit and some do not. However, civil rights commissions have the power to investigate complaints—not to harass businesses or seek out unrelated information. Also, as many civil rights experts note, many people who are victims of discrimination do not file discrimination charges. They are often concerned about the personal and financial costs of doing so, or fear that filing a lawsuit will forever saddle them with a reputation as litigious—a reputation that could interfere with their future employment prospects.

For all of his concern about potential business interference, Perkins had not developed an initiative to limit protections for other minorities. Nor did he acknowledge that antidiscrimination laws offer protection to all persons, and not solely those in the minority. Likewise, Broadus did not testify that he objected to the economic burden of civil rights laws that prohibit discrimination based on a variety of other characteristics, including race, sex, and religion.

Identifying the Gay-Specific Objections

All civil rights laws tend to generate debate. However, a special level of vehement opposition arises against laws that seek to protect lesbians, gay men, and bisexuals against discrimination. The state of Colorado, through its legal arguments and its witnesses at trial, presented the full array of these gay-specific objections in its defense of Amendment 2.

First were arguments based on visibility and definition. The state's witnesses, including CFV leaders Perkins, Tebedo, and Marco, as well as former civil rights commissioner Rodriguez, testified that it is not appropriate for lesbians and gay men to be covered by civil rights laws because gay people are not readily identifiable and because there is no agreed-upon definition of sexual orientation. In other words, the argument regarding identification went, if sexual orientation is not evident to the casual observer, how can one know whether alleged discrimination is based upon sexual orientation?

And similarly, if there is disagreement in popular culture, academic circles, and even communities of lesbians and gay men about what it means to be lesbian or gay, how can a civil rights law related to sexual orientation be administered fairly? This dispute about the meaning of "gay" parallels, in its conflict about how to define a core aspect of human identity, the long-standing debate in American society and jurisprudence concerning the meaning of race and who should be considered a person of color. In past decades, of course, the definition of race was significant for determining who would be considered "white" and who would be "colored" for segregation purposes. However, the civil rights debate about the definition of race today, like the debate about sexual orientation, focuses on whether and how antidiscrimination prohibitions should be enforced.

Second, in addition to its argument regarding the definition of sexual orientation, the state, though the same CFV witnesses, Rodriguez, and Harvard professor Harvey Mansfield, argued that people should not receive protections for "chosen" behavior. Since being gay, it maintained, is defined by a choice of behavior, sexual orientation is not a sufficiently immutable characteristic upon which to base antidiscrimination protection.

Ultimately, again relying on testimony of CFV leaders, the state argued that the citizens of Colorado did not want their state to outlaw maltreatment of lesbian and gay Coloradans and that they supported Amendment 2 as a vehicle to prevent the legislature from so doing. Banning antidiscrimination prohibitions covering gay people, the state maintained, was an acceptable way for voters to express their disapproval of a subset of Colorado's population that they disliked.

Visibility

Could sexual orientation discrimination be prohibited because there are no visible cues as to a person's sexual orientation? Could the difficulty in defining who is "lesbian" or "gay" render such laws vulnerable to abuse? Ignacio Rodriguez, former state civil rights commissioner, laid out both arguments in his testimony in response to questioning by state's attorney Jack Wesoky.

> *Wesoky:* You were testifying as to the perceived differences between sexual orientation as an identifiable group or homosexuals as an identifiable group, and what I'll call the traditional minorities as an identifiable group. Why do you not consider them the same?
>
> *Rodriguez:* I don't know how the group would be identified. There are no obvious immutable characteristics. The way I understand it, even sexual practices are very divergent. The only thing the group seems to have in common is an attraction for its own gender. It's a very heterogeneous group, very different. I don't believe that there's, quote, a homosexual lifestyle, for example.

Interestingly, this was one point on which the state's witnesses and gay people were in agreement. Many gay people asserted that the only difference between them and heterosexuals is that lesbians and gay men have same-sex partners. But other opponents of equal rights for lesbians and gay men have maintained that being gay is, in fact, a "lifestyle choice." And many gay people countered that sexual orientation is not a predictor of lifestyle and that their lifestyles are as diverse as the lifestyles of heterosexuals.

Wesoky asked how the heterogeneity of gay people that Rodriguez talked about affected enforcement of laws that prohibited discrimination against gay people. Rodriguez responded that because sexual orientation typically becomes known only after the individual in question identifies it, such laws would be "extremely difficult if not impossible to enforce . . . because just about anyone could self-identify" as gay.

"Now, obviously you can't identify what religion I am by looking at me," said Wesoky. "How do you differentiate between self-identification of religion and self-identification of sexual orientation?" Rodriguez suggested that an individual's religious identification might be "general knowledge" but conceded that, generally, self-identification would be required to identify someone's religion, too. This concession, however, did not weaken Rodriguez's conviction that laws protecting gay people are uniquely unworkable. He told the court that "authorities would be unable to appropriately address complaints from [gay] people. It's too intangible. There's nothing firm or solid there."

Rodriguez, who had helped draft Colorado's statewide antidiscrimination law, which did not include sexual orientation, expanded on these arguments later in his testimony.

> *Wesoky:* Are there any differences that come into your mind or play into your mind when you were deciding whether or not to add that group [i.e., gay people] to the protected list under Colorado law?
>
> *Rodriguez:* One of the traditional criteria had to do with identity, and being able to identify and enumerate a group, and I don't believe this can be done with a gay, homosexual, lesbian community.
>
> *Wesoky:* And why do you think that?
>
> *Rodriguez:* It's a very divergent group. It's not defined even by the groups themselves. There's a disagreement within the homosexual community about identity. . . . Most recently, I read in the paper about a lady in Boulder who indicated that she was a lesbian by choice, that she had chosen that, quote, lifestyle or whatever it is you want to call it. Others say that it is not a matter of choice, and I think the jury is still out on that.

CFV's Marco, too, testified that "even within the gay community itself there is a considerable amount of disagreement regarding whether this characteristic is innate or immutable."

Again, the state's witnesses were correct in suggesting that many gay people hold divergent views about the origins of sexual orientation. Many gay people say they feel certain that being gay is a characteristic they cannot change, regardless of whether the origins are in genetics, biology, or elsewhere. Others, including many women who came out as lesbians during the women's liberation movement in the 1970s, say they made a choice to be gay or bisexual. But what was missing in the state's testimony was any discussion of the origin of heterosexual orientation—or the choice involved in being heterosexual.

Marco also reiterated his view that sexual orientation is "not obvious." After indicating that he had a gay activist roommate while living in New York City during the late 1960s, Marco added that "I would be very confident myself, on the basis of two of the definitions of sexual orientation given by the plaintiffs and one by a leading gay militant, to claim homosexual orientation myself." Later, Marco added, that because of questions about visibility and definition, laws banning sexual orientation discrimination might lend themselves to abuse.

> For example, a person might come in under an ordinance granting protected class status through sexual orientation to apply for a job alongside an African-American person and a woman, let's say, and say, "Well, I notice you have a number of African-American people working here, you have a number of women, how many homosexuals do you have?" Can you imagine this person who's a Caucasian male and who says, "I am a homosexual and I want this job?" You have an immediate threat of a lawsuit if the employment is denied and possible grievance complaints on behalf of the other to recognized protected classes who were denied that job. In that case, the plaintiffs' definition of sexual orientation offers no grounds whatsoever for proof of one's identity in terms of sexual orientation. So the potential for fraud in cases like this is enormous.

The plaintiffs' civil rights expert, Burke Marshall, disagreed as he addressed the "visibility" question in his videotaped deposition, in response to questions from Kathryn Emmett.

> *Emmett:* Another point that has been made is that somehow or other the characteristic that qualifies a group for protection under any discrimination laws is the visibility of the trait that binds the group together or identifies members of the group. . . .
> *Marshall:* That also is clearly not correct. Someone's religion is not marked on her face. Someone's national origin is not marked on one's face. In fact, in many cases, one's race is not clearly marked on one's face. Hence, the desire [to outlaw discrimination] protects against . . . the desire to "pass," as it used to be put, and appear to be something that you are not in order to escape the discrimination that comes from what you are. But visibility is not a characteristic of any of these groups except maybe the racial groups.

Supporting Marshall's testimony, Culp, in response to Eurich's questioning, also addressed the state's argument that laws should not prohibit sexual orientation discrimination because "you can't tell by looking at somebody if they are gay or lesbian." "We don't know your marital status by looking at you," he noted. "There's lots of different categories that are not readily apparent. And the notion that [physical appearance] is the only basis or the exclusive basis or necessarily even the primary basis [for legal protection against discrimination] seems to me to be wrong." Culp also observed that part of the invisibility for many gay people comes from the fact that "social norms are so great to force [gay people] to hide their identit[ies]" and provides a "stronger reason to protect gays, lesbians, and bisexuals."

In addition, as Marshall and Culp both implied, the critical inquiry in a discrimination case is not whether the plaintiff, is, in fact, gay. It is whether the discriminator treated that person differently because the discriminator believed the person to be gay. For example, if an employer fires an employee whom the employer thought was Jewish, based on the employee's name or appearance, the fired employee could claim religious discrimination even if the employee was Baptist. Similarly, if a landlord evicts a tenant whom he or she perceives to be a lesbian, because of the friends with whom the tenant associates, the tenant can sue for sexual orientation discrimination even if she is heterosexual (so long as there is a law against sexual orientation discrimination where she lives). The illegal act occurs when the employer or landlord discriminates based on the belief that the person has a particular characteristic.

To add real-world experience to this discussion about the theory behind antidiscrimination laws, the plaintiffs' attorneys brought to court two witnesses responsible for enforcement of laws prohibiting sexual orientation discrimination. Leanna Ware, director of the Civil Rights Bureau for the State of Wisconsin, testified about enforcement issues under Wisconsin's law against sexual orientation discrimination in response to questions from Denver's attorney Darlene Ebert. Wisconsin's law was enacted in 1982 and is the oldest such state law in the country.

> *Ebert:* Have you heard the argument or been confronted with the argument that sexual orientation laws cannot be enforced because of the alleged difficulty in detecting what an individual's sexual orientation is?
> *Ware:* Yes, I have heard the argument.

Ebert: Has it been a problem in your investigation of sexual orientation cases?

Ware: It is sometimes an issue that the employer raises—that he or she was not aware of the individual's sexual orientation—just as it is in some of the other protections that are not visible. Marital status, or diabetes as a disability, is not visible, so it might be a defense that the employer raises in sexual orientation cases as in other cases.

Ebert: And how does one investigate a case, then, where the sexual orientation or other unknown cause for discrimination of an individual is at issue?

Ware: Well, in our investigative process . . . we would then go back to the complainant and say that "The employer has indicated that he or she wasn't aware that you were covered under this basis. Why do you believe that the employer was aware?" And usually the complainant will give information about some statements that the employer has made or information that their sexual orientation or marital status or whatever was generally know in the workplace, through witnesses. So it depends on the individual circumstances, but it's certainly something that we deal with in many cases.

Ebert: Is the investigation of a sexual orientation claim any different from the investigation of other types of discrimination claims?

Ware: No, it is not.

To demonstrate that investigation practices for sexual orientation–based discrimination complaints in Wisconsin were not materially different from those in Colorado, the plaintiffs called Brenda Toliver-Locke as a witness. Toliver-Locke was the compliance officer for Denver's Agency for Human Rights and Community Relations and was charged with enforcing Denver's antidiscrimination ordinance, which included a prohibition against sexual orientation discrimination. After sexual orientation was added to the antidiscrimination ordinance in 1990, she testified, over one-fourth of the complaints filed included a sexual orientation discrimination charge.

Ebert: Have you had any difficulty in the cases which you have investigated in determining whether the party against whom the complaints have been filed, whether those people or companies have been aware of the sexual orientation of the complainant?

Toliver-Locke: We have not had difficulty. Sometimes what happens is the respondent will say, "I was not aware of the sexual orientation of the charging party," and what we do in that case is we go back to the complainant, we ask them for more information about their case that will help us substantiate that allegation. We also ask witnesses and other people that we have identified. We also seek documents or anything that we can get to substantiate that.

Ebert: And what types of evidence have you uncovered when you have gone back to do that additional investigation?

Toliver-Locke: We have often gotten direct quotes that employers may have made to another employee that show that there was some knowledge or perceived knowledge of one's sexual orientation. There may have been rumors that were floating around among the employees and their employer. . . . [S]ometimes we have to look a little deeper, but we have been able to find examples that substantiate them that there was some knowledge of sexual orientation.

Ebert: Have you determined in the course of your investigations whether employers or landlords or people that run schools or whatever have some stereotypical views on visible traits of sexual orientation?

Toliver-Locke: Some people do. They have some perception of what they think are stereotypes of someone with a particular sexual orientation.

On the question of how the definition of the group of lesbians and gay men compares to definitions of other groups subjected to discrimination, civil rights expert Marshall testified that an academic or cultural disagreement over the exact parameters of what it means to be lesbian or gay does not lessen discrimination against those perceived to be gay.

Emmett: Can you tell me how, in your view, gay men, lesbians, and bisexuals as a group would compare to the other groups that— those that you've discussed and others—have been protected in law against discrimination?

Marshall: Well, they share a characteristic, which is their sexuality, that makes them into a community that, when it's known, at least, leads—this is as clear as crystal—leads to rampant discrimination and in some cases violent retaliation simply because of what they are. So that they are a group that is vulnerable once they are known, in the same way that these other groups that I've been talking about are vulnerable. Everything about our recent history says that, including the debate, of course, about gays in the military and what has happened to gays in the military. So that they share a characteristic which is common to them, which is at the core of their personality, which . . . when known, at least, leads to retaliation and discrimination by the outside community because of the characteristic. So they are sort of a classic group that should be protected, could be protected, by laws against discrimination if the voters—you know, if the people that are faced with that problem want to do something.

Civil rights expert Culp likewise illustrated that a characteristic need not be genetically immutable and physically visible to be protected by an antidiscrimination law.

Eurich: Well, but aren't the categories that are already covered readily identifiable? Isn't the concept of race a purely dichotomous variable; either you are white or you are black?

Culp: Well, I think that is a notion that no longer has much credibility in either the scientific, the historic, or humanistic communities. . . . in this country, black Americans have more genetic material in common with the average white American than white ethnic groups have in common with each other. The kind of genetic notion and the kind of notion of race as a thing that exists is commonly, and I think appropriately, challenged now.

Eurich: It's important in terms of analyzing discrimination cases, perceptions of people, or whether they have some immutable characteristics they can scientifically demonstrate?

Culp: I think the most important characteristic is their exclusion from the protections that the civil rights movement has been trying to extend—the protections of access to public accommodations, access to jobs, access to housing, access to political participation.

Identity vs. "Chosen Behavior"

In addition to charges related to the visibility of sexual orientation, the state, through its witnesses, urged that sexual orientation is a behavior and therefore not appropriate for civil rights protection. "Our argument consistently was throughout the campaign that how you have sex, for whatever reason, is not an appropriate criterion for civil rights," Will Perkins testified. This view—that laws prohibiting sexual orientation discrimination amounted to protections for sexual behavior—drove much of the Amendment 2 campaign. It surfaced consistently as a thorny question at trial, as well as in the public debate about lesbian and gay civil rights.

The argument persuaded many people, as evidenced, at least in part, by the Amendment 2 campaign's success at the polls. In fact, the equation proffered by Amendment 2's proponents, in which lesbians and gay men were defined by sexual behavior and then deemed undeserving of civil rights laws, was a powerful and widespread myth. It took full advantage of popular misconceptions about gay people as well as about the nature of discrimination and the purpose of civil rights laws.

The equation contained two sub-arguments. First, it maintained that people's *choices* are an inappropriate basis for civil rights protections—in other words, the *only* characteristics worthy of legal protection are those that are immutable and involuntary in nature. That argument failed though, in light of widespread protections against religious discrimination, with religion being neither immutable nor involuntary. Second, it assumed that being gay is a choice—and an unpopular one. As CFV's Kevin Tebedo stated, "the public out there . . . seems to be interested not only in the civil rights and ethical issues, but they are also interested in society's view of what is acceptable and what is not acceptable behavior in American society."

Opponents of gay civil rights protections urged that such laws would encourage gay men and lesbians to engage in disapproved acts. Testifying for the state, Harvey Mansfield, a government professor at Harvard University, expressed this view on cross-examination.

> *Eurich:* One of the reasons you think there's something wrong with being gay is you believe being gay is surely partly voluntary, correct?

Mansfield: Not *being* gay, but *behaving* in—I think that would come out in reference to the sexual practices of gays, which are different, as are the political beliefs of gays. . . . They have choices in their own life and they are capable of leading a moral life within the limits of the tendencies or inclinations they have which may not be voluntary.

The state's concern was that laws prohibiting sexual orientation discrimination enabled more people to feel free to reveal that they are lesbian or gay. Where antigay hostility runs rampant, lesbians and gay men are more cautious about revealing their sexual orientation. To the plaintiffs, the real question was not whether such laws give sanction to homosexuality or "homosexual sex," but instead whether they provided sanctuary for people to live openly without fear of invidious discrimination.

Real Discrimination

Were lesbians and gay men unable to live openly in Colorado? Although this question did not need to be answered for the court to decide the constitutionality of Amendment 2, it was addressed by both sides.

Plaintiffs challenging Amendment 2 had given personal testimony almost a year earlier at the preliminary injunction hearing, highlighting the impact of this antigay discrimination on their lives in Colorado. Angela Romero had testified about losing her job as school resource officer with the Denver police department when her supervisor found out she was a lesbian. She had testified, too, that she endured repeated derogatory comments and graffiti about lesbians and gay men made by other officers and received inadequate backup while on patrol, because she was a lesbian. Paul Brown had testified about being "let go" from a job by a manager who then rehired another man who had spray-painted "Paul is a fag" across the office building wall.

Toliver-Locke, Denver's antidiscrimination compliance officer, testified that the law met a real need. "We have had some cases that have demonstrated that people are definitely being discriminated against because of their sexual orientation," said Toliver-Locke, "both in employment and in housing and in public accommodations."

The evidence before the court, including police reports and records of discrimination complaints, demonstrated there could be no real question about whether lesbians and gay men in Colorado experienced discrimination and bias-motivated violence. They did. But the state, which on one hand tried to show that sexual orientation antidiscrimination laws were unnecessary, then used the existence of this discrimination to make one of its key arguments for Amendment 2—that fighting discrimination against gay people would take away from fighting discrimination against more "acceptable" minorities.

Dilution

Throughout the campaign and the trial, Amendment 2's supporters urged that laws against sexual orientation discrimination would dilute popular support for civil rights laws by adding protections for an unpopular group. At the same time, they urged that adding protections for sexual orientation would take away enforcement resources needed for combating other civil rights violations. The professed fear that enforcement of legal protections for gay people would drain resources seemed to clash directly with the state's argument that gay people did not need protection from discrimination. Still, the state pressed forward, apparently having decided to offer all possible theories to the court without regard to the contradiction.

The state's witnesses reinforced both aspects of the "dilution" argument repeatedly throughout their testimony. For example, civil rights expert Broadus was asked whether states including characteristics such as sexual orientation in civil rights laws breed disrespect for civil rights laws generally. He replied that, "to the extent that [state governments] proceed kind of indiscriminately, not as carefully as the federal government has in extending them, they will bring measures into disrepute." On the question of whether enforcement of existing civil rights laws suffers when other protected classifications are added, Broadus also endorsed the state's argument: "I think there can be a dilution of resources by expanding [the number of] groups. . . . the fact remains that the ability of the courts to assume litigation is not endless."

Former Colorado Civil Rights Commission chair Rodriguez offered similar views.

> *Wesoky:* Given your experience in the civil rights field, . . . do you
>   believe that the addition of sexual orientation to the list of

> [classes protected against] discrimination in Colorado Civil
> Rights law would or would not be a departure from the histori-
> cal aims of civil rights laws?
>
> *Rodriguez:* A drastic departure.
>
> *Wesoky:* Why do you say that, sir?
>
> *Rodriguez:* Drastic, in that I think it would weaken and dilute those
> civil rights protections that had been earned by minorities, by
> women, by the disabled over the years.
>
> *Wesoky:* Why do you say it would weaken or dilute those protec-
> tions for the enumerated groups?
>
> *Rodriguez:* I think that there's—at this point in time—a general
> acceptance and respect for civil rights laws and the need for
> them. Inasmuch as the gay, lesbian group has not demonstrated
> that need, I think that that would lower the [esteem] in which
> the general public holds civil rights law.

CFV's Will Perkins also reinforced this point, testifying that inclusion
of sexual orientation in antidiscrimination laws "will dilute the whole
meaning of civil rights and dilute the resources that are available to be
used."

And Colorado Civil Rights Division regional supervisor Tom
Duran testified that because of lack of adequate funding, "it doesn't
make sense to include another class [in the state's civil rights law]
because there is no fund[ing] available to investigate, to mediate, to
take to hearing." He added that addition of sexual orientation as a protected classification in the state law "might be injurious to those parties
that are already . . . defined protected classes." Further, he maintained
that a statewide prohibition against sexual orientation discrimination
would "probably not" receive the same respect as other protected classifications because the majority of Colorado's population have "ill
respect or a lack of respect for . . . this class of individuals."

In contrast, however, both Toliver-Locke and Ware, each with
direct experience enforcing laws against sexual orientation discrimination, testified that the laws neither put an excessive demand on their
enforcement resources nor diluted respect for other provisions of the
civil rights laws. In addition, Toliver-Locke, as chief enforcer of Denver's antidiscrimination ordinance, explained that opposition to the
law's coverage of discrimination based on sexual orientation had not
affected general opinion of the city's civil rights laws.

Toliver-Locke: We have observed that there are people who—
   employers or landlords or whatever the nature might be,
   depending on the case—who just do not feel that sexual orientation should be a protected class. So they are against that portion
   of the ordinance.

Ebert: Have you observed employers or landlords who have similar reactions to other provisions of the ordinance such as marital
   status? Military status?

Toliver-Locke: No.

Ebert: Or any of the others?

Toliver-Locke: [No.]

Ebert: Because of that observation, has that made protections . . .
   against race discrimination, sex discrimination or any of the
   other groups more difficult to enforce?

Toliver-Locke: No, ma'am.

Turning to the question of whether expansion of civil rights law coverage greatly burdens a government's resources to enforce other civil rights protections, Burke Marshall noted that while there is some increase in demand on the state, "a great deal of the enforcement of the laws is by private lawsuit, so that although there may be an added burden that is, you know, measurable, but not significant, on the court systems in any particular jurisdiction, there isn't even that increase in the demand on the resources of the state." Therefore, he concluded, "I can't see any basis for believing that it would undercut the implementation or efficacy of the prohibitions against discrimination" based on other characteristics.

The Debates Continue

Again, despite their extensive testimony, civil rights experts could not identify a single or absolute indication of what it means to be lesbian or gay. Opponents of gay civil rights sought to capitalize on this ambiguity, charging that if there is not a clear definition of who gay people are, then it is inappropriate to provide civil rights protections to those claiming to be gay. Gay advocates responded that civil rights legislation is concerned not with the victim's actual identity but rather with the discriminator's perception of the victim: if the discriminator fired someone because he or she believed the employee to be gay, that is enough. On this theory, the meaning of "gay" or "lesbian" would be determined by the individual discriminator's perceptions. Or, perhaps, genetic, psychological, historical, and political science vantage points are each independently sufficient, with sexual orientation antidiscrimination laws prohibiting antigay acts based on any of these fields' definitions of "gay." With each new witness, it was increasingly clear that no single definition of gay identity would make sense for the wide variety of contexts in which gay people's civic participation and civil rights would be evaluated.

Chapter 7

Morality Plays

The terms are loaded: morality, religion, family values. When mixed with a discussion of politics and government, they can become explosive. And that was the mix compounding the battle over Amendment 2, with morality, religion, and family values becoming constant fodder for both sides.

Amy Devine, head of the Colorado-based Citizens Project that monitors right-wing religious groups and their activities, said she would classify Colorado for Family Values "with the organizations that would like to see biblical law dictating American law" and that Amendment 2 was "their main step" down that road.[1] To support her contention, she pointed out a statement made by CFV official Kevin Tebedo that, despite the separation of church and state, "Jesus Christ is the king of kings and the lord of lords" and that "all power and authorities" belonged to him.

Opponents of Amendment 2 also evoked the church at times. The gay congregation of the Metropolitan Community Church Family in Christ published an essay opposing Amendment 2 as "contrary to the teachings and example of our Lord Jesus."[2]

The debate quickly spilled outside the borders of Colorado.

On a national PBS broadcast, the pro–Amendment 2 side saw it this way: "It's not a question of evangelical Christians trying to grab control of the levers of government here and impose some conservative Christian agenda on the community. It's basically Christian people— conservative Christian people in particular, in the case of Amendment 2—trying to prevent the government from interfering in their lives. What they oppose is the force of government being brought on them to

---

1. Interviewed in *Bill Moyers Journal*, "The New Holy War," aired on PBS stations nationwide November 19, 1993.
2. Colleen Dolan-Fullbright, "No," a companion article to "Yes," examining the arguments for and against Amendment 2; *Coloradan*, August 8, 1992, Religion page.

force them to accept and condone this life-style that violates their most basic beliefs."[3]

"While for some, 'family values' is an innocent appeal to nostalgia, for too many others it is a code for the narrow-minded, fear-inspired, hate-filled exclusion of anyone not living a 'Walton' life-style," read a *USA Today* editorial just two months before the November 1992 vote. "For them, the phrase rings with intolerance for single parents, divorced couples and women who work outside the home, and gays and lesbians."[4]

One might expect such inflammatory rhetoric about family values and morality on the campaign trail. But the debate continued in the courtroom. Why?

Primarily, the issues came up in the state's attempt to support one of the six stated reasons it had advanced for needing Amendment 2. The state said Amendment 2 was necessary to protect religious, familial, and personal privacy. According to the state, laws in some Colorado cities that prohibited discrimination based on sexual orientation encroached on the right of those parents who held a religiously based belief that homosexuality is wrong; the antidiscrimination laws, said the state, interfered with these parents' desire to teach their children to act on that belief.

The discussion about morality, religion, and family values was additionally important for Amendment 2 supporters because it offered a historical backdrop to support the argument that the majority of voters could stipulate that a minority would have fewer civil rights than other citizens. To accomplish this, the state first had to establish that laws have always been based on some notion of morality—right and wrong. Then, the question became not so much, "What is moral?" but "Whose morality shall guide the law?" In a democracy, the state contended, the answer would always be with those in the majority.

Attorneys challenging Amendment 2 tackled these same questions in a different manner and, naturally, came to different conclusions. In a democracy, they argued, society puts a moral value on equality, and on laws seeking to preserve that value. The plaintiffs' expert on civil

---

3. Dan Griswold, editor of the editorial page at *The Gazette Telegraph* in Colorado Springs, interviewed in *Bill Moyers Journal*, "The New Holy War," aired on PBS stations nationwide November 19, 1993.

4. Editorial, "Focus on Family Needs, Not Fuzzy 'Family Values,'" *USA Today*, August 20, 1992, 12A.

rights, Burke Marshall, testified that the "purpose of laws is to create a society that respects and complies by the value of equality . . . and is part of the American tradition of fairness and American culture."

In contrast, one of the state's experts, James Hunter, a professor of sociology and religious studies at the University of Virginia, stated in his affidavit that Amendment 2 was "rooted in the American public's most deeply held beliefs and values" but also in its "different and competing systems of moral understanding."

To explain the state's moral understanding of the law as it pertained to gay people, the state called on ancient Greece.

The Morality of Law

Most of Aristotle's contemporaries believed the Earth was the center of the universe and that the sun and all the other planets revolved around it. As wrong as they were, and from so far away as over 2,000 years in time, the great Greek thinkers have had enormous influence on contemporary Western thinking. And as thoughtful and influential as they were, they were also a product of their time. Consequently, some of Aristotle's ideas are scoffed at today, particularly in a democratic society.

Yet, the state of Colorado called on Aristotle, in a manner of speaking, to justify its attempts to treat gay people differently under Amendment 2. The effort provided the trial with some of its most contentious and bizarre moments.

Returning to ancient roots in a battle over a new law was a logical effort on the state's part. Just seven years earlier, in upholding Georgia's antisodomy law, the U.S. Supreme Court had said such prohibitions had "ancient roots" and that similar laws had existed "throughout the history of Western civilization." The majority in that decision, *Bowers v. Hardwick,* had even noted, in support of its holding, that "condemnation of those practices is firmly rooted in Judeo-Christian moral and ethical standards" and that sodomy between men was a crime under Roman law.

The state of Colorado's aim was to demonstrate that morality provided an equivalent basis for Amendment 2. Laws, argued the state, are inevitably based on some sense of right and wrong. If the public believes homosexuality is wrong, the argument continued, it should have the right to put that view into law.

In pretrial depositions and at the trial itself, scholars testifying on behalf of the state and Amendment 2 explained how, in their view, Aristotle, Plato, and society at large had, for centuries, discouraged sexual activities between men. And they tried to illustrate that, in the history of lawmaking, society's needs were often in conflict with, and took precedence over, the rights and morals of nonconforming individuals.

The plaintiffs did not balk at the discussion of what the Greeks thought about homosexuality. Indeed, one of their own expert witnesses testified that in today's society, "we, in general, admire" the Greek culture and see it as "a model of cultural excellence." That witness, not surprisingly, said the Greek model "supported and endorsed" homosexual relationships. But the plaintiffs' chief defense against the state's argument that there were ancient roots to laws discouraging homosexuality was to show that ancient attitudes about sexuality should not serve as an excuse to exercise prejudice against a group of people. The plaintiffs contended that the state was failing to make a crucial distinction in the debate—a distinction between *acts* that society sometimes frowned upon and the *people* who sometimes engaged in those acts.

In conjuring up the ancient Greeks at trial, the state frequently referred to an affidavit that had been filed with the court from John Finnis, a visiting professor of law at the University of Oxford.

"In my theory," said Finnis, "as in Plutarch's and at least incipiently in Plato's, homosexual sex is bad because it is inevitably and radically nonmarital in character." Marriage, he argued, can be seen only in a "committed partnership adopted not only to friendship but also to the procreation and education of children."

Finnis argued that "homosexual acts" are "morally bad" because "genital activity between same-sex partners cannot actualize or allow them to really experience any common good to which they are jointly committed." The common good to which he was referring was the procreation of children and, as he claimed in a rebuttal affidavit, could also be "the good of [a heterosexual married couple's] marriage."

The three "greatest" Greek philosophers, said Finnis, referring to Socrates, Plato, and Aristotle, "regarded homosexual conduct as intrinsically shameful, immoral, and indeed depraved or depraving." In more recent times, he wrote, a "standard modern position" concerning homosexuality has "emerged." That "standard modern position" is one that makes no law against consenting same-sex couples engaging in sex in private. "But states do have the authority," he said, "to discourage homosexual conduct and orientation . . . and typically . . . do so by various criminal and administrative laws and policies, many of which discriminate . . . between heterosexual and homosexual conduct adversely to the latter."

In another affidavit, another of the state's experts, David Novak, explained why the state wanted to discourage sexual activity between partners of the same sex. He said Amendment 2 was society's reaction to "the demand by homosexuals and bisexuals (and their sympathizers) that they be accorded the status of a persecuted minority, a minority to whom society owes special compensatory policies because of unjust discrimination in the past."

Novak, a professor of Judaic studies at the University of Virginia, acknowledged that the "special" compensation in public policy "has been biased in favor of heterosexuality." But the "real point" of the gay civil rights movement, Novak argued, was to "alleviate men of the responsibility for the care of women and children." Such a goal, he said, would undermine "much of social policy throughout our history."

"The legal repeal of Amendment 2 would, in effect," he said, "require the state to admit that it has been in moral error in its endorsement of the traditional family in such matters as restricting the rights and benefits of marriage and parenthood to heterosexuals."

This was the "family values" argument—a contention that required one to believe that "family" is a good thing but that gay people are not included in that concept and that they do not support it. And the attorneys opposing Amendment 2 had their expert witness in this area to refute this contention and that concerning the ancient roots for discouraging homosexuality.

Martha Nussbaum, who at the time was a professor of philosophy and classics at Brown University, had served for seven years as consultant to the United Nations' World Institute for Development Economics Research, investigating—particularly in Scandinavia—ways that debates over morality can contribute to policy-making concerning women and the family. A professor of philosophy and classics at Brown University, she had also been chosen by the Harvard University Press and the Loeb Classical Library trustees, a few years earlier, to assess all the translations of Greek and Roman philosophers and determine, she said, "which ones were good and bad."

Nussbaum opened her testimony by addressing the state's concern for maintaining the integrity of the family. She testified about the possible influence of homosexuality on the so-called traditional, heterosexual married couple's family.

"What impact have you observed," asked plaintiffs' attorney Greg Eurich, regarding Nussbaum's work with the United Nations, "on the stability of family structure in Scandinavia in light of the fact that they are widely tolerant of same-sex marriages or same-sex families?"

"I have to say that I think the family in Finland, as I've observed it, is in very good shape," responded Nussbaum. "Certainly the rate of households headed by single parents is much lower than in the United States—in both Finland and Sweden. And, in general, I think one can say that, although, of course, some of the families have the form of marriage and some have the form of these other forms of legalized cohabitation, the families have a great deal of stability over time, and lifelong partnerships of many kinds are making valuable social contributions."

Nussbaum noted, too, that the United Nations, in designating 1994 to be the "International Year of the Family," made it "very explicit that they were not going to offer a definition of family that ruled out same-sex families." Scandinavian countries, she noted, support such arrangements through domestic partnership registrations.

Nussbaum spent the bulk of her testimony ripping into the translations upon which Finnis relied for his conclusion that the three "greatest" Greek philosophers had "regarded homosexual conduct as intrinsically shameful, immoral, and indeed depraved or depraving."

Finnis, she said, presented a "Platonic-Aristotelian tradition" that considered "any use of another person's body for the sake of one's own personal pleasure [as] bad" and that the only sex that can avoid such use of another person's body is sex within marriage that is open to the prospects of procreation.

But, said Nussbaum, the Greeks believed that "in the original nature of human beings, there was an original wholeness of human beings."

"At some point in our prehistory," she said, the Greeks believed "we were, as it were, split into two." Sex, she said, was considered "a longing to identify and come into unity with your original other half— that's what the strength of the longing is all about. That is why it is deeply natural, and that is what is so joyful and valuable—valuable to persons and to society about fostering that kind of relationship."

Concerning Finnis's argument that sex in marriage is the only sex that can achieve a "common good," Nussbaum suggested that Finnis failed to investigate the common good that comes with "the expression of love, the expression of friendship, the expression of joy and pleasure that individuals might share mutually in a sexual relationship without exploiting one another's bodies for the purpose of their solitary pleasure."

She also dismissed Finnis's expertise in the classics outright, saying he used "some of the worst translations" of the ancient texts that she had ever seen.

"The particular translation of Plato's laws which Finnis used," noted Nussbaum, "was made in 1926. I think one can see in that period that there was a great deal of shame and embarrassment about homosexuality in the British and American cultures" that made some of the translations suspect. She illustrated her point with some examples.

A neutral phrase such as "those who first venture to do this," said Nussbaum, was, in the translation Finnis used, interpreted as "those who were first guilty of such abominations."

"In Greek cultures of the fifth and fourth centuries B.C. and on, really, through to the first century A.D. where Christianity starts to have a big impact," said Nussbaum, "homosexual acts between consenting males, and in rarer cases between consenting females, are attested as received with great approval. . . . There is a good deal of evidence that such acts not only took place but took place with social approval and that they were regarded not as subverting the fabric of society but rather as tending to reinforce the fabric of society."

"A Lot of Argument"

On cross-examination, state's attorney Terrance Gillespie quizzed Nussbaum about the work of Kenneth Dover on ancient Greek attitudes about homosexuality, and, in particular, about anal intercourse. Dover's study of the thinking of the great Greeks on homosexuality, entitled *Greek Homosexuality,* is well respected in the field, as is Dover himself. Nussbaum acknowledged that there was "a lot of argument" about the Greeks' attitudes concerning anal intercourse, but generally speaking, she said, it was condemned only if a man took "only the passive role in anal sex throughout."

"There is some evidence," she said, "that that would be held against you because it might be taken as evidence that you were incapable of arousal yourself." Dover, said Nussbaum, had concluded that the Greeks did not condemn sex between men and that anal intercourse "was a common form of sexual conduct."

Robert George, a witness later called by the state, vigorously disputed Nussbaum's interpretations and conclusions in this area. Their disagreement eventually turned into a full-fledged controversy outside the courtroom, in Greek classicist scholarship. An article in one academic magazine, examining the controversy, noted that Dover seemed to come out somewhere in the middle, going on record "as saying that although Socrates condemned homosexual copulation, it was not because he thought it was 'wicked, shameful, and depraving.'"[5]

Regardless of whether the Greeks condemned homosexuality, the ancient roots for laws today that treat gay people differently did not condemn certain *people* but certain *acts*. The fact that heterosexual couples, as well as gay couples, engage in anal intercourse was not explored by the testimony at trial, despite the fact that neither form begets children. This distinction was repeatedly ignored in the debate or blurred beyond comprehension.

The next expert on the stand concerning morality and law was a scholar for the state, Harvey Mansfield, professor of government at Harvard University. Mansfield, who testified three days after Nussbaum, argued that every law has a moral base and that, "in a free society, it's important to maintain the greatest possible range of freedom morally."

Mansfield's testimony grew long and labored because he seemed to be recasting his views more softly than he had in pretrial deposition. In deposition, for instance, he said that homosexuality was bad and that Amendment 2 reflected that notion. But in the courtroom, he seemed to be claiming that homosexuality was not bad, it was just not as respectable as heterosexuality.

Again, terms were used loosely with no distinction made between acts and people.

Amendment 2, said Mansfield, "represents a solution which permits a kind of live-and-let-live policy, which offers the least intrusion into our lives and morals." Amendment 2, he said, limits the degree to which local or state government can use an antidiscrimination law to impose its own sense of right and wrong onto people's behavior and

---

5. Daniel Mendelsohn, "The Stand," *Lingua Franca,* September/October 1996, 34–46.

attitudes. Under antidiscrimination laws, he said, "right" is treating everyone equally, "wrong" is discriminating against gay people. Amendment 2, said Mansfield, "provides more respect for the realm of the private" individual's sense of right and wrong, "both politically and morally" because homosexuality was, to many, wrong.

Mansfield's view ran up against the reality that society, for the most part, has accepted laws that prohibit discrimination based on race and sex as a necessary intrusion on this private realm. When Mansfield tried to argue that the different treatment of homosexuality rested on a difference between being female or black and engaging in "homosexual activity," plaintiffs' attorney Eurich, who was conducting the cross-examination, read into the trial record Mansfield's pretrial statement suggesting that homosexual orientation, like sex and race, is not a chosen characteristic, much less an activity or behavior: "There's nothing wrong with being black or being a woman, but it is perfectly reasonable to think that there is something wrong with being gay. Whether or not the defect is the fault of gays, it is not a life that makes for individual happiness or for social responsibility. And the sexual practices that go with that life can well be regarded as shameful."

Mansfield hedged. *Being* gay might not be voluntary, he now explained, but gay people are "capable of leading a moral life."

"If, in your deposition, the question was framed in terms of *being* gay," noted Eurich, "you are at least telling us now that you intended to be talking about *conduct?*"

"Yes," replied Mansfield.

Eurich then went on to dissect the rest of Mansfield's controversial statement.

"You say being gay is not a life that makes for individual happiness," said Eurich. "To begin with, you have never made an academic study whether gays are happy, have you?"

"I speak—you are right," said Mansfield. "I have not actively qualified as an expert on gays. I speak of the reading I have done in the classics of moral and political philosophy. I heard some testimony last week from Professor Nussbaum. I have read some of the same books she has read."

"The basis for your opinion that gays are not happy in life is from ancient Platonism and Freud and Don Quixote and also conversations with one student of yours and your own experience [of] heterosexuality?" asked Eurich.

"Together with having read articles in both the newspapers and magazines, yes," said Mansfield.

"But you say that being gay is not a life that makes for individual happiness, knowing that there are gay people who are happy. That you know, right?"

"I don't think that they are as happy as they would be if they weren't gay."

Eurich then quizzed Mansfield about a deposition statement that gay people are socially irresponsible.

"As a group," said Eurich, "you say that gays are not socially responsible, correct? That's what you said in your statement?"

Mansfield acknowledged making the statement and explained that he considers gay people socially irresponsible because of "their inability to raise families or at least the extreme difficulty that they have in raising families."

"That's an example of being self-centered and not trying to help others?" asked Eurich.

"No," said Mansfield, "it's more specific than simply being self-centered. I think a lot of gays are not self-centered especially, for example, when they organize politically in defense of gay rights."

Eurich again showed Mansfield the text of his deposition, pointing to an exchange in which Mansfield had been asked whether it was his opinion that "gays as a group are self-centered, as opposed to being oriented toward trying to help others." In response to that question, Mansfield, in deposition, had answered, "Yes. This might not be entirely their fault to the extent their behavior is not voluntary."

Once shown the text of the deposition, Mansfield explained that his statement had arisen out of his discussion of "the family."

"Let's talk about your view on the family," said Eurich. "You think a major way to be socially responsible is to raise children, correct?"

"Yes," said Mansfield.

"In fact," said Eurich, "you believe married heterosexual people who do not have children are not socially responsible."

"No," replied Mansfield. "They are *less* responsible in that way than they could be."

Again Eurich directed Mansfield to look at his deposition where, to a nearly identical question—one for which Mansfield, in deposition, had answered simply "Yes."

"If a gay person raised a child," said Eurich, "that person would be socially responsible as much as he or she could be—that's your view, right?"

"Yes," said Mansfield.

Eurich then took on Mansfield's contention that many sexual practices associated with gay people are shameful.

"Now, the sexual practices that you identified by gays are sodomy and anal intercourse and mutual masturbation and fellatio, right?" asked Eurich. "And the reasons that these particular sexual practices are shameful is because they are for the sole purpose of pleasure and they can't be procreative, right?"

"Yes," said Mansfield.

"And I assume those same practices by heterosexuals would be shameful for the same reasons, true?" asked Eurich.

"Yes, I think so," said Mansfield.

Eurich had finally drawn the distinction, and Mansfield searched for a way out.

"You know, it's hard to—it's hard to draw a sharp line in these questions of what constitutes shameful and what doesn't," said Mansfield. "What I think can be said with assurance is that the question of shame is always involved. . . ."

". . . You believe it's not possible for human beings to engage in sex at all without having a sense of shame," said Eurich, "because it's part of our nature and it's part of the way we practice sex, right?"

"Without having shame involved," said Mansfield, "you might feel that what you are doing is perfectly correct, but, for example, you wouldn't do it in public. Why not? Because it's considered shameful to have sex in public."

"Although one of the reasons you believe that gays—being gay— is bad is because of their sexual practices that you regard as shameful, it's not just their sexual practices you regard as shameful," said Eurich. "You regard all sex as shameful, correct?"

"Oh, no," said Mansfield, explaining that what he meant was that "shame is always involved" in sex.

"For gays and heterosexuals, right?" asked Eurich.

"For gays and heterosexuals. But that doesn't mean that it's always shameful to have sex. It's always involved in sex because it's something which we seem all of us to want to do in private."

Eurich also took Mansfield to a statement in his deposition where he said that homosexuality should be tolerated but disapproved.

"That's my position," said Mansfield, "and I don't think Amendment 2 takes a stand on that question."

"You say that you don't think Amendment 2 takes a stand on that question, although you believe that, in passing it, it can repudiate respectability for homosexuals, correct?" asked Eurich.

"It repudiated the moral equivalence of homosexuality and heterosexuality," said Mansfield. "It doesn't take a stand on the question in the sense that it permits people to practice homosexuality without its being made criminal or without their being punished in any way."

Eurich asked his question again, more directly: "Your view is that in passing Amendment 2, Colorado voters repudiated respectability for homosexuality?"

"They repudiated *perfect* respectability for homosexuality," said Mansfield, "Yes."

Eurich again noted that that was not the same answer Mansfield had offered in deposition. In deposition, Mansfield did not distinguish between respectability and perfect respectability. And again, in court, Mansfield explained that "what I meant was perfect respectability."

"There is still that respectability" for homosexuality, said Mansfield in court, "—that respectability that goes with being tolerated."

"You think being tolerated gives one respectability?" asked Eurich.

"Not perfect respectability, but a certain degree," said Mansfield. "It means that other people are respecting your rights."

"To the extent there is stigmatization of homosexuals in America," said Eurich, "you would agree that Amendment 2 tends to support that stigma, correct?"

"What I meant," said Mansfield, "was that—"

"Did you say that?" asked Eurich.

"Yes, I said that, and what I meant was that those who were most extreme in their opposition to gay rights would have felt that they had a great success when Amendment 2 passed."

"You didn't provide that clarification in your deposition, did you?" asked Eurich.

"That's right."

"And in addition to those views," continued Eurich, "you think that Amendment 2 reinforces prejudice against gays, right?"

"No," said Mansfield, "I don't think it reinforces prejudice against gays, even though I may have said that."

The Paper Fights

In addition to the dueling testimony of plaintiffs' and defendants' witnesses, this contorted, confusing debate over the relationship between Amendment 2—or any law—and morality occurred in many of the sworn affidavits that the trial judge had taken under advisement.

The plaintiffs' key affidavit came from John Boswell, an openly gay scholar. A professor at Yale, Boswell had conducted studies and written award-winning books on religious attitudes toward gay people. In attempting to link Amendment 2 to religious-based discrimination, Boswell, in his affidavit, said that most prejudice against gay people has originated with the "triumph of Christianity."

The state secured a number of scholars to submit affidavits to dispute Boswell's claims. One of them was Richard B. Hays, an associate professor of the New Testament at Duke University. He characterized Boswell's book, *Christianity, Social Tolerance, and Homosexuality*, as "seriously misleading in its assessment of early Christian attitudes toward homosexuality." Boswell, as Hays noted, asserted that "homosexual acts" were not seen as *immoral* by the early Christians but as *unusual*, and that "homosexual acts" were condemned only when performed by "apparently heterosexual persons." Boswell had interpreted the text of the Bible as saying that "homosexual acts" are not "against" God's design or nature but "beyond" it.

But to state's expert Hays, the early Christians considered the teachings of their messiah and his apostles as more than just "a moral or philosophical teaching which adherents may accept or reject as they choose." It was, said Hays, "the eschatological instrument through which God is working his purpose out in the world."

The apostle Paul, according to Hays, portrayed "homosexual behavior" as not just an act but an "antireligion" followed by people "who refuse to honor God as creator" and who flout the "sexual distinctions" between man and woman. The distinctions between man and woman, said Hays, "are fundamental to God's creative design."

However inadvertently, the argument sounded like one put forth by the state of Virginia in defending its laws prohibiting interracial marriages. One purpose of such laws, argued Virginia in a 1955 case,

Naim v. Naim, was "to preserve the racial integrity" sought by a creator who, in Virginia's view, put the races on different continents.[6] The U.S. Supreme Court, in striking down those laws, said such arguments amounted to "an endorsement of White Supremacy."[7]

Although often brought into the political fray during the campaign to pass Amendment 2, and discussed liberally through the affidavits of experts, the alleged conflict between religious freedom and laws prohibiting antigay discrimination seldom entered the discourse at the trial itself—only during the brief testimony of one witness, Rev. Hansford Van Jr.

With Van, the state focused attention on the human rights ordinance of Boulder, which prohibited discrimination based on various categories including sexual orientation. The law also permitted religious organizations, such as churches, "to restrict hiring to individuals who are members of the same religious denomination." In other words, based on the law's text, a Baptist church could reject for employment a qualified person who was Catholic, but not a qualified Baptist person who was gay. If Amendment 2 went into effect, however, Boulder's law would no longer prohibit discrimination against gay men, lesbians, and bisexuals, for churches or anyone else.

Van was pastor of the Second Baptist Church in Boulder, and he, apparently, was chosen by the state to make the case that the current human rights ordinance in Boulder interfered with his free exercise of religious-based beliefs that homosexuality is against God's will.

But Van did not really illustrate the point in his 11 minutes on the witness stand. Van said his church can have gay people in the congregation but that, because of "church doctrine," it cannot let a gay person hold an office or job within the church.

"If we did that," said Van, "we would sanction that type of action. We could not have that."

"What would you do," asked Colorado Solicitor General Tim Tymkovich, "if faced with a conflict between the Boulder ordinance and the church doctrine of your organization?"

Van said he would "look at Romans chapter 13 in the Bible." That, he explained, says that governments "are instituted by God" and "ordained of God," and that Christians "obey all the laws of the land, but then there is a higher law. And any time the laws that we find in

---

6. *Naim v. Naim,* 197 Va. 80, 87 S.E.2d 749 (1955).
7. *Loving v. Virginia* 388 U.S. 1 (1967).

'The Word' are contrary to the laws that man makes, there is a scripture that says it is better to obey God than to obey man, so we would have to honor God."

"And does the policy of the Boulder ordinance conflict with the ability of your church to follow its religious doctrine?" asked Tymkovich.

"So far, it hasn't been a problem," said Van, although that clearly was not the answer Tymkovich was seeking. He tried again.

"But it could be, couldn't it?"

"It could certainly be a problem."

Anticipating this sort of religious freedom argument, the plaintiffs had called on Burke Marshall, in his videotaped testimony, to rebut Colorado's claim that Amendment 2 was necessary to protect the First Amendment guarantee of freedom of religion for citizens with a religious belief hostile to homosexuality. Marshall discussed the landmark U.S. Supreme Court case of *Bob Jones University v. United States.*[8] In that case, a private university got into a tax dispute with the federal government over its admission policy, which forbade interracial dating and marriage, based on a fundamentalist religious view that the Bible forbade such relationships.

Bob Jones University had argued that its racially discriminatory admissions policy was an exercise of the school's religious mission. Marshall noted that the U.S. Supreme Court's 1983 ruling—that the government's interest in eradicating racial discrimination justified its action in denying the school tax-exempt status—suggested it was possible for antidiscrimination laws and religious freedom to coexist.

Traditional Values

Because the First Amendment prohibits the state from establishing an official religion *and* protects the right of each citizen to exercise any religion or no religion at all, proponents of Amendment 2 could not simply argue that the initiative reflected the religious beliefs of some people and should be upheld on that basis. However, the state could argue that Amendment 2 gave effect to "traditional moral values." Opponents could argue that the government's reliance on these values to justify Amendment 2's discrimination was just a mask for prejudice and that prejudice was not a legitimate basis for lawmaking.

---

8. *Bob Jones University v. United States,* 461 U.S. 574 (1983).

The term *traditional values* had actually been around for a very long time and was generally interpreted to represent the presumed views of a churchgoing heterosexual married couple with children—including belief in God, marital fidelity, and having children. History books show that, over the decades, various things have been labeled as threats to such "traditional" values. Around the 1920s, the wave of migration to cities was seen as a threat to traditional values. Alcoholic beverages were considered a threat, as was the teaching of evolution. In some cases, people who were most afraid of losing traditional values sought and succeeded in passing laws as a way of protecting these values themselves. For instance, the Eighteenth Amendment to the U.S. Constitution was passed to prohibit the sale of liquor. And some states passed laws prohibiting the teaching of evolution.

By the 1990s, the existence and visibility of gay people were, like evolution, liquor, and urbanization, seen as threats to traditional values. This belief that gay people lived in a manner contrary to these values was captured by a rhetorical shift in which the term "traditional values" became more commonly invoked as "traditional family values" or "family values."

Whether called "family values" or "traditional values," the concept was gaining a new visibility by the time the campaign for Amendment 2 was in full swing. *USA Today* noted in August 1992 that "family values" had become "the most popular phrase" in the 1992 presidential race for both parties. For the Democrats at that time, family values included all types of families—single parents with children and gay couples among them—and no discrimination. As New York governor Mario Cuomo said from the 1992 Democratic National Convention podium where he nominated Clinton for the presidency, "the first principle of our commitment" is the "politics of inclusion" of American citizens, regardless of "from wherever [they came], no matter how recently, of whatever color, whatever creed, whatever sex, of whatever sexual orientation, all of them are equal members of the American family."

For Republicans, "family values" meant the heterosexual married couple with children, and opposition to laws that prohibited discrimination against gay people. One Republican candidate for the nomination, Patrick Buchanan, gave a high profile to the disparity between the two parties in his address to the Republican National Convention in Houston in August 1992. He called the dispute a "cultural war," and he put gay people on one side and Republicans on the other.

By the time of the trial, in October 1993, Democratic candidate Bill Clinton had won the election, and the Republicans' high-profile "cultural" hostility to gay people and unmarried mothers was seen as a significant factor in incumbent president George Bush's loss of reelection. But the culmination of the presidential campaign did not end the national dispute over whose morality should prevail in politics.

As the intense positioning of each side made evident, there was no easy way out of this conflict between those who desired to discriminate on religious grounds and those who believed that discrimination, regardless of religious or moral viewpoint, had no place in a commercial setting. By the end of the testimony from both sides on this issue, neither the position of the Greek philosophers nor the real impact of antidiscrimination laws on those whose religious beliefs advised discrimination shed conclusive light on the subject.

Chapter 8

The Colorado Verdicts

The much awaited ruling of the Colorado district court was announced on December 14, 1993, just three months after the trial concluded. Amendment 2 was declared unconstitutional.

Given the high legal standard the Colorado Supreme Court had imposed on the state—to show that Amendment 2 was narrowly drawn to support at least one compelling government interest—Judge Jeffrey Bayless's determination was not surprising. Instead, the key questions for interested observers concerned how Bayless would evaluate the extensive and wide-ranging testimony. Would he offer a fact-based assessment of Amendment 2's impact on gay people, and, in doing so, define the terms *lesbian* and *gay?* Would he decide that any of the state's interests could justify the measure's disparate treatment? If so, would he find that Amendment 2 was narrowly tailored to accomplish that interest? Would he find that Amendment 2 made a suspect classification by singling out gay people for discriminatory treatment?

Bayless dealt methodically with the task of ruling on Amendment 2's constitutionality in his 16-page ruling. He adhered closely to the Colorado Supreme Court's guideline as he reviewed Colorado's six justifications for the amendment and the evidence introduced at trial regarding history, science, politics, civil rights, religion, and moral philosophy to support each interest. These interests—the deterrence of factionalism, protection of the state's political functions, protection of the state's ability to remedy discrimination against suspect classes, prevention of interference with familial and religious privacy, prevention of state subsidies to special interest groups, and promotion of the physical and psychological well-being of children—demonstrated the compelling need for Amendment 2, according to the state.

Reviewing the first argument and the cases cited in its support, Judge Bayless concluded the state was not trying to deter "factionalism" caused by city-by-city battles over homosexuality but was trying to deter "difference[s] of opinion on a controversial political question." Even the cases cited by the state to support its factionalism defense, wrote Bayless, stood for the principle that the Constitution values and protects diversity of opinion.

" 'Competition in ideas and governmental policies is at the core of our electoral process and of the First Amendment freedoms,' " Bayless said, quoting one of the cases.[1] "The 'factionalism' which defendants here argue about was found [by the Supreme Court] to be a great strength of the American political process," he added.

Bayless explained that the country is best served by a "market-place of ideas" in which diversity and competition among ideas thrive: "The history and policy of this country has been to encourage that which defendants seek to deter." Therefore, he concluded, the "first claimed compelling state interest is not a compelling state interest. The opposite of defendants' first claimed compelling interest is probably most compelling."

Second, concerning the state's claim that Amendment 2 protected Colorado's initiative process from being undermined by legal challenges, Bayless looked at the testimony of the leaders of Colorado for Family Values to ascertain Amendment 2's purpose and effect. Will Perkins had testified that Amendment 2 "was intended to deny protected status to homosexuals and bisexuals." Kevin Tebedo had expressed concern that, without Amendment 2 in place, affirmative action programs for gay people would be implemented in Colorado. Tony Marco had insisted that Amendment 2 "was a defensive measure to fend off statewide militant gay aggression." In his opinion, Bayless wrote that "the court's notes contain [Marco's] term *militant gay aggression* no less than six times in his direct testimony alone." However, Bayless held, the evidence presented at trial "does not satisfy this court that there is militant gay aggression in this state which endangers the state's political functions."

Bayless made clear that, although the people have great power, they may not alter the state constitution in ways that would violate the U.S. Constitution. On this point, he quoted familiar U.S. Supreme Court doctrine: "The facts remain that 'one's right to life, liberty, and property . . . and other fundamental rights may not be submitted to vote; they depend on the outcome of no elections,' " and that " 'a citi-

---

1. Bayless's ruling quoted *Anderson v. Celebrezze*, 460 U.S. 780, 794 (1983), on this point.

zen's constitutional rights can hardly be infringed simply because a majority of the people choose that it be.'"[2]

The state's third argument was that Amendment 2 was necessary to preserve limited financial resources available "to remedy discrimination against suspect classes." Bayless described the claim as contending "basically that there are insufficient fiscal resources available to the state to add another group to the rolls of those protected by existing civil rights laws or ordinances." At trial, the state's witnesses had also claimed that adding sexual orientation would diminish respect for existing civil rights laws.

Bayless noted that "the absence of this amendment does not mean that gays have been added as a protected class to any statute." There is no mandate that governments anywhere in the country must add sexual orientation protections to their antidiscrimination laws or policies. In deliberating on this point, Bayless was also apparently unimpressed by the testimony of George Mason University School of Law professor Joseph Broadus, who had urged that, in addition to decreasing resources available to enforce those laws, prohibiting discrimination against gay people would also dilute the public's respect for existing civil rights laws. Bayless noted that the testimony of Denver mayor Wellington Webb and Denver antidiscrimination ordinance compliance officer Brenda Toliver-Locke revealed that Denver's ordinance prohibiting sexual orientation discrimination had not raised costs, did not require increased staff, and had not otherwise taken away from enforcement of other civil rights laws. Bayless also noted that Leanna Ware, of the Wisconsin Civil Rights Bureau, had testified that Wisconsin's prohibition of sexual orientation discrimination, in place since 1982, had not limited Wisconsin's enforcement of any other laws.

"The facts don't support defendant's position," concluded Bayless. "Defendants' evidence was principally in the form of opinion and theory as to what *would* occur" if the state legislature adopted a law generally prohibiting sexual orientation discrimination. "There is no such statute, nor is one proposed," Bayless wrote. The state's witnesses offered no more than speculation as to increased cost, he said, in contrast to the "actual experiences" of the plaintiffs' witnesses "that the presence of a sexual orientation provision has *not* increased costs or

---

2. Bayless quoted the Colorado Supreme Court, which quoted *West Virginia State Bd. of Educ. v. Barnett*, 319 U.S. 624, 638 (1943), and *Lucas v. Forty-Fourth Gen. Assembly of Colo.*, 377 U.S. 713, 736 (1964).

impaired the enforcement of other civil rights statutes or ordinances."
Furthermore, Bayless ruled, based on prior U.S. Supreme Court precedent, that fiscal concerns are insufficient to justify a state's infringement
of fundamental rights. The state's evidence on this argument, he wrote,
was "unpersuasive in all respects," he wrote.

The state's fourth justification for Amendment 2 was essentially a
claim that people should be free to discriminate against gay people for
any reason—be it personal, familial, or religious—and that antidiscrimination laws interfered with personal and familial rights of privacy.
Taking on the religious exercise prong first, Bayless agreed that "preserving religious freedom is a compelling state interest" because freedom of religion is explicitly protected by both the U.S. and Colorado
constitutions. Noting the testimony of Boulder pastor Hansford Van
regarding the potential for conflict between Van's church and Boulder's ordinance prohibiting sexual orientation discrimination, Bayless
looked to the U.S. Supreme Court for guidance in balancing the competing interests of religious freedom and antidiscrimination laws. In
particular, he considered the case of *Bob Jones University v. United
States*,[3] discussed by the plaintiffs' expert Burke Marshall, in which the
government's interest in prohibiting race discrimination was held to
justify denying tax-exempt status to a private school that prohibited
interracial dating for religious reasons.

Bayless had to determine, in this case, whether Amendment 2's
discriminatory classification of gay people was *narrowly tailored* to
achieve the state's "compelling" interest of preserving religious freedom. Here, Bayless noted that "the religious belief urged by defendants
is that homosexuals are condemned by scripture and therefore discrimination based on that religious teaching is protected within freedom of
religion." But he added, "in this case, it is obvious that the amendment
is not narrowly drawn to protect religious freedom." Amendment 2
could be narrowly tailored to exempt religious organizations from
compliance with antidiscrimination laws, but he said it could "not . . .
deny gays and bisexuals their fundamental right of participation in the
political process."

Turning next to the aspect of the argument that alleged a denial of
familial privacy, Bayless noted that several witnesses testified on this
point, including CFV leaders Tebedo, Perkins, and Marco, and Robert

---

3. *Bob Jones University v. United States*, 461 U.S. 574 (1983).

Knight, Director of Cultural Studies for the Family Research Council, a self-described "profamily" lobbying organization with an antigay platform. Knight had testified that "gay rights advocates are seeking to destroy the family by, in part, seeking to remove special societal protections from the family." Bayless was unconvinced.

> The court would have to assume or speculate what the family is, according to Mr. Knight. He never defined the family, nor was he asked to provide a definition. If the Court assumes the family consists of a mother and father who are married and living together, and children from that marriage who live with their parents, more questions are raised than are answered. Does the family include parents who are divorced? Does it include a family where the parents are divorced and remarried? Does it include single parent families, or families created by second marriages with stepparents and stepchildren?

Bayless said the state also failed to explain satisfactorily the connection between protecting personal and familial privacy and Amendment 2's restriction on the political participation of lesbians, gay men, and bisexuals.

"Seemingly, if one wished to promote family values, action would be taken that is profamily rather than anti some other group," wrote Bayless.

As to the state's argument that Amendment 2 was necessary to protect "personal privacy," Bayless found that the state had also failed adequately to explain this argument: "The court can only speculate as to what defendants mean by personal privacy and how Amendment 2 protects such a right." Without more, Bayless rejected this third prong of the "privacy" defense.

For its fifth justification, the state urged that Amendment 2 served a compelling interest by preventing government subsidies to "special interest groups." The state argued that, by prohibiting sexual orientation discrimination, the government was subsidizing the agenda of gay political groups. In his opinion, Bayless quoted what he identified as the state's "strongest" argument in this regard—"For example, if a landlord is forced to rent an apartment to a homosexual couple, the landlord is being forced to accept, at least implicitly, a particular ideology." But, Bayless called this a "fairly remarkable" contention, noted that the state cited no authority to support it, and rejected it as a compelling interest.

The sixth and final claim from the state was that Amendment 2 was necessary to protect Colorado's children from physical and psychological harm. At trial, however, the state had not presented any evidence to support this point. Bayless relied on Dr. Carole Jenny, who testified for the plaintiffs that the disproportionate number of perpetrators of child sexual abuse are heterosexual. "If the compelling interest relates to protecting children physically from pedophiles, . . . [Dr. Jenny's testimony] is more persuasive than anything presented by defendants," he said. "If the compelling interest is in protecting the psychological well-being of homosexual youth, the Court is unable to discern how allowing discrimination against them by virtue of the Colorado Constitution promotes their welfare." Finding that the defendants had failed to provide sufficient evidence to support its alleged concern for protecting children, Bayless rejected the last of the state's six proposed justifications for blocking government from ever prohibiting discrimination against lesbians, gay men, and bisexuals.

Suspect Classification?

Rejection of the state's arguments was "not the end of the matter," said Bayless, who next turned his attention to the plaintiffs' contention that laws discriminating based on sexual orientation should require a heightened level of judicial scrutiny, whether or not they infringe upon a fundamental right, because such laws are more likely than not to reflect invidious prejudice and outmoded stereotypes. Bayless first noted that no federal appellate court had ever declared homosexuals and bisexuals to be a "suspect" or "quasi-suspect" class. To date, he noted, the U.S. Supreme Court had recognized only five classifications as meriting either the strict or intermediate level scrutiny that comes with suspect and quasi-suspect classification designation: race, alienage, national origin, gender, and illegitimacy.

He then identified elements the Supreme Court has indicated would trigger these forms of close scrutiny. The characteristic in question must be or have been: (1) the basis of a history of discrimination; (2) obvious, immutable, or distinguishing, so as to define the group as a discrete one; and (3) a basis for the group in question being rendered relatively politically powerless. Bayless noted that "to persuade the court, plaintiffs filled the witness stand with doctors, psychiatrists, genetic explorers, historians, philosophers, and political scientists."

He started with the so-called immutability question, calling the conflict over the origins of sexual orientation one of the trial's "hot debates." Contrasting the plaintiffs' argument that homosexuality is inborn with the defendants' argument that it is chosen, Bayless noted that "even Dr. Hamer, the witness who testified that he is 99.5 percent sure there is *some* genetic influence in forming sexual orientation, admits that sexual orientation is not completely genetic." But, ultimately, Bayless said, this was not a debate for him to settle. "The ultimate decision on 'nature' vs. 'nurture,'" he wrote, "is a decision for another forum, not this court."

In one quick paragraph, without any reference to historian George Chauncey's testimony, Bayless agreed that gay men and lesbians have experienced a history of discrimination. He noted that, in this respect, his finding accorded with that of a federal appeals court in a case called *High Tech Gays v. Defense Industrial Security Clearance Office*,[4] which also recognized gay people as having suffered a history of discrimination.

As to the question of whether gay people are relatively politically powerless, however, Bayless disagreed with the plaintiffs. He reasoned that the failure of gay people to prevail in the Amendment 2 voting did not demonstrate that they were politically powerless because this small group of people was able to get more than 46 percent of Coloradans to vote against the measure.

"Testimony placed the percentage of homosexuals in our society at not more than 4 percent. If 4 percent of the population gathers the support of an additional 42 percent of the population, that is a demonstration of power, not powerlessness," he wrote. Further, he cited the growing number of laws prohibiting sexual orientation discrimination and—apparently disregarding the outcome of the "gays in the military" debate—noted that President Clinton "has taken an active and leading role in support of gays."[5] Additionally, Bayless said that gay people are "skilled at building coalitions which is the key to political

---

4. *High Tech Gays v. Defense Industrial Security Clearance Office*, 895 F.2d 593 (9th Cir. 1990).

5. Notably, and despite Bayless's conviction that President Clinton was a leader in support of the rights of gay people, the Clinton administration declined to file a friend-of-the-court brief in support of the plaintiffs when this case reached the U.S. Supreme Court.

power." The plaintiffs had targeted the testimony of their political science expert, Kenneth Sherrill, specifically to overcome these common assumptions. Their effort did not succeed. Lesbians and gay men are not "politically vulnerable or powerless," Bayless wrote.

Based on his conclusion that "homosexuals fail to meet the element of the political powerlessness prong" and his view that it was necessary for the plaintiffs to satisfy each prong of the suspect classification analysis he had identified, Bayless held that gay people "therefore fail to meet the elements to be found a suspect class." He did not address the related question of whether quasi-suspect classification would have been appropriate.

Aware that the case would almost certainly be appealed again to the Colorado Supreme Court and then to the U.S. Supreme Court, both sides had also asked the trial court to give a final answer to the question of Amendment 2's validity under the lowest level of judicial review, known as the "rational basis" test—that is, whether there was *any* legitimate purpose to explain the measure. However, sticking closely to the Colorado Supreme Court's instruction to evaluate by "strict scrutiny" whether the state had a *compelling* interest in infringing the plaintiffs' fundamental rights, Judge Bayless "decline[d] to apply" what he termed "a legally inappropriate test to this case." He invalidated Amendment 2 under the highest level of judicial scrutiny only.

Moving up the Appeals Ladder

Within hours of Bayless's invalidation of Amendment 2 becoming public, the state announced its intention to appeal.

After a several month period of rebriefing the case followed by oral argument, the Colorado Supreme Court again heard oral argument in *Evans v. Romer*. This time, the state asked the court to reverse the fundamental rights analysis it had adopted a year earlier and to find, instead, that Amendment 2 did not violate any fundamental right and that it could, therefore, be justified by a rational interest, rather than a compelling one. The plaintiffs urged the court to maintain its original fundamental rights analysis but they, too, asked the court to consider whether there was any rational justification for Amendment 2. Although the plaintiffs knew the rational basis standard would be easier for the state to satisfy, they also believed the case was strong enough to win on either theory and wanted a final resolution of all questions before reaching the U.S. Supreme Court.

In its October 11, 1994, ruling, the Colorado Supreme Court took up neither side on its request for a modified approach. Instead, in an opinion authored by Chief Justice Luis Rovira and joined by justices Howard Kirshbaum, George Lohr, Mary Mullarkey, Gregory Scott, and Anthony Vollock, the court reiterated its view that Amendment 2's ultimate effect infringed the plaintiffs' fundamental right by prohibiting the adoption of laws, regulations, ordinances, and policies against sexual orientation discrimination. It reasserted, too, the flaw in Amendment 2 it had identified in the last round of the litigation.

> The right to participate equally in the political process is clearly affected by Amendment 2, because it bars gay men, lesbians, and bisexuals from having an effective voice in government affairs insofar as those persons deem it beneficial to seek legislation that would protect them from discrimination based on their sexual orientation. Amendment 2 alters the political process so that a targeted class is prohibited from obtaining legislative, executive, and judicial protection or redress from discrimination absent the consent of a majority of the electorate through the adoption of a constitutional amendment. Rather than attempting to withdraw antidiscrimination issues as a whole from state and local control, Amendment 2 singles out one form of discrimination and removes its redress from consideration by the normal political processes.

Like the trial court, the Colorado Supreme Court engaged in a step-by-step analysis of whether each of the state's proffered rationales for Amendment 2 was compelling, and if so, whether Amendment 2 was narrowly tailored to achieve that goal. To do so, it waded through the substantial testimony regarding history, science, politics, religion, and morality that Judge Bayless had heard at trial.

First, the court considered the state's claimed interest in "protecting the sanctity of religious, familial, and personal privacy" and reached the same conclusion as Bayless: that protection of religious freedom is "among the highest values of our society" and constitutes a compelling governmental interest. But, the court agreed, even if ordinances prohibiting discrimination against lesbians, gay men, and bisexuals burden the religious liberty of those who object to employing gay people or renting homes to them, Amendment 2 was not "narrowly tailored" to preserve religious liberty. And, like Judge Bayless, the state supreme court concluded that "an equally effective, and substantially less onerous way of accomplishing that purpose simply would be to require that antidiscrimination laws which include provisions for sexual orientation also include exceptions for religiously based objections." The court also pointed out that the existing antidiscrimination ordinances in Denver, and federal laws prohibiting employment discrimination, such as Title VII of the Civil Rights Act of 1964, provide such an exemption for religious organizations.

The Colorado Supreme Court was not swayed, either, by the state's claim that Amendment 2 was necessary to protect "familial privacy," or the right of "some parents to teach traditional moral values to their children." The court characterized these claims as asserting that "if a child hears one thing from his parents and the exact opposite message from the government, parental authority will inevitably be undermined." However, the court wrote, "this argument fails because it rests on the assumption that the right of familial privacy engenders an interest in having government endorse certain values as moral or immoral." While parents have a right to inculcate their values in their children, said the court, they do not have a right to have government reinforce those beliefs: "It is clear that the government does not burden an individual's constitutional rights merely because it endorses views with which that individual may disagree." The court continued:

> Consequently, fully recognizing that parents have a "privacy" right to instruct their children that homosexuality is immoral, we find that nothing in the laws or policies which Amendment 2 is intended to prohibit interferes with that right. With or without Amendment 2, parents retain full authority to express their views about homosexuality to their children. We believe that Amendment 2 is neither necessary nor narrowly tailored to preserve familial privacy because that right is not implicated by the laws and policies which Amendment 2 proscribes.

The Colorado Supreme Court, like Bayless, determined that the meaning of the "personal privacy" prong of the state's "privacy" argument was not entirely clear, but surmised that the phrase referred to the constitutional protection for freedom of association.

Over the years, the U.S. Supreme Court has defined associational privacy to cover those "deep commitments and attachments to the necessarily few other individuals with whom one shares not only a special community of thoughts, experiences, and beliefs but also distinctively personal aspects of one's life."[6] Looking again to Amendment 2's breadth, the Colorado Supreme Court concluded that "while preserving associational privacy may rise to the level of a compelling state interest, Amendment 2 is not narrowly tailored to serve that interest." It noted that the measure affects "a vast array of affiliations which in no way implicate associational privacy." For support, it cited a U.S. Supreme Court observation that "the Constitution undoubtedly imposes constraints on the State's power to control the selection of one's spouse that would not apply to regulations affecting the choice of one's fellow employees."[7] Further, the court reasoned that, to the extent laws prohibiting discrimination against gay people could potentially infringe associational rights, as in the context of owner-occupied rental housing, the narrowly tailored solution would be to exempt such situations from the law. Amendment 2, the court found, "does no such thing."

The court turned next to the state's argument that Amendment 2 was necessary and appropriate to conserve the limited available government resources for those who "really" need remedies for discrimination. The court first noted that "it is well-settled that the preservation of fiscal resources, administrative convenience, and the reduction of the workload of government bodies are not compelling state interests." Therefore, the court concluded, the state's alleged interest in conserving financial resources to protect "suspect classes" was not compelling. Even if the state's concern about having sufficient resources to enforce antidiscrimination laws for other minorities was legitimate, said the Colorado Supreme Court, the evidence indicated Amendment 2 was not necessary to achieve that aim. Reviewing testimony that sexual orientation antidiscrimination laws in Denver, Wisconsin, and elsewhere had not interfered with those governments' ability to protect other

---

6. *Roberts v. United States Jaycees*, 468 U.S. 609, 620 (1984).
7. *Id.*

groups, the court affirmed the trial court's finding that Amendment 2 was not constructed to save scarce resources. If the government wants to preserve funds to protect certain classes, the "narrowly tailored" way to accomplish that goal, said the court, would be to earmark funds for specific enforcement. "The governmental interest in ensuring adequate resources for the enforcement of civil rights laws designed to protect suspect classes from discrimination need not be accomplished by denying the right of gay men, lesbians, and bisexuals from participating equally in the political process," the court wrote.

Next, the court turned to the state's asserted interest in "allowing the people themselves to establish public social and moral norms," an interest that seemed to grow out of the earlier-advanced privacy justification. The state had divided this interest into two parts: Amendment 2 "preserves heterosexual families and heterosexual marriage, and, more generally, it sends the societal message condemning gay men, lesbians, and bisexuals as immoral." The state had relied on only one case to support these arguments. In that case, the U.S. Supreme Court upheld a state law that proscribed public nudity and required dancers to wear "G-strings" and "pasties," which, in essence, banned nude dancing establishments.[8] However, the Court noted that, although four of the nine justices in the majority in that case found that Indiana's public indecency statute "further[ed] a substantial government interest in protecting order and morality," the fifth justice to make up the majority did not rely on a moral justification for the law. In any event, the Court remarked, public morality was not a "compelling" government interest. "Consequently," the Colorado Supreme Court wrote, "defendants have cited no authority to support the proposition that the promotion of public morality constitutes a compelling governmental interest, and we are aware of none."

Further, the state high court found, "even recognizing the legitimacy of promoting public morals as a government interest, it is clear to us that Amendment 2 is not necessary to preserve heterosexual families, marriage, or to express disapproval of gay men, lesbians, and bisexuals." Marriage and divorce rates appeared unaffected by the existence of laws prohibiting sexual orientation discrimination, noted the court, and it rejected the state's notion that married heterosexuals

8. *Barnes v. Glen Theatre*, 501 U.S. 560 (1991).

"might 'choose' to 'become homosexual' if discrimination against homosexuals is prohibited."

The court also rejected the state's argument that sexual orientation antidiscrimination laws implicitly "endorse" homosexuality and will also undermine marriage and heterosexual families. "We do not believe that antidiscrimination laws constitute an endorsement of the characteristics that are deemed an unlawful basis upon which to discriminate against individuals," it said.

The court swept aside the state's argument that Amendment 2 was necessary to prevent the state from supporting the political objectives of "special interest groups" such as gay activists, saying this argument "would justify striking down almost any legislative enactment imaginable." Practically all laws could be said to benefit some "special interest group," it reasoned. Indeed, the state exists in order to implement the political objectives of its constituents, it added.

As with the state's other defenses, the Colorado Supreme Court found little merit in the argument that Amendment 2 was necessary to restrain factionalism in Colorado and to "ensure that the deeply divisive issue of homosexuality's place in our society does not serve to fragment Colorado's body politic." Echoing fears expressed by James Madison during the framing of the Constitution of unrestrained factionalism—the breakdown of government by relentless competition among differing interest groups—the state had urged that public debate at the local government level over equal rights for lesbians and gay men threatened to produce this sort of debilitating turn of events. The Colorado Supreme Court did not agree.

"Political debate," the court wrote, "even if characterized as 'factionalism,' is not an evil which the state has a legitimate interest in deterring but rather, constitutes the foundation of democracy." The court reasoned that the state, whose role is to serve its constituents, cannot have a legitimate interest in foreclosing one side of a difficult debate from seeking response by government solely because the group's interest sparks controversy. It found no precedent to support the state's proposition "that there is a compelling government interest in preventing divisive issues from being debated at all levels of government by prohibiting one side of the debate from seeking desirable legislation in those [forums]."

The state had also introduced a new argument in its briefs to the

Colorado high court—that even if the court struck down Amendment 2's restrictions on antidiscrimination protections based on sexual *orientation,* the amendment's other proscriptions of protections for "homosexual, lesbian, or bisexual . . . *conduct, practices, or relationships"* are valid. It pressed the argument that *Bowers v. Hardwick,* the U.S. Supreme Court case that upheld a Georgia "sodomy" law as applied to same-sex sexual relations, justified differential treatment by government based on sexual "conduct." Colorado had argued strenuously that at least the proscription of antidiscrimination protections based on "conduct" should stand in Amendment 2.

Again, the Colorado Supreme Court said no. First, it concluded that each of the designated classifications—orientation, conduct, practices, or relationships—"provides nothing more than a different way for identifying the same class of persons"—gay men, lesbians, and bisexuals. Then, the court distinguished the *Hardwick* case, explaining that "while it is true that [an antisodomy] law could be passed and found constitutional under the United States' constitution, it does not follow from that fact that denying the right of an identifiable group (who may or may not engage in homosexual sodomy) to participate equally in the political process is also constitutionally permissible." On this thorny point, the court added, "the government's ability to criminalize certain conduct does not justify a corresponding abatement of an independent fundamental right."

Finally, the court turned to the state's argument that the Tenth Amendment gave Colorado the right to amend its state constitution in any way the voters saw fit. The Tenth Amendment to the U.S. Constitution reserves to the states and the people the powers not delegated by the Constitution to the federal government. The court relied on the well-established principle that states "have no compelling interest in amending their constitutions in a way that violates fundamental rights."

Colorado had identified no interest or argument that persuaded the court. Bayless's declaration that Amendment 2 was unconstitutional was affirmed.

A Concurring Opinion

Justice Gregory Scott, who joined the majority's opinion, added his own analysis of the case through a concurring opinion that focused on the core rights of citizenship denied by Amendment 2. The amendment, he wrote, "impermissibly burdens the right peaceably to assemble and to petition the government for redress of grievances" guaranteed to every citizen based on the "privileges or immunities" clause of the Fourteenth Amendment to the U.S. Constitution.

"Citizenship, not the good graces of the electorate, is the currency of our republican form of government," Scott wrote. Although each state is sovereign, Scott explained, it is also part of a greater union, and neither the states nor their voters may intrude upon fundamental guaranteed rights of the U.S. Constitution. Reminding the court that Madison found the "cure" for tyranny of the majority in a republican form of government which would protect society from itself as well as the oppression of its rulers, Scott recalled the first Justice John Marshall Harlan's famous words in dissent from an 1896 U.S. Supreme Court ruling, *Plessy v. Ferguson*,[9] that separate train cars for different races constituted "equal" treatment, and said the Constitution will not tolerate "classes among citizens."

Scott wrote that the constitutional guarantee that "no State shall make or enforce any law which shall abridge the privileges or immunities of citizens of the United States" was intended to apply to situations just like that presented by Amendment 2, in which one set of citizens was denied a political participation right available to others. He reasoned that the right to petition the government for redress of grievances, guaranteed by the Constitution, was a right of national citizenship "that the states could never have a legitimate interest in terminating." The fundamental right to participate in the political process, Scott said, is also an attribute of national citizenship. The privileges and immunities clause extends its guarantees to *every* citizen, Scott emphasized. He continued, "like the right to vote which assumes the right to have one's vote counted, the right peaceably to assemble and petition is meaningless if by law government is powerless to act."

And a Dissent

The sole justice to dissent from the Colorado Supreme Court's first ruling in the case upholding the trial court's preliminary injunction dissented again from the court's final decision striking down Amendment

---

9. *Plessy v. Ferguson,* 163 U.S. 537 (1896).

2. Maintaining his analysis from the earlier dissent, Justice William Erickson reiterated his view that the Colorado Supreme Court had fashioned a new and indefensible right to equal political participation. The court, he said, had effectively given a higher level of legal scrutiny to laws and policies discriminating against gay people. He argued that the majority had misinterpreted the cases on which it had relied. Those cases, he wrote, had applied heightened judicial scrutiny because they involved race discrimination—not because of a fundamental right to political participation.

Erickson analyzed Amendment 2 under the lowest level of judicial review—the rational basis standard—which requires that government classifications must be upheld if "there is any reasonably conceivable state of facts that could provide a rational basis for the classification."

Reviewing the same set of rationales from the state that were rejected by a majority of the court, Erickson found that at least three of Colorado's proffered interests satisfied the rational basis standard. First, he said, individual religious freedom is "among the highest values in our society" and "no government official or body may delineate what is a 'proper' form of faith and require citizens to act in accordance with government-mandated religious standards."

Second, Erickson found that, even if it did not have a compelling interest in deterring factionalism per se, the state did have a "legitimate interest in promoting statewide uniformity." According to Erickson, Amendment 2 "involves a matter of statewide concern because the public is deeply divided over the issue of homosexuality," and so the state had a legitimate interest in restricting to the statewide level laws related to homosexuality.

Third, Erickson said he would have accepted the state's argument that Amendment 2 was a legitimate means of allocating the state's resources to protect "traditionally suspect classes" and to avoid diminishing respect for "traditional" civil rights categories. He noted in particular the testimony of law professor Joseph Broadus that "the addition of homosexuals to civil rights statutes or ordinances would lessen the public's respect for historic civil rights categories." He relied, too, on testimony that gay men, lesbians, and bisexuals are a "relatively politically powerful and privileged special interest group." Concluding his dissent, Erickson urged that Amendment 2 was constitutional and should be permitted to take effect.

The End of the Road?

Typically, a state supreme court ruling represents the end of the road for even the most difficult cases. As the highest court in the state, a state supreme court, such as Colorado's, ordinarily makes the final pronouncement on cases filed in the state court system about controversies implicating the state constitution. But, when a ruling rests on an interpretation of the federal constitution and concerns an issue of national importance, one more court has the power to review the case—the Supreme Court of the United States. The state filed its notice of appeal.

Chapter 9

The U.S. Supreme Court

When the U.S. Supreme Court announced on February 21, 1995, that it would review the Colorado Supreme Court's decision, the news came as no surprise to most court watchers. The Colorado court's ruling had the requisites of a classic high court case: It involved an "important question of federal law," and there was a proliferation of similar conflicts that ensured the issue would not go away. And it was no surprise on October 10, 1995, the morning the Court set to hear *Romer v. Evans,* that hundreds of people hoping to get into the courtroom to listen to attorneys for both sides present their arguments had formed a line so long it ran down the front steps, across the Court's vast plaza and around the block. Many of those observers expressed surprise at the vigor with which some of the justices pursued the arguments—to the point that the justices were debating each other more than questioning the attorneys.

The issue before the Court as Colorado originally stated it in its brief requesting review was:

> Whether a popularly enacted state constitutional amendment precluding special state or local legal protections for homosexuals and bisexuals violates a fundamental right of independently identifiable, yet non-suspect, classes to seek such special protections.

On October 10, 1995, the issue on the Court's own docket summary put it this way:

> Does popularly enacted state constitutional amendment that prohibits state and local governments from conferring protected status on persons of 'homosexual, lesbian or bisexual orientation' violate Equal Protection Clause?

During the months before the oral argument, numerous briefs were filed with the Court laying out legal and policy arguments implicated in this question. In addition to the two primary parties in the case—the state of Colorado and the group of plaintiffs challenging the initiative—a large number of other people and organizations sought to shape the Court's ultimate decision. The Court accepted more than two dozen friend-of-the-court briefs representing the official views of almost 100 organizations, cities, and individuals. The extraordinary array of organizations filing briefs in this case underscored the intensity and scope of the debate prompted by the case—civil rights organizations, teachers' groups, religious denominations, unions, state and city governments. And the briefs themselves tackled the full range of issues examined at trial—the origin and immutability of sexual orientation, the history of discrimination, moral and religious views, the relative power of gay people politically, the purpose of civil rights legislation.

Best known among the authors of these friend-of-the-court briefs in support of Amendment 2 was Robert H. Bork, a former federal appeals court judge and solicitor general, as well as an unsuccessful nominee for the U.S. Supreme Court. Bork became involved in the case when Colorado first filed its petition to the U.S. Supreme Court seeking review. His brief, filed on behalf of Alabama, Idaho, and Virginia, had urged the Court to accept Colorado's appeal, saying the Colorado Supreme Court ruling had created a "new fundamental right of breathtaking scope" (an argument that the state made in its own petition to the Court). He defended Amendment 2 as doing no more than removing "one issue"—which he identified as "homosexual and bisexual rights"—from the political process. And he argued that the equal protection claim being made by gay people in the *Romer* case was "identical in all material respects" to the claim made in a previous case, *James v. Valtierra*,[1] which the Supreme Court rejected in 1971. The *James* case, out of California, also involved a voter-approved initiative to amend the state constitution—this one to block the enactment of any low-rent housing project unless the project first won approval by a majority of voters in a popular referendum. The U.S. Supreme Court had rejected the plaintiffs' challenge in that case, ruling that the California initiative satisfied the requirements of the Constitution's Equal Protection clause.

---

1. *James v. Valtierra*, 402 U.S. 137 (1971).

Bork's brief in support of Colorado's petition for review was largely reiterated in a final friend-of-the-court, or amicus curiae, brief filed for those three states and four others (California, Nebraska, South Carolina, and South Dakota) after the Court agreed to take the *Romer* case. The essential point of both briefs was that the Constitution guarantees the people the right to govern through majority rule as they see fit.

Several of the other briefs filed in support of Amendment 2 contended that the U.S. Supreme Court's ruling in the *Bowers v. Hardwick* case—allowing states to outlaw some types of same-sex sexual relations—by extension meant that states could also outlaw protections for gay people.

Also filing in support of Amendment 2 were the Oregon Citizens' Alliance and a group called Equal Rights, Not Special Rights, based in Cincinnati, each of which was promoting its own antigay initiative. In addition, several groups often linked to the religious right submitted their defenses of Amendment 2 to the high court, including the American Center for Law and Justice Family Life Project (a Pat Robertson affiliate), the Family Research Council, Concerned Women for America, the Christian Legal Society, Focus on the Family, and Colorado for Family Values. While presenting an array of arguments to the Court, these groups were united in the theme that recognition of civil rights for gay people would threaten religious freedom and the moral fiber of American society.

More than half of the amicus briefs submitted in the case took positions against Amendment 2. Represented in these were seven states (Oregon, Iowa, Maryland, Massachusetts, Minnesota, Nevada, and Washington) plus the District of Columbia, numerous cities, and such prestigious organizations as the American Bar Association, the National Association for the Advancement of Colored People's (NAACP) Legal Defense and Educational Fund, a variety of religious groups, the National Education Association, and the Anti-Defamation League. They urged the Court that Amendment 2 was motivated by bias and prejudice and that it lacked a legitimate governmental purpose for its discriminatory impact.

Clearly responding to the Bork characterization of the case, one brief, from a group of state bar associations, organizations of lawyers, and others, argued that "no 'breathtaking'" principles were being foisted upon the public by the Colorado Supreme Court and no injury was being done to the right of the majority to govern as it sees fit.

Bork's counterpart on the opposite side of the case, constitutional law professor Laurence Tribe, also argued that the issue of whether sexual orientation is immutable was irrelevant to the legal conflict. What matters, said Tribe and other law professors who joined him in the brief, is that the Constitution's guarantee of equal protection applies to "every person within the state's jurisdiction, regardless of what the person might have done, and certainly regardless of what the person might be inclined to do."

"Never since the enactment of the Fourteenth Amendment," wrote Tribe, "has this Court confronted a measure quite like Amendment 2—a measure that, by its express terms, flatly excludes some of a state's people from eligibility for legal protection from a category of wrongs."

Echoing the trial testimony concerning scientific understanding of sexual orientation, the American Psychiatric Association, the American Psychological Association, and similar groups filed a brief opposing Amendment 2, arguing that "there is no basis for such discrimination" and that the initiative "rests on baseless stereotypes about gay people." And in discussing which characteristics define the class of gay people, a brief filed by a number of national civil rights and gay political organizations, including the Human Rights Campaign Fund and the National Gay and Lesbian Task Force, argued that "logically, what defines the class of homosexuals and heterosexuals . . . is the gender of one's partner."

The American Bar Association's brief, ghostwritten by Ruth Harlow, who at the time was on the staff of the ACLU's Gay and Lesbian Rights Project, urged the Supreme Court to consider an argument that the Colorado courts did not consider: that Amendment 2 lacked any rational justification. Referring the Court to its 1985 decision in *City of Cleburne v. Cleburne Living Center*, the ABA further argued that "state purposes that embody such prejudice against a disfavored group cannot be countenanced."

A coalition of religious organizations, including the American Jewish Committee, the United Church of Christ, and the Unitarian Universalist Association, submitted a brief arguing that the "avowed religious belief" of Amendment 2 proponents "that homosexual persons should be singled out for discrimination is not a universal religious belief and, in fact, is contrary to the religious beliefs" of the organizations filing the brief.

A coalition comprised of organizations fighting racial and ethnic discrimination, including the National Council of La Raza, the Asian

American Legal Defense and Education Fund, and the Japanese American Citizens League, filed a brief against Amendment 2, saying that it violated the rights of gay people in ways similar to how African-Americans were treated before the Civil War, and "as aliens, women, and illegitimate offspring were traditionally denied legal protection by the common law to varying degrees and under varying circumstances."

"Our own history, and the bloody course of the twentieth century, have taught us all too well what happens when minorities are denied legal protection—sooner or later individuals' very existence is at stake," wrote Pamela S. Karlan and Eben Moglen, attorneys for the seven groups that signed onto the brief. "The process of dehumanization begins with laws like this one."

A separate brief filed by the NAACP and Mexican American Legal Defense and Educational Funds and the Women's Legal Defense Fund argued that the claim by Colorado that Amendment 2 would help "assure that sufficient funds were available to enforce existing" civil rights laws was "utterly implausible." It likened the CFV's claims that Amendment 2 was necessary to fight "militant gay aggression" to "the canard voiced half a century ago that Jews . . . were somehow covertly exercising control over the nation's policies."

"Not since the heyday of Jim Crow," stated the brief, "have state officials attacked as a threat to the 'body politic' the enactment of minimal protections for an unpopular group."

The large and well-established set of groups lining up against Amendment 2 provided for an interesting contrast to the plaintiffs' arguments at trial that gay people lacked political power. Here, some of the nation's most respected and mainstream professional, political, and religious associations, along with a diverse set of civil rights supporters, had not backed off from the issue at hand simply because gay people were the targets. Certainly, some of the groups were involved because of their concern that Amendment 2 could lead to the erosion of civil rights for other minorities. But they were there and on the plaintiffs' side in this crucial dispute. Whether this support would translate into actual political power was unclear, but, however ironic, the message sent was a powerful one.

There was, at the same time, fallout over at least one powerful entity that did *not* file a brief in the case: the U.S. Department of Justice. President Clinton's administration was said to have been in a "raging" debate over whether to submit a brief in the case on the side of those opposing Amendment 2.[2] Eventually, U.S. Attorney Janet Reno announced the department would not file a brief because there "was not a federal statute or federal program involved" in the case. But most political observers speculated that the Clinton administration was simply trying to avoid any further political fallout for being publicly supportive of gay people.[3]

Not surprisingly, there was significant debate among both legal teams about who would present each side's argument in court. But, on the morning of October 10, the stage was set: Timothy Tymkovich, the Colorado Solicitor General who presented much of the state's case at trial and before the Colorado Supreme Court, was in place to speak for Colorado's majority of voters. Jean Dubofsky, who had acted as the lead attorney for the plaintiffs throughout the litigation, would represent the minority. The courtroom was packed with members of the legal teams, a number of the plaintiffs named in the case, interested attorneys and activists from both sides, and a full media galley.

Both parties were prepared to train their attention particularly on associate justices Sandra Day O'Connor and Anthony Kennedy, two Reagan appointees. Chief Justice William Rehnquist and associate justices Antonin Scalia and Clarence Thomas were the Court's consistently conservative members, particularly on gay-related issues. By contrast, associate justices John Paul Stevens, David Souter, Ruth Bader Ginsburg, and Stephen Breyer were consistently more liberal. O'Connor and Kennedy were widely regarded by court observers as critical "swing" votes on cases, such as this one, where the Court was expected to be closely divided.

For the State

Timothy Tymkovich, for the state, came to the podium first to address the bench. He began his argument by saying that Amendment 2 simply "reserves to the state the decision of whether to extend special protections under state law on the basis of homosexual or bisexual conduct or orientation." Making the same point that Bork's brief had pressed, he

---

2. Lisa Keen and Lou Chibbaro Jr., "White House in Raging Debate over Support in Colorado Case," *Washington Blade*, June 2, 1995, 1.

3. Lisa Keen, "Attorney General 'Pulled the Rug Out from Under Us,'" *Washington Blade*, June 9, 1995, 1. See also Neil A. Lewis, "Administration, Burned in Past, Declines to Join Challenge to Gay Rights Ban," *New York Times*, June 9, 1995, A22.

said the issue at stake in the 1971 *James v. Valtierra* case was "indistinguishable" from the issue in the *Romer* case and, consequently, that Supreme Court ruling "controls here."

Barely a minute into this opening argument, Justice Anthony Kennedy interrupted. Usually, he said, judges pondering the constitutionality of legislation such as Amendment 2 "measure the objective" of the legislation "against the class" that is singled out for discrimination by the law. In other words, courts consider why *this* particular class of people is singled out to bear the burden imposed by the legislation.

"Here," said Kennedy, "the classification seems to be adopted for its own sake," and not for the sake of any governmental objective. "I've never seen a case like this," he said. "Is there any precedent that you can cite to the court where we've upheld a law such as this?" In the view of many observers, the question was prompted by Tribe's amicus brief that stated that a measure has "never" before attempted the exclusion Amendment 2 attempted.

Again Tymkovich pointed to *James*.

"But the whole point of *James* was that we knew that it was low-income housing, and we could measure the need, the importance, the objectives of the legislature to control low-cost housing against the classification that was adopted. Here," Kennedy repeated, "the classification is just adopted for its own sake, with reference to all purposes of the law, so *James* doesn't work."

It was a serious blow to Colorado's argument, delivered only five minutes into Tymkovich's allotted half-hour. Tymkovich tried to save the *James* precedent by suggesting, as Bork had, that rather than targeting homosexual and bisexual people for "all purposes," Amendment 2 sought to resolve only "an issue of whether or not to extend special protections to homosexuals and bisexuals." That reference to "special protections" would soon come back to haunt him, but first he had to field a question from Justice Sandra Day O'Connor. She said the text of Amendment 2 was vague and that it "has never been actually interpreted" by the state courts.

"Does it mean that homosexuals are not covered by Colorado's laws of general applicability?" asked O'Connor, referring to laws that prohibit mistreatment generally, rather than laws that prohibit discrimination based on specific characteristics.

"No," they would not be excluded, said Tymkovich.

"How do we know that?" pressed O'Connor. "I mean, the literal language would indicate that, for example, a public library could refuse to allow books to be borrowed by homosexuals and there would be no relief from that, apparently."

Tymkovich said the Colorado Supreme Court decision indicated that laws of general applicability would not be "displaced" by Amendment 2: "It absolutely changes no provisions under federal law in access to the court or vindication of one's equal protection rights, nor does it affect the state. . . ."

"Well, how do we know that?" asked O'Connor again. Again, she expressed her sense that the amendment's text left the intent and reach of the measure unclear.

Tymkovich said the intent and reach was clear from the "legislative history" of the Amendment 2 campaign and the "intent of the proponents." It affected only laws within the state of Colorado, not federal law, said Tymkovich.

But, interjected Justice Ruth Bader Ginsburg, "federal law is, of course, supreme." She was apparently reminding him that state laws must comply with the U.S. Constitution's mandates and with federal statutes written under the federal government's legislative power. Continuing, Ginsburg underscored Justice Kennedy's point about *James*, seeming to reject Tymkovich's contention that Amendment 2 dealt with only one issue—that of antidiscrimination protections for gay people.

"*James v. Valtierra*," she said, "dealt with one issue, low-cost housing. . . . But here, it's everything. Thou shalt not have access to the ordinary legislative process for anything that will improve the condition of this particular group. And I would like to know whether in all of U.S. history, there has been any legislation like this that earmarks a group and says, 'You will not be able to appeal to your state legislature to improve your status. You will need a constitutional change to do that'?"

Tymkovich conceded that Amendment 2 was "unusual," but he said earlier Supreme Court decisions have allowed states to "withdraw authority over certain issues" from government decision makers.

Justice Antonin Scalia interrupted the discussion briefly to ask a question that seemed off that point at first. He wanted to know whether Amendment 2 applied to people with a homosexual "orientation" or just those who engage in sex with someone of the same gender. Tymkovich, who seemed somewhat bewildered by the question, said,

"It's unclear from this text." That was an odd answer. The text mentioned "homosexual, lesbian or bisexual orientation, conduct, practices or relationships."

Tymkovich's response thwarted Scalia's apparent aim, which was to come to Tymkovich's aid in finding a precedent for Amendment 2 in established law. So Scalia simply forged his point alone.

"If all 'orientation' means" is conduct, "then you have plenty of precedent," he said bluntly. "Namely, state laws that absolutely criminalize such activity—bigamy, homosexuality. . . ."

"That's right," said Tymkovich, realizing Scalia's point.

Then Ginsburg came back, speaking to Tymkovich, but clearly responding to Scalia.

"Colorado has no law that prohibits consensual homosexual conduct," she noted.

"No," Tymkovich conceded, and then he tried to fall back into the discussion about whom Amendment 2 affects, ultimately mumbling something about believing that "conduct is the best indicator of . . ."

"Is it the sole indicator?" asked Souter, in a swift and aggressive pounce. "Are you representing to this Court that Colorado's position is that the class-defining characteristic is conduct as opposed to preference or proclivity or whatnot?" He seemed incredulous.

"No, your honor," replied Tymkovich. That issue had been considered "immaterial" in the state courts' discussion. Again, the answer seemed odd. The trial court had heard hours of testimony trying to define what "homosexual orientation" meant, distinguishing feelings from fantasy from conduct. Tymkovich did acknowledge this discussion briefly, but said it came up simply as part of "an attempt" by attorneys challenging Amendment 2 to prove that homosexual orientation constituted a suspect classification.

Defining the Class

"If the class of people affected by Amendment 2 is defined by more than just their conduct," said Souter, then the Court has to assume that "orientation means something more than conduct or . . . I suppose we would have to send [the case] back and ask the courts of Colorado to tell us." Then he asked if there was "a serious question" about whether orientation means something different from conduct.

Tymkovich said no.

"So orientation means something more than conduct," said Souter, "and we have to assume that in ruling on this challenge, don't we?"

Souter then quizzed Tymkovich about his opening remark—that Amendment 2 was simply withdrawing one issue from local levels of government and reserving it for statewide action.

"It seems to me that there are two things wrong with that characterization," said Souter. "One of them has already been brought up—and that is, this is not merely a reservation for this particular subject to be dealt with, for example, by statewide referendum. It is, in fact, a provision that no law may be made addressing, or addressing for protective purposes, this kind of discrimination." That statement appeared to align Souter's concerns with those of Kennedy and Ginsburg, against Amendment 2.

"The second thing that seems to me inaccurate about the characterization you're giving us," said Souter, "is that this is not merely a reservation of a subject matter" because the subject matter was being reserved only for a certain class of people, raising a question of equal protection under the law.

"Your honor, there is a classification involved," said Tymkovich, "but there is no invidious discrimination" in identifying that class. "That is not the case here. I think we've shown that there are reasons for the classification." And because there are reasons, he said, the law can stand unless gay people are considered a suspect class or unless Amendment 2 is deemed to violate some fundamental constitutional right.

Souter repeated his original point—that the question at issue is more than just a "mere reservation" of an issue for "action at one level rather than another." Tymkovich resisted, and soon Ginsburg jumped back in, reminding Tymkovich that, under the amendment, even the state legislature cannot address any issue involving protection or recognition of gay people. That, too, seemed to weaken his contention that Amendment 2 was merely reserving to the state the right to act on this issue.

"I was trying to think of something comparable to this," said Ginsburg, "and what occurred to me is that this political means of going at the local level first is familiar in American politics. In fact, it was the way that the suffragists worked. When they were unable to achieve the vote statewide, they did it on a cities-first approach. And I take it from what you are arguing that if there had been a referendum that said no local ordinance can give women the vote, that that would have been constitutional?"

Tymkovich said no.

"What is the difference?" asked Ginsburg.

"I think that that classification would be analyzed under this Court's equal protection jurisprudence as a suspect . . ."

"Well, cast your mind back to the days before the Nineteenth Amendment," said Ginsburg, referring to the constitutional amendment which, in 1920, gave women the right to vote. Her remark provoked laughter in the quiet courtroom audience.

The analogy seemed to sting. Chief Justice William Rehnquist changed the subject. If Amendment 2 is upheld, he asked, it could be changed through another statewide referendum, right?

"That's right, your honor." Tymkovich added that opponents of Amendment 2 would have to do the same—and no more—to remove the law than proponents of Amendment 2 had to do to put the amendment in place. He then appeared to try to undermine Ginsburg's analogy by suggesting that the antigay activists who won passage of Amendment 2 were more comparable to the suffragists than the gay activists who fought it.

"What the [opponents of Amendment 2] are saying is that those who oppose certain types of special protections here cannot get their policy preference vindicated through the legislative process unless they are able to successfully preempt or repeal such laws at the local level," said Tymkovich.

What Is Special?

Scalia used Tymkovich's mention of "special protections" to change the subject again.

"When you talk about 'special protection,'" said Justice Scalia, ". . . how do you interpret the term 'minority status, quota preferences, protected status'?" Amendment 2 prohibited any governmental entity within Colorado from enacting any law or policy which "shall constitute . . . or entitle" a gay or bisexual person to "have or claim any minority status, quota preferences, protected status or claim of discrimination."

"Protected status," said Tymkovich, "would be a particular affirmative positive piece of legislation that granted some type of protection. . . ."

Scalia interrupted: "Special protection beyond what?"

"Beyond the Fourteenth Amendment," said Tymkovich.

"Why wouldn't that have been your answer?" asked Scalia, to Justice O'Connor's early question about whether Amendment 2 would mean that libraries could prohibit gay people from checking out books. "No homosexual can be treated differently from other people," said Scalia. "He simply cannot be given special protection by reason of that status."

"That's right," said Tymkovich, again accepting an assist from Scalia. But the question was not settled. Justice John Paul Stevens was concerned about what "special protection" would mean in the context of places open to the public.

"Could an innkeeper refuse accommodations to a homosexual who was not engaging in any homosexual conduct but had admitted that he had that type of tendency?" asked Stevens.

"To the extent there was some tort law of general applicability in those circumstances about innkeeper's duty," Tymkovich said, "we don't think that Amendment 2 would knock that out." Stevens tried to translate Tymkovich's point.

"So you would say the public accommodations protection is still available to homosexuals?"

Tymkovich's answer was muddled: "Amendment 2 would carve out any special protections in the public accommodation area that had been extended to homosexuals." Stevens seemed frustrated. Now, it seemed Tymkovich was saying gay people could be refused public accommodation.

"What would the rule be in Colorado?" Stevens asked again. "How do you understand the law there? Now, would a homosexual have a right to be served in a restaurant?" he asked, perhaps alluding to the days when restaurants commonly refused service to African-Americans.

"A homosexual would not have any claim of discrimination or special liability theory in a private setting after Amendment 2," said Tymkovich. That seemed more clear. Stevens seemed satisfied. But then Tymkovich muddled the answer with an addendum: "Unless the court . . . and again we haven't had a full construction of Amendment 2 yet from our state courts," said Tymkovich. "Unless a state court construed the innkeeper's duty to be a law of general applicability to . . ."

"Do you know what the law of Colorado is on that point?" asked Stevens.

"I do not," conceded Tymkovich.

"So we don't know whether homosexuals have a right to be served or not," concluded Stevens.

Tymkovich agreed, and that response seemed to throw Stevens into O'Connor's position of thinking the language of Amendment 2 had not been adequately interpreted by the state courts. It appeared there might be enough support on the bench to send the case back to the state courts for a more definitive interpretation, an option that would keep antigay initiatives alive for months to come. But Stevens was not finished. He took a swipe at Scalia's characterization of protection for gay people as being "special" protection.

"If they do have a right to be served" in a hotel or restaurant, asked Stevens, "would that be an affirmative right, then, as in the distinction Justice Scalia was drawing, or would that be just being treated like everybody else?"

"I think it would be treated just like any other characteristic or classification that has not gotten the special benefits of the civil rights law," said Tymkovich.

Stevens's question, and Tymkovich's response, seemed to puncture Scalia's "special protections" balloon. But again, Stevens wasn't finished.

What Is the Purpose?

"One last question: What is the rational basis for this statute?" It was the question opponents of Amendment 2 most wanted asked.

"The purpose of this statute," said Tymkovich, "was to preempt state and local laws that extended special protections. It was a response to political activism by a political group that wanted to seek special affirmative protections under the law."

"Well, it went further" than preemption, noted Stevens, "because there were political groups that had already—as I understand it, Aspen had a protective statute of some kind."

"That's correct," conceded Tymkovich.

So what, asked Stevens, is the rational basis for "the people outside of Aspen telling the people in Aspen they cannot have that statute?"

When Tymkovich tried to sidestep the question, Stevens repeated it: "What's the rational basis for the people outside of Aspen telling the people in Aspen they cannot have this nondiscriminatory provision?"

Tymkovich fumbled, then asserted that "the rational basis for that substantive decision in our view was a political response to what the people [of the entire state] might have perceived as laws going too far or being too intrusive."

This time, Rehnquist rescued Tymkovich.

"The state of Virginia has a very broad state preemption doctrine," he noted. The law there prevents any local government from passing laws that provide rights beyond what the state law already dictates. Called the Dillon Rule, it has been used by some to argue that localities cannot prohibit discrimination based on any category, such as sexual orientation, not already recognized by state law. "I suppose the rational basis for that is just that the people generally would prefer to have the rules set by the state at large rather than by local governments," remarked Rehnquist.

"That's correct, your honor," said Tymkovich, again jumping on the assist. "And there's nothing wrong, especially in this area of civil rights and statewide protections, in making that an issue of statewide concern. And that's simply what Colorado was. . . ."

But Souter jumped on what he apparently saw as a flaw in that argument. Yes, generally speaking, a state can reserve certain subject matters to itself, as Virginia does. But that is not what Colorado was doing with Amendment 2. Colorado was reserving to the constitutional amendment process all subject matters pertaining to gay people but not to other people, such as senior citizens or people with disabilities. The question, said Souter, is what is the rational basis for making that distinction and singling out gay people?

"Your honor," said Tymkovich, "that's a quintessential political judgment on how you provide protection to relative groups."

"Well, it's a judgment that is made *politically*, but that doesn't state a *rational* basis," said Souter. "The question that's being asked here is: Why is discrimination against one group dealt with under state law differently from discrimination against other groups? And your rational basis answer, it seems to me, has got to go to a justification for the classification. It isn't enough simply to say, 'Oh, well, that's what politics decided.'"

Tymkovich fell back on two of the reasons the state had offered at trial: that the state wanted "uniformity" in its laws on this matter, and that there were "other liberty interests," such as the religious liberty of people who objected to homosexuality. But then he conceded that the state courts also felt that Amendment 2 had not been "narrowly tailored" to advance the religious liberty concern. Scalia interrupted.

"Mr. Tymkovich," said Scalia. "If this is an ordinary equal protection challenge and there's no heightened scrutiny, isn't it an adequate answer to Justice Souter's question to say, 'This is the only area in which we've had a problem'?"

Tymkovich, again, agreed, but Justice Souter challenged him to explain what "the problem" with gay people had been.

"I think the problem that the voters saw—they were presented with an opportunity to preempt and make a decision at a statewide level for laws that raise particular and sensitive liberty concerns," said Tymkovich. He was fumbling again, with no clear response. And again, Scalia came to the rescue.

"State subdivisions giving preferences which the majority of the people in the state did not think desirable for social reasons—isn't that the problem that was seen?" asked Scalia, though his "question" was clearly a response to Souter's question.

"That's right," said Tymkovich.

Scalia continued the argument.

"And if they should start giving preferences for some other reason that the majority of the state did not consider desirable—let's say bigamy, special preferences to bigamist couples—there would be a law on that subject as well. Isn't that your answer? This is the only area where the people apparently saw a problem, which is enough [of a rational basis] for equal protection."

"It is," said Tymkovich, trying to pick up the ball Scalia had given him. "And this is an area where there have been piecemeal additions of special protections."

"What is the special preference at stake here?" asked Stevens, again undercutting Tymkovich's attempt to regain composure. "What is the special preference that a homosexual gets?"

Tymkovich said "homosexuals are entitled to every other protection" available to others plus "a cause of action on the basis" of sexual orientation "that's not available" to others.

But, noted Ginsburg, Tymkovich had already conceded that a restaurant could refuse service to gay people. Presumably a hospital could, she said, refuse a gay person treatment on a kidney dialysis machine, saying that the machine was a scarce resource. What if some wanted to ration its use by cutting only gay people off the waiting list? What cause of action, she asked, would a gay person have?

Tymkovich had to concede again: He did not know.

The final question for Tymkovich came from Justice Steven Breyer. Only he and Justice Clarence Thomas had stayed out of the discussion thus far, and Thomas would, as he typically had in the Supreme Court oral arguments, not become engaged in the discussion.

Like O'Connor, Breyer was confused about some of the amendment's specific language. He wanted to know what the initiative language meant when it said that no entity of the state could adopt or enforce "any statute, regulation, ordinance or policy" concerning protections for gay people. If a local police department has a "policy" against gay bashing or a librarian has a "policy" of allowing gay people to use the library, he asked, does Amendment 2 undo those policies? Tymkovich said Amendment 2 "would not prohibit that."

"Then what does the word 'policy' prohibit?" asked Breyer.

Again, Tymkovich fell back on Scalia's "special" preferences mantra.

"Policy," he said, "prohibits the enactment of some special entitlement . . ."

But Breyer interrupted him.

"What is 'policy,'" he asked, "if it isn't the policy of the department saying, 'Do not discriminate against gays'?"

Scalia tried to help.

"Mr. Tymkovich," he prompted, "I assume in your state you're not allowed to bash nongays either, are you?"

"No," said Tymkovich, following Scalia's lead. But by that point, Scalia seemed to have given up on Tymkovich being able to follow his lead adequately. When Tymkovich tried to continue that thought, Scalia simply interrupted him.

"The criminal law," said Tymkovich, "is . . ."

"So prohibiting the bashing of gays," continued Scalia, "would not be a special protection, would it? It would just be enforcing the general law."

"Yes," said Tymkovich, who tried again to pursue the point. "And Amendment 2 does nothing to restrict the applicable . . ."

"Isn't that," interrupted Scalia again, "the response to Justice . . ."

"That's right," said Tymkovich.

"Fine," said Scalia, and the courtroom again erupted in laughter.

But Breyer clearly felt he had not gotten an answer to his question about "policy." What does the word "policy" prohibit, then?

"It prohibits any type of special protection or a liability claim that somebody might have under that policy," said Tymkovich.

Kennedy reentered the fray at this point to note that Tymkovich's answer was "inconsistent" with the Colorado Supreme Court ruling, which said Amendment 2 would void state health insurance antidiscrimination policies as they pertain to gay people.

When Breyer went back to his police department example again, Tymkovich inexplicably suggested that police policy could prohibit discrimination against lesbians and gay men. His time was nearly up, and he stepped down from the podium, saving his final minute for rebuttal of Dubofsky's arguments on behalf of plaintiffs.

For the Plaintiffs

As she went to the podium, plaintiffs' counsel Jean Dubofsky felt confident the case had already been won against Amendment 2. Justice Kennedy's comment to Tymkovich that *James* "doesn't work" in the *Romer* case, was, she believed, tantamount to victory. A respected attorney with experience before the Supreme Court had advised her, she said, "that the argument in the Supreme Court would be about what Amendment 2 means." And that advice had already proven itself on the mark.

But when Dubofsky launched her argument against Amendment 2 by saying that the initiative is "vertically broad"—that it prohibits "all levels of government in the state," including police departments, from providing protection to gay people, both Rehnquist and Kennedy immediately shot two holes in the argument, noting that voters can and the state courts may be able to take action.

Breyer picked up on Dubofsky's disagreement with Tymkovich's sudden claim that Amendment 2 did not prevent a police department policy and asked her about it. In response, Dubofsky pointed out that the Colorado Supreme Court ruling noted examples of such policies as among those that would be repealed by the measure and precluded from future enactment.

Scalia then suggested that Dubofsky was overreaching with these examples. The proper interpretation of the Colorado Supreme Court ruling, he said, was that Amendment 2 would prohibit only "special protection" for gay people. He asked whether Dubofsky was suggesting that, under Amendment 2, no general laws—such as those criminalizing murder and "bashing"—could protect gay people the same as they protect all citizens.

Dubofsky said she thought Amendment 2 could, in fact, undo the application of general laws to gay people but conceded that the Colorado Supreme Court did not "go that far in its interpretation."

"I think they interpreted it to refer to special protections accorded to homosexuals," said Scalia, "and not to [general protections for] the public at large."

"I think we're having trouble a little bit with semantics," said Dubofsky. Part of the trouble, she said, was Scalia's use of the term *special protection*.

"I don't think there is such a thing as special rights or special protections," said Dubofsky. "I think there's a right which everyone has to be free from arbitrary discrimination."

"No, but if I go and ask a homeowner to take me in on a bed and breakfast or boarding house, and the homeowner says, 'I don't like Italians,' that's my tough luck," said Scalia, "unless there's a law against it. It's that person's house and that person is entitled not to like Italians and not to rent rooms to Italians."

Returning to Scalia's "special protections" terminology, Dubofsky argued that laws that prohibit discrimination based on sexual orientation provide protection generally, to "everyone"; Amendment 2 preempts these laws, Dubofsky said, "only on the basis that they" protect gay or bisexual people.

"But they are laws that provide special protection for that particular category of person," said Scalia, "which they don't provide to people at large. . . . Special protection is given by this law which [gay people] cite by reason of homosexual orientation or conduct. Is that not special?"

Justice Kennedy soon jumped in to explore ways in which Amendment 2 might *not* preclude protection for gay people. If a city has a law against barring people from a public accommodation for any "arbitrary or unreasonable" reason, could not a court in Colorado still declare, under Amendment 2, that barring a person because of sexual orientation constitutes such an "unreasonable or arbitrary" reason?, he wondered.

Dubofsky said she thought a court could do that. But if the person was denied the accommodation because he or she is a gay person, then a court might not be able to grant relief.

Ginsburg apparently felt Dubofsky was straying.

"But isn't the very purpose of [Amendment 2] to say, 'It's *not* arbitrary to leave out of a catalog of protection against discrimination, it's *not* arbitrary to leave out . . . persons of homosexual, lesbian, or bisexual orientation?'" she asked.

"Amendment 2, if interpreted at its broadest, would authorize that type of discrimination," said Dubofsky.

Now Souter seemed to think she had misstepped.

"But even on a narrower interpretation, even for example if Amendment 2 didn't touch the courts," said Souter, "wouldn't it be very difficult for the courts of Colorado to say that that was an irrational or an arbitrary basis for discrimination with Amendment 2 on the books—even if Amendment 2 was narrowly construed?"

"Yes," said Dubofsky, "it would be, I believe. . . . But the Colorado Supreme Court," she pointed out eventually, "didn't think it was necessary to go that far in order to find the amendment unconstitutional."

How Far the Reach?

That prompted Justice O'Connor to reiterate her concern: that the state courts had not given Amendment 2 a "definitive interpretation . . . of how far this amendment would go."

"I think the arguments and responses this morning," she said, "are illustrative of the fact that we're not sure."

Dubofsky tried to disagree, pointing out one section of the Colorado Supreme Court ruling, but O'Connor dismissed that section.

"I looked at that," she said, "and I just thought that that wasn't definitive. There are still questions about how far it would go and the extent to which it reaches courts, and so forth and so on."

Specifically how far the amendment reaches, suggested Rehnquist, might not be important given that the case challenges the measure's constitutionality on its own—and not as applied to any specific instance. Dubofsky agreed.

Scalia saw a hole. If this was a so-called facial argument, he noted, then Dubofsky would have to show that "there are not applications in which the statute can be constitutional."

"It doesn't necessarily mean that there are *no* applications that would be constitutional," said Dubofsky, apparently fearing that Scalia would proffer one. "It just means that those are irrelevant."

"Well, that's not what our case law involving facial challenges says," said Scalia.

This time, Ginsburg held out an assist.

"Ms. Dubofsky," she said, "do I understand correctly what you're saying about what the Colorado Supreme Court said—at a minimum, this amendment immediately repeals all of the laws that are listed, and this group of people cannot be reinstated into this group of laws without a constitutional amendment—and that is what you say is unconstitutional under federal equal protection?"

Dubofsky attempted to respond, then found herself in another skirmish with Scalia, who pointed out that Colorado's antidiscrimination laws did not prohibit all forms of arbitrary discrimination. After saying that Scalia "could be right," Dubofsky described antidiscrimination ordinances as "general prophylactic rules" and attempted to distinguish such rules from Scalia's critique.

Breyer jumped in, suggesting that Dubofsky meant to explain that laws against arbitrary discrimination are still undone, as they apply to gay people, under Amendment 2.

"That's correct," said Dubofsky.

"Seems a Little Odd"

Kennedy again sought a way of interpreting Amendment 2 that might not preclude general protection for gay people.

"Suppose that Colorado is concerned that one city has passed an ordinance giving preference to gays in employment hiring, and, for any number of reasons, the citizens of Colorado do not want that. Some people say they want 'uniform' laws because it's easier on employers," suggested Justice Kennedy. "Could the citizens of Colorado, by referendum, repeal that ordinance?"

"Yes, they could repeal that ordinance," said Dubofsky.

"Could they also provide that no such ordinance shall be adopted in the future?"

No, said Dubofsky, and that was the crux of the argument for opponents of Amendment 2—that the prohibition on future laws interfered with the right of gay people to participate equally in the political process. She did not get a chance, however, to explain that argument.

"Well, it would seem a little odd," said Justice Kennedy; "there could be an ordinance enacted, then repealed by the referendum, then the ordinance is enacted again, then repealed. It just goes back and forth. That seems a little odd."

Then Justice O'Connor offered a hypothetical: "Could Colorado adopt a law that says any law in our state dealing with discrimination on any ground has to be passed at the state level?"

"It could," conceded Dubofsky. "There are other problems with dealing with civil rights protections and generally, but let's say they passed Amendment 2 but it didn't target gay people; it simply said that no one can obtain any protection from discrimination, arbitrary discrimination, for any reason. That," said Dubofsky, "would not present the problem that Amendment 2 presents. Amendment 2 is very selective. It targets only one group of people, and that's where it encounters equal protection difficulties."

"What group does it target?" asked Scalia, saying he was reiterating to her his question to Tymkovich about what does "orientation" mean—to whom does it apply?

Dubofsky said that, since "heterosexual people are not identified exclusively by heterosexual conduct," homosexual orientation would include more than just those people who engage in homosexual sex.

But Ginsburg interrupted this discourse to point out that the language of Amendment 2 refers to people with both a homosexual "orientation" and "conduct." And Souter returned Dubofsky to her "political participation" argument.

"Let's say there were an ordinance in a given city saying there will be no discrimination based on age, handicap, or sexual orientation," said Souter, "and there were a political move in that city to repeal the reference to sexual orientation. That would be targeted at homosexuals, but it would not run afoul of what I understand your position to be here, is that correct?"

"No," said Dubofsky, after a long pause. But before Dubofsky could take up the opportunity to discuss political participation, Rehnquist interrupted with yet another hypothetical. If "dissident Mormons" wanted to repeal a law against polygamy, he said, and the Constitution says polygamy will always be a felony, "does that fence out these people?"

"Not necessarily," said Dubofsky, because that law or constitutional provision deals with "much more of a discrete issue. It's not restructuring the political process."

"That is different from this case," she elaborated, "because this case is targeting a particular group of people on a personal characteristic."

As Dubofsky seemed to settle that hypothetical, Scalia took his final swipe. He wanted to know whether she was asking the Supreme Court to overrule its 1986 decision in *Bowers v. Hardwick*, upholding Georgia's sodomy law as it applied to same-sex partners. Although the plaintiffs would certainly have welcomed such an action by the Court, they had not asked for that in their briefs, believing it was both risky and unnecessary to winning their case in *Romer*. But Scalia apparently wanted a clear statement on the record to that effect.

"No, I am not," said Dubofsky.

Since the Supreme Court said in *Hardwick* that "homosexual conduct" can be made criminal, said Scalia, "Why can't a state not take a step short of that and say, 'We're certainly not going to make it criminal but on the other hand, we certainly don't want to encourage it, and therefore, we will neither have a state law giving it special protection, nor will we allow any municipalities to give it special protection."

"It seems to me," said Scalia, ". . . if you can criminalize it, surely you can take that latter step, can't you?"

"What you've done," said Dubofsky, "is deprived people, based on their homosexual orientation, of a whole opportunity to seek protection from discrimination, which is a very different thing."

Amendment 2, interjected Justice Stevens, applies to gay people "even if they abstain from the prohibited conduct."

Justice Ginsburg returned Dubofsky to Justice Kennedy's point that, if Amendment 2 could not prevent the enactment of future legislation, then the state might be in a situation where a city council passed antidiscrimination and voters repealed it, over and over again.

"Isn't the state entitled to end a ping-pong game?" asked Ginsburg.

Dubofsky tried again to suggest simply that preempting future legislation is "different" than repealing existing legislation. Then Justice Souter jumped in with the answer: The state, he suggested, could "end the ping-pong" game if it ends it with respect to protection against all people, not just gay people.

Dubofsky's time was up. Tymkovich had one minute remaining and tried again to emphasize that Amendment 2 was taking one "issue"—and not gay people—out of the political process. But again Souter made clear he was unpersuaded, saying the initiative "speaks both in terms of issue, i.e., basis for claim, and group."

"It refers to both, doesn't it?" asked Souter. "You can't have one without the other. . . ."

"It Refers to Both"

Seven months later, on May 20, 1996, the U.S. Supreme Court agreed that the initiative was excluding "both"—gay people and protections for gay people—from the political process. It affirmed the Colorado Supreme Court decision, striking down Amendment 2 as unconstitutional. But where the state court said the initiative violated a fundamental constitutional right to participate in the political process, the Supreme Court noted that it was deciding the case on "other grounds." In a 6 to 3 decision, the Court held Amendment 2 violated the constitutional right to equal protection because it violated the literal guarantee to equal protection of the laws and because it lacked a rational basis for its classification of gay people. The reasons the state offered to justify its infringement of gay people's ability to seek protection against discrimination from government, said the majority, were "implausible." The initiative seemed to be motivated by nothing but "animus" for gay people, and animosity could not be a legitimate reason to discriminate against any group.

Justice Kennedy wrote the majority opinion and was joined by Justices John Paul Stevens, Sandra Day O'Connor, David Souter, Ruth Bader Ginsburg, and Stephen Breyer. The majority opinion was 14 pages long, approximately the same length as the majority opinion ten years earlier in *Bowers v. Hardwick* and, following an eloquent and symbolically significant nod to previous cases, it explained the Amendment's constitutional flaw.

"One century ago," wrote Kennedy, in the ruling's first paragraph, "the first Justice Harlan admonished this Court [in his dissent to *Plessy v. Ferguson,* a ruling upholding racial segregation] that the Constitution 'neither knows nor tolerates classes among citizens.'

Unheeded then, those words now are understood to state a commitment to the law's neutrality where the rights of persons are at stake.
The Equal Protection Clause enforces this principle and today
requires us to hold invalid a provision of Colorado's Constitution." (It
is interesting to note that, of all the briefs filed in the case—citing
numerous cases from the history of the civil rights struggle of
African-Americans from the earliest civil rights cases to school deseg-
regation cases to cases challenging antimiscegenation laws—only one
brief [and the concurring opinion at the Colorado Supreme Court]
mentioned *Plessy v. Ferguson.* That brief, a secondary brief from attorneys for the City of Aspen, quoted the same statement from Harlan's
dissent.) By invoking this powerful, historic lesson at the outset of the
opinion, the majority was sending a clear message that the Court considered the type of discrimination imposed by Amendment 2 as
offensive as society now considers the racial segregation permitted by
the *Plessy* majority.

The opinion then turned quickly to the present to explore the
meaning of Amendment 2. Noting that the state had argued Amendment 2 simply denies gay people "special rights," Kennedy wrote,
"This reading of the amendment's language is implausible." Instead,
said Kennedy, the amendment's impact is "sweeping and comprehensive." Through Amendment 2, gay people would be "put in a solitary
class" in relation to government and in private activities.

"The amendment withdraws from homosexuals, but no others,
specific legal protection from the injuries caused by discrimination, and
it forbids reinstatement of these laws and policies," said the majority.
The impact of this is "far-reaching" and has "a severe consequence."

The initiative would not only bar gay people from securing protection under laws prohibiting discrimination based on sexual orientation, but it also "deprives gays and lesbians even of the protection of
general laws and policies that prohibit arbitrary discrimination in governmental and private settings."

"Even if, as we doubt, homosexuals could find some safe harbor in
laws of general application, we cannot accept the view that Amendment 2's prohibition on specific legal protections does no more than
deprive homosexuals of special rights," said the majority. "To the contrary, the amendment imposes a special disability upon those persons
alone. Homosexuals are forbidden the safeguards that others enjoy or
may seek without constraint."

Turning its full force on the "special rights" rhetoric that had been successfully used to promote Amendment 2, the Court said, "We find nothing special in the protections Amendment 2 withholds. These are protections taken for granted by most people either because they already have them or do not need them; these are protections against exclusion from an almost limitless number of transactions and endeavors that constitute ordinary civic life in a free society."

Having identified the amendment's effect, the Court then turned to assess its constitutionality. The state of Colorado, said the majority, failed to satisfy the judicial system's most lenient equal protection scrutiny applied to laws that single out a group of people for discriminatory treatment.

"First," wrote Kennedy, "the amendment has the peculiar property of imposing a broad and undifferentiated disability on a single named group. . . ." And, "second, its sheer breadth is so discontinuous with the reasons offered for it that the amendment seems inexplicable by anything but animus toward the class that it affects; it lacks a rational relationship to legitimate state interests."

Concerning the singling out of a group, noted the majority, courts must see a nexus between the class singled out and "the object" of the law affecting that class differently.

"In the ordinary case," wrote Kennedy, "a law will be sustained if it can be said to advance a legitimate government interest, even if the law seems unwise or works to the disadvantage of a particular group, or if the rationale for it seems tenuous. . . . By requiring that the classification bear a rational relationship to an independent and legitimate legislative end, we ensure that classifications are not drawn for the purpose of disadvantaging the group burdened by the law."

On the first point—targeting a "single named group," Amendment 2, which the Court characterized as "unprecedented in our jurisprudence," "identifies persons by a single trait and then denies them protection across the board." The Court said, "A law declaring in general that it shall be more difficult for one group of citizens than for all others to seek aid from government is itself a denial of equal protection of the laws in the most literal sense."

On the second point—targeting for reasons of "animus"—the majority said that Amendment 2 "inflicts on [gay people] immediate, continuing, and real injuries that outrun and belie any legitimate justifications that may be claimed for it."

In short, "a law must bear a rational relationship to a legitimate governmental purpose, and Amendment 2 does not."

The Court noted that Colorado claimed that Amendment 2 respects the religious freedom and freedom of association of those people who have "personal or religious objections to homosexuality." It also noted Colorado's claim that Amendment 2 helped conserve the state's financial resources for fighting discrimination against other groups. But the breadth of the initiative, said the Court, "is so far removed from these particular justifications that we find it impossible to credit them."

"We cannot say that Amendment 2 is directed at any identifiable legitimate purpose or discrete objective," wrote Kennedy. "It is a status-based enactment divorced from any factual context from which we could discern a relationship to legitimate state interests; it is a classification of persons undertaken for its own sake, something the Equal Protection Clause does not permit. . . .

"We must conclude that Amendment 2 classifies homosexuals not to further a proper legislative end but to make them unequal to everyone else," concluded Kennedy. "This Colorado cannot do. A state cannot so deem a class of persons a stranger to its laws."

Impassioned Dissent

In dissent, three justices made prominent mention of their upset over the legal and political consequences of the decision.

"In holding that homosexuality cannot be singled out for disfavorable treatment, the Court contradicts a decision [*Bowers v. Hardwick*], unchallenged here, pronounced only 10 years ago, and places the prestige of this institution behind the proposition that opposition to homosexuality is as reprehensible as racial or religious bias," wrote Justice Antonin Scalia.

Scalia, joined by Chief Justice William Rehnquist and Justice Clarence Thomas, accused the majority of taking sides in the "Kulturkampf"—cultural war—over homosexuality.

Amendment 2, wrote Scalia, was not an expression of hatred toward gay people but "rather a modest attempt by seemingly tolerant Coloradans to preserve traditional sexual mores against the efforts of a politically powerful minority to revise those mores through use of the laws."

The cultural war, wrote Scalia, revolves around the question of whether discrimination against gay people "is as reprehensible as racial or religious bias." Since there is "nothing about this subject" in the Constitution, he said, "it is left to be resolved by normal democratic means," such as through initiatives.

"This Court," wrote Scalia, "has no business imposing upon all Americans the resolution favored by the elite class from which the Members of this institution are selected, pronouncing that 'animosity' toward homosexuality is evil." (The notion of an "elite" class being "free of democracy in order to impose the values of an elite upon the rest of us" was proffered in 1989 by Robert Bork.)[4]

"The amendment prohibits *special treatment* of homosexuals, and nothing more," said Scalia. If a gay person worked for the state, he said, that person would, like all other employees, be eligible for a pension at retirement. All Amendment 2 would do, he said, would be to prevent the state from paying the "life partner" of a gay employee a death benefit "when it does not make such payments to the longtime roommate of a nonhomosexual employee."

Scalia did not mention that the "nonhomosexual employee," unlike the gay one, has the option of making his or her longtime roommate a legally married spouse to obtain those death benefits.

To the dissent, the problem was not Amendment 2 but laws prohibiting discrimination based on sexual orientation, or presumably any other characteristic. These laws, said Scalia, bestow "*preferential* treatment" on certain groups, since these groups, like all Americans, already have the Constitution's guarantee of equal protection of the laws. He made this viewpoint even clearer later when he explained that Amendment 2 did not "prohibit giving favored status to people who are *homosexuals*; they can be favored for many reasons—for example, because they are senior citizens or members of racial minorities. But it prohibits giving them favored status *because of their homosexual conduct*—that is, it prohibits favored status for homosexuality." What Scalia did not address was that human rights laws do not address just discrimination against racial minorities, but discrimination based on the characteristic of race—any race. And they do not prohibit discrimination against only those people with a homosexual orientation but

4. Robert H. Bork, "The Case against Political Judging," *National Review,* December 8, 1989, 24.

rather discrimination based on sexual orientation itself—any sexual orientation. What Amendment 2 sought to do was limit the law so that it would protect only those people with a heterosexual orientation. Under Amendment 2, if any group was getting "special" protection or treatment, it was, in fact, people with a heterosexual orientation.

Nevertheless, Scalia said Colorado had ample basis for withdrawing "special protection" from gay people. First, he said, the Court's ruling in *Bowers v. Hardwick* justifies treating gay people differently.

"If it is constitutionally permissible for a State to make homosexual conduct criminal," wrote Scalia, "surely it is constitutionally permissible for a State to enact other laws merely *disfavoring* homosexual conduct." (His words closely paralleled those in a brief filed in support of Amendment 2 by the Concerned Women for America: "It follows that if Colorado may criminalize sodomy . . . it may constitutionally preclude the adoption of special homosexual rights laws.")

Where the majority of justices saw a "status-based" targeting, Scalia saw no distinction between a person who is gay and a person who engages in "homosexual conduct." Even if a person with a homosexual orientation did not engage in "homosexual conduct," said Scalia, the *Hardwick* rationale for upholding Amendment 2 suffices.

"If it is rational to criminalize the conduct, surely it is rational to deny special favor and protection to those with a self-avowed tendency or desire to engage in the conduct."

"Amendment 2 is unquestionably constitutional as applied to those who engage in homosexual conduct," asserted Scalia. Because the lawsuit was a "facial" challenge to the initiative, he reasoned, the plaintiffs could not prove, as required by law, that there was no set of circumstances under which Amendment 2 would be valid.

Concerning the majority opinion's claim that Amendment 2 was motivated by "animus," Scalia argued that "our moral heritage" teaches that "one could consider certain conduct reprehensible—murder, for example, or polygamy, or cruelty to animals—and could exhibit even 'animus' toward such conduct."

"Surely," wrote Scalia, "that is the only sort of 'animus' at issue here: moral disapproval of homosexual conduct."

Scalia acknowledged that Colorado had repealed its law against sodomy—or, as he put it, "homosexual conduct"—in 1971. But, he said, "the society that eliminates criminal punishment for homosexual acts does not necessarily abandon the view that homosexuality is morally wrong and socially harmful." The repeal of sodomy laws often reflects the view that enforcement of such laws "involves unseemly intrusion into the intimate lives of citizens," he said. The problem in such societies, he wrote, is that gay activists organize to pass laws to prohibit discrimination based on sexual orientation, using the legal system "for reinforcement of their moral sentiments." People who do not approve of homosexuality, he said, indicating that he believes they constitute the majority of people, counter this with measures like Amendment 2.

Scalia argued that this sort of majority countermove to "preserve traditional American moral values" was at work with laws that prohibit polygamy.

"Polygamists, and those who have a polygamous 'orientation,' have been 'singled out' by these provisions for much more severe treatment than merely denial of favored status," wrote Scalia. The only remedy polygamists have to regain legal favor is to amend state constitutions and U.S. law that required that state constitutions ban polygamy, he added.

While the political branches are in the business to "take sides in this culture war," said Scalia, the courts should not. "But the Court today has done so," said Scalia, "by verbally disparaging as bigotry adherence to traditional attitudes."

"When the Court takes sides in the culture wars," it tends to be with "the knights rather than the villeins [commoners]," wrote Scalia.

"Amendment 2 is designed to prevent piecemeal deterioration of the sexual morality favored by a majority of Coloradans, and is not only an appropriate means to that legitimate end, but a means that Americans have employed before. Striking it down is an act, not of judicial judgment, but of political will."

Some immediately hailed Justice Scalia as a truth-sayer, while others saw his scathing words as the venomous tirade of a defeated jurist. Likewise, some saluted Justice Kennedy as a great defender of core constitutional principles, while others critiqued the majority opinion as long on rhetoric but short on law. Responding to that critique, some scholars observed in the aftermath that, when it is writing to convey a principle not only to other lawyers but also to the public at large, the high court will deliberately craft an opinion that is brief and easily understood by nonlawyers to alert readers to the dramatic import of its ruling. One thing was certain, however: Despite Scalia's passionate oration in announcing his dissent from the bench, his points had been firmly rejected by a majority of the Supreme Court.

The *Romer* decision was a strong, stunning legal victory for the gay civil rights movement. Though Colorado Solicitor General Tymkovich and Colorado for Family Values officials said they might try to rewrite the initiative to pass constitutional muster, the decision did not offer hope that such an effort would succeed. The Court had found the proffered reasons for the initiative—whether religious, moral, or economic—to be not just weak but "implausible." The measure was clearly motivated by hatred for gay people and designed to put gay people at disadvantage—to make them "strangers to the law." That, said the high court, a state cannot do.

Chapter 10

The Law and Social Change

While the battle over Amendment 2 was being waged in the legal system, copycat initiatives emerged—from Arizona to Florida, and Alaska to Maine. Each became a lightning rod for religious right organizing efforts. In an attempt to fend them off, lesbians, gay men, and civil rights advocates had to embark on a whole new level of organizing to respond to these assaults.

As the number of initiatives increased and their geographic reach expanded, it became increasingly clear that lesbians and gay men had been targeted for the first line of attack in the religious right's stepped-up "cultural war." The initiative campaigns, when they were not directly attacking gay people, couched their messages carefully in deceptive rhetoric. Appealing to voters, they offered seemingly fair messages that everyone should be free to employ or to rent to whomever they wish. They did not underscore, at least publicly, that this freedom would preserve the "freedom" to discriminate.

The initiative campaigns also contained subliminal appeals to racial hatred among whites and to a sense of vulnerability among people of color. The measures, for example, sought to forbid "quota preferences" and affirmative action. Although "quota preferences" was a legally meaningless phrase, both it and affirmative action were commonly associated in the public's mind with issues of race discrimination. Likewise, by labeling civil rights as "special rights," the leaders of initiative campaigns tapped into a popular although incorrect view that people of color receive "special" benefits under civil rights laws. To white audiences, these references aimed to suggest that gay people were trying to get "something more" than the average American. And to people of color, these campaign slogans were intended to imply that gay people were trying to take away or take advantage of the hard-earned rights of racial minorities. The campaigns succeeded. This rhetoric, along with the measures themselves, began to change the course of the American debate about civil rights for the 1990s and beyond.

In addition, although gay people had long been confronted with vicious attacks on their civil rights and basic humanity, the carefully organized, highly sophisticated, and well-funded new round of assaults looked to be the most difficult battle to date. Myriad new gay and lesbian organizations emerged to enter the ever-changing battleground. Both nascent and long-standing organizations found themselves engaged in rapid-fire public exchanges about many of the complex questions raised at trial regarding what it means to be gay as well as what it means to be "equal." A typical antagonistic talk radio host might ask, "Why do you people deserve special protection for your immoral, harmful, and disgusting sexual behavior?" Even friendly hosts would pose questions such as, "Why do gay people want to be singled out for special benefits instead of just being equal like everyone else?" Interviewers on both ends of the political spectrum would inquire, "How do we even know when someone is gay and is eligible for the protection of these laws?" As the experts at trial illustrated, many different answers could be offered in response to these questions, depending on whether one gives a historical, scientific, political, or yet another perspective. Still, activists and community members had little choice but to develop their best answers, learn quickly from their errors, and move on to the next debate.

The Onslaught

Not surprisingly, Amendment 2's passage in Colorado spawned a series of copycat measures all over the country. Just a year later, and barely weeks after closing arguments in the Amendment 2 trial, election day 1993 arrived. With it, one Amendment 2 look-alike in Cincinnati, Ohio, scores of local amendments in Oregon municipalities, and one local initiative to repeal Lewiston, Maine's ordinance prohibiting sexual orientation discrimination appeared on ballots in their respective communities. All of them passed.[1] The number of antigay amend-

---

1. The Oregon legislature enacted a law that prevented the local charter amendments from taking effect. The Cincinnati enactment was immediately challenged in court. At the time of publication, enforcement of the charter amendment was enjoined but the amendment remained in litigation. The Lewiston, Maine ordinance was repealed.

ments on the books grew exponentially and with more battles unfolding.

Religious right national organizers, encouraged by these solid successes and seeing a potent vehicle for fund-raising and identification of political supporters, launched ambitious plans to reproduce antigay measures throughout the United States. Local religious right activists from all parts of the country began to announce plans for antigay initiatives in their own cities and states. Their campaign strategies picked up on many of the same themes addressed by expert witnesses at the Amendment 2 trial regarding the nature and origins of homosexuality, the political power of gay people, issues of morality and religion, and the historical status of gay people compared to other minority populations. Each campaign attempted to show that being gay was a dangerous behavior, that gay people comprised a wealthy and politically powerful group, and that providing civil rights protections to gay people would endanger respect for and enforcement of existing civil rights legislation.

The Amendment 2 pilot model appeared to be a favorite of antigay activists. Measures introduced in Michigan and Missouri copied Amendment 2 word for word. The proposed measures there sought to stop those states from ever prohibiting discrimination against lesbians, gay men, and bisexuals. Arizonan organizers put their own provocative spin on their initiative. In addition to targeting gay people, the Arizona measure added pedophiles to the list of those who would be deemed ineligible for antidiscrimination protection. This strategy appeared aimed to sweep in wavering voters and to play on the myth that gay people disproportionately commit child sexual abuse.

In other states, initiatives expressed antigay hostility even more overtly. The Oregon Citizens Alliance, sponsor of the failed 1992 antigay measure, introduced the "Minority Status and Child Protection Act" in 1994. This measure, like the others, sought to bar state and local governments from prohibiting discrimination against gay people and provided that "the people find that to be morally opposed to certain sexual behaviors such as homosexuality . . . is a Right of Conscience in accord with . . . [the Oregon] Constitution." It contained several additional provisions, including prohibition of legal recognition of the relationships of gay couples through marriage or other means, and banning use of public funds "in a manner that ha[d] the purpose or effect of expressing approval of homosexuality." The initiative also sought to allow employers to consider "private sexual behaviors" as relevant factors in making personnel decisions. In addition to Oregon, "Citizens Alliance" groups in Idaho and Nevada promoted this text. Washington state had two groups and two initiatives in 1994: One paralleled the Oregon measure and, among other aims, sought to repeal and block laws and policies that would prohibit discrimination against gay people, bisexuals, transsexuals, and transvestites, and to prohibit teachers from discussing homosexuality as acceptable. The second sought to do all this plus prohibit recognition of same-sex marriages or domestic partnerships, prohibit the use of public funds to express approval of homosexuality, limit the borrowing of public library books on the topic of homosexuality to adults only, ban gay people from being parents, bar legal recognition for a person's sex change operation, and allow personnel decisions based on private sexual conduct.

Finally, in Florida in 1994, and in Maine in 1995, more stealth-like measures were introduced. Never once mentioning the word *homosexual*, these measures sought to impose a blanket limitation on government's ability to pass civil rights laws and simultaneously to repeal all existing laws that provided protections beyond those specified in the initiatives. In Florida, the proposed amendment would have permitted the state government to pass antidiscrimination legislation covering race, gender, age, disability, and six other characteristics. Notably, sexual orientation was not among them. Neither were veteran's status, source of income, or student status, all of which were governed by existing Florida laws that the amendment would have repealed and forever barred. But the rhetoric surrounding the measure's introduction left no question as to its target. To obtain a petition, interested voters were told to dial 1–800-GAY-LAWS. And the pamphlet circulated with the petition addressed only the "special rights" sought by gay people and the wealth and privilege of lesbians and gay men.

Rumbles of similar initiatives in California, Montana, Ohio, Wyoming, and elsewhere also kept gay activists wary. Although measures were not ultimately introduced in those states, most onlookers speculated that antigay forces were only awaiting the outcome of the Amendment 2 litigation in the U.S. Supreme Court before introducing their own. The litigation did not halt every effort though—Amendment 2–type measures were introduced in several legislatures, including in New Mexico and Oklahoma.

Antigay attacks were not limited to the initiative and legislative processes, either. Apparently as an alternative to an antigay amendment, Ohio religious right organizers opted for an electoral strategy as Cincinnati's Issue 3 remained stymied in the courts. Rather than squelch already-passed laws that would prohibit discrimination against gay men and lesbians, these organizers decided to develop a strategy to fight the reelection of legislators who supported legal protections for gay people. Called Project Spotlight, and backed by religious right activists in and outside of the state, this plan aimed to excoriate publicly and retaliate in an organized fashion against any elected official who showed support for the rights of gay people. Indeed, any elected official who refused to go "on the record" against equal rights for gay people would be a target under this plan for recall efforts and future challenges.

In addition to activity on the statewide level, antigay activists worked fervently in local communities to repeal, and in some cases prohibit, future passage of ordinances perceived to benefit gay people. Oregon, as it had for many years, faced yet another wave of municipal charter amendments to ban local governments from protecting their lesbian and gay constituents against discrimination. Florida's campaign moved to the local level. While a court ruling kept off the ballot an effort to repeal Tampa's ordinance prohibiting sexual orientation discrimination, another antigay effort, this time spearheaded by the "Concerned Citizens of Alachua County," met with election day success. By an overwhelming margin, voters passed an amendment to the county charter in November 1994 barring the county government from passing any ordinance that included the classification "sexual orientation, sexual preference or similar characteristics." Voters also approved a companion ballot measure that repealed provisions in the county's human rights and fair housing ordinances prohibiting discrimination based on sexual orientation.[2]

In Austin, Texas, the antigay effort took the form of a campaign by "Concerned Texans" to repeal a city law providing health insurance coverage to unmarried city employees with domestic partners. Several months earlier, at the behest mainly of lesbian and gay groups in Austin, the city had passed an ordinance authorizing dependent health

---

2. The Alachua County charter amendment banning ordinances that would prohibit sexual orientation discrimination was invalidated by a Florida district court. However, the county's sexual orientation protections were repealed pursuant to the voters' mandate.

benefits to city employees with domestic partners equal to those provided to married employees. Religious right organizations struck back
with a powerful campaign to undo the many years of advocacy that
had led to adoption of the equal compensation plan. Their effort succeeded: Domestic partnership benefits for Austin employees were
repealed in May 1994.

And in Springfield, Missouri, in February 1994, 71 percent of voters repealed a city law that enhanced penalties for bias crimes motivated by the race, gender, religion, and other traits, including sexual
orientation, of the victim. Opponents of the hate crimes law focused
their efforts on portraying the law as creating a "mini–gay rights bill."

In still other venues, the fights were not about laws protecting gay
people from discrimination or providing benefits to employees with
unmarried partners but over who would control the school board and
other local government entities. The years of the stealth candidate had
arrived. From small town to large city, candidates with unpublicized
ties to religious right organizations launched campaigns for public
office and often won. Once in office, they began pushing their own
agenda to rid schools of gay-positive programming, including multi-
cultural education. In place of such programs, these candidates promoted curricula that highlighted as their role models an English-speak-
ing nuclear family headed by a married heterosexual couple. Although
these school board races were quite distinct from the campaigns for
antigay ballot measures on the surface, both were driven by similar
rhetoric that appealed to popular fears about gay people, diversity, and
civil rights. And many of the themes sounded by the expert witnesses
during the Amendment 2 trial—including the historical entrenchment
of antigay bias and the limited yet feared political power of lesbians
and gay men—continued to surface in the public debate.

Reading between the Lines

Through their texts and supporting rhetoric, the statewide ballot measures revealed an important refinement of the radical right's strategy
and marked the contours of this new era of backlash against lesbian
and gay civil rights. Whether or not a particular measure appeared on
the ballot, its introduction forced discussion in each state about the
rights of gay people, and, ultimately, about whether civil rights protections should exist at all.

On the surface, these measures appealed to people's fears, igno-rance, and hatred of lesbian and gay people. By offering the general public an opportunity to vote away basic rights for gay men and les-bians while leaving those same rights available for all others, the mea-sures left little question that their promoters believed much mileage could be had from popular disapproval and dislike of gay people.

But the impact of these initiatives was intended to reach much fur-ther. They offered the public an opportunity to oppose civil rights pro-tections generally. While the apparent aims were limited to gay people, the format of these proposals appeared intended to pave the way for redefining and ultimately eradicating the framework of civil rights. The very process of holding an election on a minority group's ability to obtain protection against discrimination from government ran contrary to a fundamental tenet safeguarded by earlier Supreme Court interpre-tations of the Constitution—that basic rights should not be put to pop-ular vote. If the ability of one minority group to obtain legal protection could be put on the electoral chopping block, there was little reason to think that any other group's rights might not be similarly vulnerable.

Fighting Back

It was a daunting time. Many of the lesbians and gay men leading cam-paigns against initiatives in their states had not previously been involved in any sort of political battles or were just beginning to learn how to address gay issues in the political arena. In Idaho, for example, prior to the Idaho Citizens Alliance proposal of antigay legislation, only a handful of gay people were willing to be seen on television or use their names when speaking with reporters about gay issues. The 1994 gay pride march and festival held in Boise, for example, attracted a large proportion of nongay people, which reflected both the political success of gay leaders at building bridges and the debilitating fear of many gay people who refused to march out of concern that an employer or family member might witness the parade and identify them as lesbian or gay.

In other states, such as Florida and Washington, statewide gay organizations had existed for many years. For the most part, however, these groups had been sustained by a small handful of dedicated vol-unteers who did not have the capacity to organize a major statewide opposition campaign. In both of those states, as well as in Arizona, Missouri, Nevada, and elsewhere, activists familiar with working in their own communities quickly had to develop statewide networks. In particular, activists working in states with large, conservative rural populations that could weigh heavily in an election had to develop strategies for organizing in towns and villages where they had few contacts, let alone organizational support.

Adding to the stress of organizing were early polls in most states showing that without an enormous and successful education campaign, gay people had virtually no chance of success at the polls. Before the passage of Cincinnati's antigay amendment in November 1993, and just after the overwhelming defeat of lesbians and gay men in the national battle about whether the military should accept openly lesbian and gay servicemembers, three of the then-largest national gay political organizations—National Gay and Lesbian Task Force (NGLTF), the Human Rights Campaign Fund, and the Gay and Lesbian Victory Fund—launched plans for a series of intensive skills-building courses in political campaigns for lesbian and gay statewide organizers. At NGLTF's annual Creating Change conference for lesbian and gay activists, for example, "Fight the Right" programs took over many slots previously reserved for other programming, as activists, intent on gathering and sharing information, met in large hotel ballrooms to discuss the immediate threats they faced. At training conferences hosted by other organizations, campaign members came together to learn how to identify voters, construct a "message," and develop literature to carry out a campaign against an antigay measure.

Despite organizers' tireless efforts, the campaigns were rarely smooth. In addition to intrastate geographic rifts, basic strategy differences emerged, both within gay groups and in the campaigns themselves. The question of how visible gay people should be and how prominently equal rights for gay people should be highlighted surfaced in virtually every campaign. Since the measures being fought were targeted at lesbians, gay men, and bisexuals, gay people naturally became active in staffing the initiative opposition teams. But whether the campaign message should have an antigovernment or a progay slant proved to be a difficult call state-by-state. In some states, pollsters showed that campaign messages that depicted the antigay initiative as creating "more" government appealed to voters more than messages depicting it as hostile to lesbian and gay residents. In most campaigns, including the one against Amendment 2, gay people were rarely featured in television advertisements opposing the amendment. Much more frequently, nongay community leaders were pictured or quoted as opposing the proposed measures.

One notable exception to this trend was a group known as the "Lesbian Avengers" that embarked on bus trips throughout the United States to focus attention and organizing efforts on various embattled states. They, as well as local organizations including some groups of cross-dressing performers in local bars and nightclubs, insisted that the anti-initiative campaigns present gay people in all their diversity. Still others viewed the campaigns as efforts not just to win at election time but also as an invaluable opportunity to debunk myths about civil rights and gay people in many different communities.

In addition to the political battles, new legal battles also formed part of the response to the onslaught. In virtually every state where an initiative was introduced, local attorneys coordinated with staff attorneys of Lambda Legal Defense and Education Fund and the ACLU to launch preelection challenges to keep measures off the ballot. Working on the premise that the civil rights and political participation of a minority group, or indeed, of any group of people, should not be put to popular vote, lawsuits were prepared and filed throughout the country asking courts to strike these measures from the ballot. The challenges typically argued that the measures did not comply with procedural requirements for initiatives because their texts were unclear or their ballot summaries were misleading or inaccurate. In addition, the suits alleged the measures were unconstitutional and should be struck from the ballot because they plainly violated the fundamental constitutional rights of lesbians and gay men. The great majority of these lawsuits were not successful as a legal matter as courts seemed reluctant to be perceived as "taking away" the voters' right to decide. Florida was a notable exception. There, the state supreme court struck the proposed amendment from the ballot as inaccurate and misleading to voters.

Even when the preemptive legal challenges failed, however, many activists believed they contributed importantly to the overall fight against the initiatives because they slowed down the process of collecting signatures necessary for placement on the ballot. Other organizers felt differently, maintaining that the lawsuits slowed fund-raising and organizing efforts by creating the impression that the problem posed by the initiative could be resolved in court.

At a minimum, it was clear that they provided organizers with an opportunity to call public attention to legal flaws of each measure. The media and education campaigns that accompanied the legal challenges underscored that these measures were divisive as well as unconstitutional. Lawyers for the challengers told reporters that the antigay proposals would waste taxpayer money and would make all people vulnerable by subjecting the rights of the minority to the majority. By framing their comments in this way, the lawyers sought to appeal to popular concerns about government spending and harm to the state's reputation in addition to the political dangers posed by the measure.

To the great relief of many lesbians and gay men, most of these initiatives failed to gather the signatures necessary to be placed on their state's ballots. By the time the last deadline for signature gathering in 1994 came and went, only two statewide antigay measures were going to voters: one in Oregon and the other in Idaho. After difficult campaigns in both states, both were defeated—albeit narrowly—at the polls.

But even as activists celebrated the narrow defeats of antigay measures in Oregon and Idaho in November 1994, serious concern underlay the festivities. The proposed antigay amendment to the Alachua County, Florida, charter had passed overwhelmingly, despite the efforts of gay activists and others in this county that includes the university town of Gainesville. Additionally, antigay organizations in Oregon, Idaho, and elsewhere immediately announced they would be back. Several variations on an amendment to Oregon's constitution were proposed swiftly, most of them known as "The Minority Status and Child Protection Act," appealing explicitly to the same themes discussed above. Idaho's antigay organization introduced a similar measure. Maine activists confronted a stealth-style antigay initiative proposed by "Concerned Maine Families." The measure, although clearly aimed at limiting the rights of gay people, was not explicitly antigay. It had garnered enough signatures to achieve a place on the November 1995 ballot, but intensive organizing efforts by Maine civil rights supporters defeated the measure at the polls. Replete with the rhetoric refined in initiative battles, themes of "special rights" and the "immorality" of gay people remained prominent on the national stage as these next battles over the dignity and equality of gay people took shape.

Looking to the Future

As soon as the U.S. Supreme Court's decision striking down Amendment 2 was announced, both antigay commentators and gay activists identified the ruling as a watershed in the public struggle over gay and lesbian equality.

Within hours, leaders of some of the nation's most virulently antigay groups were not only condemning the Court's action but also grappling with the new landscape presented by the ruling. On radio shows and in news media soundbites, they acknowledged that the debate had shifted out from under them. This far-reaching type of antigay initiative, one of the religious right's most popular vehicles ever for garnering support and grassroots activism, had just been trounced by a solid majority of the highest court in the country. Even worse, from their perspective, the Court had condemned antigay animus as a basis for lawmaking.

Gay people, on the other hand, both individually and in groups, raced to call each other to share the news, uncorked champagne, and joined in large rallies in cities throughout the country. Speaking to each other and to the media, the message was clear: The tide was turning and, for the first time in history, the U.S. Supreme Court had acknowledged the prejudice behind an antigay law and had rejected it.

But what was in this ruling that so devastated the religious right? Certainly, the principle that government cannot legislate based on a desire to harm a group of people was not a new one and had been made clear in several non–gay related cases.[3] But, since 1986, when the Court upheld Georgia's "sodomy" law, saying that "majority sentiments about homosexuality" were a sufficient basis for legislation, governments had frequently justified antigay discrimination with a simple reference to those "majority sentiments." Taking a cue from that case, *Bowers v. Hardwick*, in which the Court called a gay man's claim to constitutional privacy rights "at best facetious," governments had typically seen little need to convey respect to their lesbian and gay constituents, much less to adopt laws and policies to provide meaningful equality.

Lower courts had treated the *Hardwick* decision as a signal that

---

3. *Cleburne v. Cleburne Living Center*, 473 U.S. 432 (1985); *U.S. Department of Agriculture v. Moreno*, 413 U.S. 528 (1973).

they, too, should reject the legal claims of gay people challenging discrimination. For years, lesbians and gay men had been going to court when nonjudicial remedies had failed, challenging everything from government denial of security clearances to judicial denials of custody and visitation to gay and lesbian parents. And for years, courts had been rejecting those claims, ruling that since states could criminalize consensual sexual relations of same-sex couples, they could also ban gay people from holding certain jobs or from parenting their children. Gay people bringing these challenges were met with skepticism at best and overt hostility at worst. Most of these courts assumed that gay people, as a group, could be defined by their sexual conduct. Therefore, they concluded, following the "logic" of the *Hardwick* ruling, that courts should not demand substantial justifications for antigay discrimination by government when the "conduct that defines the class of gay people" could be criminalized. Even where lawyers did try to challenge the popular view that *Hardwick* gave states authority for all forms of antigay discrimination, they gained little ground.

And when six members of the Court declared that the state could not legislate with an aim of making gay people "unequal to everyone else," religious right-wing commentators realized how dramatically the tide had changed and how the legacy of *Bowers v. Hardwick* might soon draw to a close. Some went so far as to demand the impeachment of several Supreme Court justices, characterizing the Supreme Court as a liberal elite body subject to pressure by the "militant homosexual minority."

The Court's ruling made this shift in several important ways that had as much to do with political and social realities as with law. First, the majority recognized that gay people are more than sex acts. In contrast to *Hardwick* and the cases that followed—cases that treated gay people and "sodomy" as interchangeable concepts—the Court in *Romer* telegraphed the message that "homosexuals" are people and that they are entitled to full constitutional rights.

Second, the majority recognized that antigay animus had motivated Amendment 2—and rebuffed it. Whereas previously such animus might have been labeled "presumed moral disapproval of the majority" as in *Hardwick,* the Court now refused to countenance a measure that was so blatantly motivated by prejudice.

Third, after many years of battles in which the religious right had hammered the message that gay people were somehow seeking "special rights" when advocating for laws prohibiting sexual orientation discrimination, the Court added its authoritative view that the "special rights" rhetoric was meaningless. Appearing to speak directly to the general public in an effort to clear up any misunderstanding, the Court's opinion stated plainly that

> we find nothing special in the protections Amendment 2 withholds. These are protections taken for granted by most people either because they already have them or do not need them; these are protections against exclusion from an almost limitless number of transactions and endeavors that constitute ordinary civic life in a free society.[4]

Almost immediately, the Court's ruling had several important effects. Within three weeks of its ruling, the Supreme Court took up a case challenging Cincinnati's Amendment 2 clone, known as Issue 3. The petition for review of the federal appeals court ruling upholding that antigay city charter amendment had been sitting in the Court for nearly a year, awaiting the outcome of *Romer*. On June 17, 1996, the Supreme Court acted. It granted review of the case, vacated the appeals court ruling, and sent the case back to the appeals court for a new ruling in light of *Romer*. Justice Scalia, joined by Chief Justice Rehnquist and Justice Thomas, dissented from the Court's decision. Insisting that the Cincinnati case was different because it involved a city charter amendment rather than a statewide amendment, Scalia argued that the Court should have either let the appeals court ruling stand or set the case for argument before the Court. Again, however, his views did not prevail.[5]

Shortly thereafter, the Oregon Citizens Alliance, the group that had promoted antigay initiatives in Oregon for nearly a decade, announced it would be withdrawing a series of antigay amendments it had been circulating for placement on the state's 1996 ballot. The proposed amendments, most of which were known as "The Minority Status and Child Protection Act," paralleled Amendment 2's ban on civil

---

4. *Id.* at 1627.
5. *Equality Foundation of Greater Cincinnati v. City of Cincinnati*, 116 S.Ct. 2519 (1996).

rights protections for gay people and included a variety of other provisions restricting gay people's rights in family recognition and access to public funding. A few weeks later, on July 1, 1996, an announcement in Idaho further illustrated the *Romer* ruling's ability to topple other antigay measures. There, the Idaho Citizens Alliance announced that it, too, was withdrawing the antigay "Family and Child Protection Act" proposed for voter initiative on the 1996 ballot. After years of political and legal warfare in the voter initiative process over the basic rights of lesbians and gay men, *Romer* appeared to have edged to a close this era of gay politics in which popular initiatives took direct aim at gay people's ability to obtain protection against discrimination.[6]

Romer's immediate effect on other antigay initiatives in the political arena was matched by a renewed sense of strength among lesbian and gay civil rights advocates. During the previous several years, the silver lining of the antigay initiative battles for many lesbians and gay men had been in the dramatic growth of community organizing and the greatly increased numbers of gay and nongay people speaking out publicly in support of gay people's equality. With the authoritative weight of a Supreme Court ruling supporting the rights of gay people, both seasoned and newly minted activists experienced a tremendous boost of moral and legal force. At the moment of the ruling, gay civil rights advocates were immersed in many difficult battles over the issues of equal marriage rights, the "don't ask, don't tell" law restricting the rights of lesbian and gay servicemembers, advocacy efforts for passage of sexual orientation antidiscrimination laws, efforts to defund AIDS-related services, and myriad other arenas in which the struggle for equality and freedom from discrimination and bias-motivated violence was taking place. With the backing of the Supreme Court, the tone of the lobbying, discussions, and political warfare could shift. The Supreme Court's message, after all, was a clear one—laws cannot be created with the sole goal of giving legal effect to popular dislike of gay people. Even the most virulently antigay lawmakers would have to be more careful in pursuing their goals because any indications of animus would make their handiwork vulnerable to legal challenge.

---

6. At publication time, the last of the Colorado-style antigay initiatives, Cincinnati's "Issue 3," had been upheld again by the federal court of appeals but remained in litigation.

But the political struggle for the rights of gay people was not over. Just two days after the *Romer* ruling, President Clinton disregarded the decision's clear message when he announced his support for the "Defense of Marriage Act," also known as DOMA, a bill in Congress that sought to ban federal recognition of same-sex couples' marriages and to authorize states to do the same. The bill was crafted to respond to the initial success of a Hawaii lawsuit seeking the right to marry for same-sex couples. This announcement, both in timing and substance, was unsettling to many supporters of the rights of gay people. In addition to being a deliberate political setback to gay people in the wake of a landmark legal victory, Clinton's announcement reinforced antigay opponents in their most recent efforts to ban recognition of "gay marriage" on a state-by-state basis. Bills had already been introduced in 38 states around the country to deny recognition to same-sex couples' marriages solemnized out of state and, in some cases, to ban solemnization of marriages of same-sex couples in that state. (Of these, 16 had been enacted by the end of 1996, 25 by mid-1997.)

Although nothing could take the sting out of Clinton's quick announcement of support for the antigay marriage measure, the Court's ruling provided activists with a new and more solid base from which to ground a response to these legislative assaults. Antigay sentiment was behind DOMA, activists charged. And, they added, it was precisely this sort of lawmaking based on antigay sentiment that the Supreme Court had just rejected. While Congress moved forward with the proposed legislation and Clinton signed it in September 1996, all parties were on notice that the legislation would be measured against the *Romer* decision.

Similarly, courts reviewing the military's "don't ask, don't tell" law that places severe restrictions on lesbian and gay servicemembers also had *Romer* to consider. While laws and policies related to the military typically receive great deference from courts, it is unclear how the discrimination of "don't ask, don't tell" will be reconciled with the principles proclaimed in *Romer*. Courts inclined to defer to the military's judgment might now face a stark challenge, because the government has defended the "don't ask, don't tell" law based on a need to protect nongay soldiers from discomfort at working closely with lesbians and gay men. That justification appears to run squarely counter to *Romer*'s rejection of such animus in legislation.

So, too, "sodomy" laws,[7] bars to recognition of gay youth groups in public schools, and other forms of state-sponsored discrimination should increasingly be called into question.

It remains difficult to predict the impact *Romer* will have on these—and other—laws. The decision's core principle should, in theory, mean the end to all antigay discrimination by government because, lesbian and gay rights advocates argue, there is no reason other than dislike or disapproval of gay people for government to treat gay people differently from nongay people. However, *Romer* will not likely be such an across-the-board panacea; many judges continue to hold deeply biased views about lesbians and gay men, and other judges, who lack information about gay people, base their rulings on unquestioned fears and myths. Also, particularly in the contexts of the military and marriage, knee-jerk reactions rather than rational reasoning frequently control outcomes both in courts and in legislatures.

The majority's opinion in *Romer* does not attempt to educate readers about gay people to overcome these biases or correct misinformation. It does not offer a definitive explanation of who gay people are—indeed, it does not even attempt to take on that complex question. Perhaps appropriately, that question remains open to multifaceted answers that take into account that being gay means one thing when analyzed from a political perspective, another when considered from a scientific vantage point, and still another when viewed throughout history. Instead, the Court's opinion, and the demise of Colorado's Amendment 2, make the simple yet profound point that lesbians and gay men may not, by virtue of being members of a socially vulnerable minority, be separated out from their neighbors and rendered strangers to the law.

---

7. As of 1996, at least 19 states had "sodomy" laws in force to prohibit certain private, noncommercial, sexual acts between consenting adults. These states included Alabama, Arkansas, Arizona, Florida, Georgia, Idaho, Kansas, Louisiana, Maryland, Minnesota, Mississippi, Missouri, North Carolina, Oklahoma, Rhode Island, South Carolina, Texas, Utah, and Virginia. Of these, 5 (Arkansas, Kansas, Maryland, Missouri, Oklahoma, and Texas) prohibit private sexual relations only when they take place between adults of the same sex. Over time, these laws have come to have a tremendous stigmatizing effect on gay people. Frequently they are relied upon to justify employment discrimination against lesbians and gay men and sometimes to justify depriving gay parents of custody of or visitation with their children.

Appendix

Roy ROMER, Governor of Colorado, et al., Petitioners,
v.
Richard G. EVANS et al.
No. 94-1039.
Supreme Court of the United States
Argued Oct. 10, 1995.
Decided May 20, 1996.

Justice KENNEDY delivered the opinion of the Court.

One century ago, the first Justice Harlan admonished this Court that the Constitution "neither knows nor tolerates classes among citizens." *Plessy v. Ferguson*, 163 U.S. 537, 559, 16 S.Ct. 1138, 1146, 41 L.Ed. 256 (1896) (dissenting opinion). Unheeded then, those words now are understood to state a commitment to the law's neutrality where the rights of persons are at stake. The Equal Protection Clause enforces this principle and today requires us to hold invalid a provision of Colorado's Constitution.

I

The enactment challenged in this case is an amendment to the Constitution of the State of Colorado, adopted in a 1992 statewide referendum. The parties and the state courts refer to it as "Amendment 2," its designation when submitted to the voters. The impetus for the amendment and the contentious campaign that preceded its adoption came in large part from ordinances that had been passed in various Colorado municipalities. For example, the cities of Aspen and Boulder and the City and County of Denver each had enacted ordinances which banned discrimination in many transactions and activities, including housing, employment, education, public accommodations, and health and welfare services. Denver Rev. Municipal Code, Art. IV §§ 28-91 to 28-116 (1991); Aspen Municipal Code § 13-98 (1977); Boulder Rev.Code §§ 12-1-1 to 12-1-11 (1987). What gave rise to the statewide controversy was the protection the ordinances afforded to persons discriminated against by reason of their sexual orientation. See Boulder Rev.Code § 12-1-1 (defining "sexual orientation" as "the choice of sexual partners, i.e., bisexual, homosexual or heterosexual"); Denver Rev. Municipal Code, Art. IV § 28-92 (defining "sexual orientation" as "[t]he status of an individual as to his or her heterosexuality, homosexuality or bisexuality"). Amendment 2 repeals these ordinances to the extent they prohibit discrimination on the basis of "homosexual, lesbian or bisexual orientation, conduct, practices or relationships." Colo. Const., Art. II, § 30b.

Yet Amendment 2, in explicit terms, does more than repeal or rescind these provisions. It prohibits all legislative, executive or judicial action at any level of state or local government designed to protect the named class, a class we shall refer to as homosexual persons or gays and lesbians. The amendment reads:

> No Protected Status Based on Homosexual, Lesbian, or Bisexual Orientation. Neither the State of Colorado, through any of its branches or departments, nor any of its agencies, political subdivisions, municipalities or school districts, shall enact, adopt or enforce any statute, regulation, ordinance or policy whereby homosexual, lesbian or bisexual orientation, conduct, practices or relationships shall constitute or otherwise be the basis of or entitle any person or class of persons to have or claim any minority status, quota preferences, protected status or claim of discrimination. This Section of the Constitution shall be in all respects self-executing. (*Ibid*).

Soon after Amendment 2 was adopted, this litigation to declare its invalidity and enjoin its enforcement was commenced in the District Court for the City and County of Denver. Among the plaintiffs (respondents here) were homosexual persons, some of them government employees. They alleged that enforcement of Amendment 2 would subject them to immediate and substantial risk of discrimination on the basis of their sexual orientation. Other plaintiffs (also respondents here) included the three municipalities whose ordinances we have cited and certain other governmental entities which had acted earlier to protect homosexuals from discrimination but would be prevented by Amendment 2 from continuing to do so. Although Governor Romer had been on record opposing the adoption of Amendment 2, he was named in his official capacity as a defendant, together with the Colorado Attorney General and the State of Colorado.

The trial court granted a preliminary injunction to stay enforcement of Amendment 2, and an appeal was taken to the Supreme Court of Colorado. Sustaining the interim injunction and remanding the case for further proceedings, the State Supreme Court held that Amendment 2 was subject to strict scrutiny under the Fourteenth Amendment because it infringed the fundamental right of gays and lesbians to participate in the political process. *Evans v. Romer*, 854 P.2d 1270 (Colo.1993) (*Evans I*). To reach this conclusion, the state court relied on our voting rights cases, *e.g., Reynolds v. Sims*, 377 U.S. 533, 84 S.Ct. 1362, 12 L.Ed.2d 506 (1964); *Carrington v. Rash*, 380 U.S. 89, 85 S.Ct. 775, 13 L.Ed.2d 675 (1965); *Harper v. Virginia Bd. of Elections*, 383 U.S. 663, 86 S.Ct. 1079, 16 L.Ed.2d 169 (1966); *Williams v. Rhodes*, 393 U.S. 23, 89 S.Ct. 5, 21 L.Ed.2d 24 (1968), and on our precedents involving discriminatory restructuring of governmental decisionmaking, see, *e.g., Hunter v. Erickson*, 393 U.S. 385, 89 S.Ct. 557, 21 L.Ed.2d 616 (1969); *Reitman v. Mulkey*, 387 U.S. 369, 87 S.Ct. 1627, 18 L.Ed.2d 830 (1967); *Washington v. Seattle School Dist. No. 1*, 458 U.S. 457, 102 S.Ct. 3187, 73 L.Ed.2d 896 (1982); *Gordon v. Lance*, 403 U.S. 1, 91 S.Ct. 1889, 29 L.Ed.2d 273 (1971). On remand, the State advanced various arguments in an effort to show that Amendment 2 was narrowly tailored to serve compelling interests, but the trial court found none sufficient. It enjoined enforcement of Amendment 2, and the Supreme Court of Colorado, in a second opinion, affirmed the ruling. *Evans v. Romer*, 882 P.2d 1335 (Colo.1994) (*Evans II*). We granted certiorari and now affirm the judgment, but on a rationale different from that adopted by the State Supreme Court.

II

The State's principal argument in defense of Amendment 2 is that it puts gays and lesbians in the same position as all other persons. So, the State says, the measure does no more than deny homosexuals special rights. This reading of the amendment's language is implausible. We rely not upon our own interpretation of the amendment but upon the authoritative construction of Colorado's Supreme Court. The state court, deeming it unnecessary to determine the full extent of the amendment's reach, found it invalid even on a modest reading of its implications. The critical discussion of the amendment, set out in *Evans I*, is as follows:

> The immediate objective of Amendment 2 is, at a minimum, to repeal existing statutes, regulations, ordinances, and policies of state and local entities that barred discrimination based on sexual orientation. *See* Aspen, Colo., Mun.Code § 13-98 (1977) (prohibiting discrimination in employment, housing and public accommodations on the basis of sexual orientation); Boulder, Colo., Rev.Code §§ 12-1-2 to -4 (1987) (same); Denver, Colo., Rev. Mun.Code art. IV, §§ 28-91 to -116 (1991) (same); Executive Order No. D0035 (December 10, 1990) (prohibiting employment discrimination for 'all state employees, classified and exempt' on the basis of sexual orientation); Colorado Insurance Code, § 10-3-1104, 4A C.R.S. (1992 Supp.) (forbidding health insurance providers from determining insurability and premiums based on an applicant's, a beneficiary's, or an insured's sexual orientation); and various provisions prohibiting discrimination based on sexual orientation at state colleges.[26]

"The 'ultimate effect' of Amendment 2 is to prohibit any governmental entity from adopting similar, or more protective statutes, regulations, ordinances, or policies in the future unless the state constitution is first amended to permit such measures." 854 P.2d, at 1284–1285, and n. 26.

Sweeping and comprehensive is the change in legal status effected by this law. So much is evident from the ordinances that the Colorado Supreme Court declared would be void by operation of Amendment 2. Homosexuals, by state decree, are put in a solitary class with respect to transactions and relations in both the private and governmental spheres. The amendment withdraws from homosexuals, but no others, specific legal protection from the injuries caused by discrimination, and it forbids reinstatement of these laws and policies.

---

26. Metropolitan State College of Denver prohibits college sponsored social clubs from discriminating in membership on the basis of sexual orientation and Colorado State University has an antidiscrimination policy which encompasses sexual orientation.

The change that Amendment 2 works in the legal status of gays and lesbians in the private sphere is far-reaching, both on its own terms and when considered in light of the structure and operation of modern anti-discrimination laws. That structure is well illustrated by contemporary statutes and ordinances prohibiting discrimination by providers of public accommodations. "At common law, innkeepers, smiths, and others who 'made profession of a public employment,' were prohibited from refusing, without good reason, to serve a customer." *Hurley v. Irish-American Gay, Lesbian and Bisexual Group of Boston, Inc.*, 515 U.S. ——, ——, 115 S.Ct. 2338, 2346, 132 L.Ed.2d 487 (1995). The duty was a general one and did not specify protection for particular groups. The common law rules, however, proved insufficient in many instances, and it was settled early that the Fourteenth Amendment did not give Congress a general power to prohibit discrimination in public accommodations, *Civil Rights Cases*, 109 U.S. 3, 25, 3 S.Ct. 18, 31-32, 27 L.Ed. 835 (1883). In consequence, most States have chosen to counter discrimination by enacting detailed statutory schemes. See, *e.g.*, S.D. Codified Laws §§ 20-13-10, 20-13-22, 20-13-23 (1995); Iowa Code §§ 216.6- 216.8 (1994); Okla. Stat., Tit. 25, §§ 1302, 1402 (1987); 43 Pa. Cons.Stat. §§ 953, 955 (Supp.1995); N.J. Stat. Ann. §§ 10:5-3, 10:5-4 (West Supp.1995); N.H.Rev.Stat. Ann. § 354-A:7, 354-A:10, 354-A:17 (1995); Minn.Stat. § 363.03 (1991 and Supp.1995).

Colorado's state and municipal laws typify this emerging tradition of statutory protection and follow a consistent pattern. The laws first enumerate the persons or entities subject to a duty not to discriminate. The list goes well beyond the entities covered by the common law. The Boulder ordinance, for example, has a comprehensive definition of entities deemed places of "public accommodation." They include "any place of business engaged in any sales to the general public and any place that offers services, facilities, privileges, or advantages to the general public or that receives financial support through solicitation of the general public or through governmental subsidy of any kind." Boulder Rev.Code § 12-1-1(j) (1987). The Denver ordinance is of similar breadth, applying, for example, to hotels, restaurants, hospitals, dental clinics, theaters, banks, common carriers, travel and insurance agencies, and "shops and stores dealing with goods or services of any kind," Denver Rev. Municipal Code, Art. IV, § 28-92.

These statutes and ordinances also depart from the common law by enumerating the groups or persons within their ambit of protection.

Enumeration is the essential device used to make the duty not to discriminate concrete and to provide guidance for those who must comply. In following this approach, Colorado's state and local governments have not limited anti-discrimination laws to groups that have so far been given the protection of heightened equal protection scrutiny under our cases. See, *e.g.*, *J.E.B. v. Alabama ex rel. T.B.*, 511 U.S. ———, ———, 114 S.Ct. 1419, 1425, 128 L.Ed.2d 89 (1994) (sex); *Lalli v. Lalli*, 439 U.S. 259, 265, 99 S.Ct. 518, 523, 58 L.Ed.2d 503 (1978) (illegitimacy); *McLaughlin v. Florida*, 379 U.S. 184, 191–192, 85 S.Ct. 283, 288–289, 13 L.Ed.2d 222 (1964) (race); *Oyama v. California*, 332 U.S. 633, 68 S.Ct. 269, 92 L.Ed. 249 (1948) (ancestry). Rather, they set forth an extensive catalogue of traits which cannot be the basis for discrimination, including age, military status, marital status, pregnancy, parenthood, custody of a minor child, political affiliation, physical or mental disability of an individual or of his or her associates—and, in recent times, sexual orientation. Aspen Municipal Code § 13-98(a)(1) (1977); Boulder Rev.Code §§ 12-1-1 to 12-1-4 (1987); Denver Rev. Municipal Code, Art. IV, §§ 28-92 to 28-119 (1991); Colo.Rev.Stat. §§ 24-34-401 to 24-34-707 (1988 and Supp.1995).

Amendment 2 bars homosexuals from securing protection against the injuries that these public-accommodations laws address. That in itself is a severe consequence, but there is more. Amendment 2, in addition, nullifies specific legal protections for this targeted class in all transactions in housing, sale of real estate, insurance, health and welfare services, private education, and employment. See, *e.g.*, Aspen Municipal Code §§ 13-98(b), (c) (1977); Boulder Rev.Code §§ 12-1-2, 12-1-3 (1987); Denver Rev. Municipal Code, Art. IV §§ 28-93 to 28-95, § 28-97 (1991).

Not confined to the private sphere, Amendment 2 also operates to repeal and forbid all laws or policies providing specific protection for gays or lesbians from discrimination by every level of Colorado government. The State Supreme Court cited two examples of protections in the governmental sphere that are now rescinded and may not be reintroduced. The first is Colorado Executive Order D0035 (1990), which forbids employment discrimination against " 'all state employees, classified and exempt' on the basis of sexual orientation." 854 P.2d, at 1284. Also repealed, and now forbidden, are "various provisions prohibiting discrimination based on sexual orientation at state colleges." *Id.*, at 1284, 1285. The repeal of these measures and the prohibition against their future reenactment demonstrates that Amendment 2 has the same force and effect in Colorado's governmental sector as it does elsewhere and that it applies to policies as well as ordinary legislation.

Amendment 2's reach may not be limited to specific laws passed for the benefit of gays and lesbians. It is a fair, if not necessary, inference from the broad language of the amendment that it deprives gays and lesbians even of the protection of general laws and policies that prohibit arbitrary discrimination in governmental and private settings. See, *e.g.*, Colo.Rev.Stat. § 24-4-106(7) (1988) (agency action subject to judicial review under arbitrary and capricious standard); § 18-8-405 (making it a criminal offense for a public servant knowingly, arbitrarily or capriciously to refrain from performing a duty imposed on him by law); § 10-3-1104(1)(f) (prohibiting "unfair discrimination" in insurance); 4 Colo.Code of Regulations 801-1, Policy 11-1 (1983) (prohibiting discrimination in state employment on grounds of specified traits or "other non-merit factor"). At some point in the systematic administration of these laws, an official must determine whether homosexuality is an arbitrary and thus forbidden basis for decision. Yet a decision to that effect would itself amount to a policy prohibiting discrimination on the basis of homosexuality, and so would appear to be no more valid under Amendment 2 than the specific prohibitions against discrimination the state court held invalid.

If this consequence follows from Amendment 2, as its broad language suggests, it would compound the constitutional difficulties the law creates. The state court did not decide whether the amendment has this effect, however, and neither need we. In the course of rejecting the argument that Amendment 2 is intended to conserve resources to fight discrimination against suspect classes, the Colorado Supreme Court made the limited observation that the amendment is not intended to affect many anti-discrimination laws protecting non-suspect classes, *Romer II,* 882 P.2d at 1346, n. 9. In our view that does not resolve the issue. In any event, even if, as we doubt, homosexuals could find some safe harbor in laws of general application, we cannot accept the view that Amendment 2's prohibition on specific legal protections does no more than deprive homosexuals of special rights. To the contrary, the amendment imposes a special disability upon those persons alone. Homosexuals are forbidden the safeguards that others enjoy or may seek without constraint. They can obtain specific protection against discrimination only by enlisting the citizenry of Colorado to amend the state constitution or perhaps, on the State's view, by trying to pass helpful laws of general applicability. This is so no matter how local or discrete the harm, no matter how public and widespread the injury. We find nothing special in the protections Amendment 2 withholds. These are protections taken for granted by most people either because they already have them or do not need them; these are protections against exclusion from an almost limitless number of transactions and endeavors that constitute ordinary civic life in a free society.

III

The Fourteenth Amendment's promise that no person shall be denied the equal protection of the laws must co-exist with the practical necessity that most legislation classifies for one purpose or another, with resulting disadvantage to various groups or persons. *Personnel Administrator of Mass. v. Feeney*, 442 U.S. 256, 271–272, 99 S.Ct. 2282, 2292, 60 L.Ed.2d 870 (1979); *F.S. Royster Guano Co. v. Virginia*, 253 U.S. 412, 415, 40 S.Ct. 560, 561–562, 64 L.Ed. 989 (1920). We have attempted to reconcile the principle with the reality by stating that, if a law neither burdens a fundamental right nor targets a suspect class, we will uphold the legislative classification so long as it bears a rational relation to some legitimate end. See, *e.g., Heller v. Doe*, 509 U.S. ———, ———, 113 S.Ct. 2637, 2642–2643, 125 L.Ed.2d 257 (1993).

Amendment 2 fails, indeed defies, even this conventional inquiry. First, the amendment has the peculiar property of imposing a broad and undifferentiated disability on a single named group, an exceptional and, as we shall explain, invalid form of legislation. Second, its sheer breadth is so discontinuous with the reasons offered for it that the amendment seems inexplicable by anything but animus toward the class that it affects; it lacks a rational relationship to legitimate state interests.

Taking the first point, even in the ordinary equal protection case calling for the most deferential of standards, we insist on knowing the relation between the classification adopted and the object to be attained. The search for the link between classification and objective gives substance to the Equal Protection Clause; it provides guidance and discipline for the legislature, which is entitled to know what sorts of laws it can pass; and it marks the limits of our own authority. In the ordinary case, a law will be sustained if it can be said to advance a legitimate government interest, even if the law seems unwise or works to the disadvantage of a particular group, or if the rationale for it seems tenuous. See *New Orleans v. Dukes*, 427 U.S. 297, 96 S.Ct. 2513, 49 L.Ed.2d 511 (1976) (tourism benefits justified classification favoring pushcart vendors of certain longevity); *Williamson v. Lee Optical of Okla., Inc.*, 348 U.S. 483, 75 S.Ct. 461, 99 L.Ed. 563 (1955) (assumed health concerns justified law favoring optometrists over opticians); *Railway Express Agency, Inc. v. New York*, 336 U.S. 106, 69 S.Ct. 463, 93 L.Ed. 533 (1949) (potential traffic hazards justified exemption of vehicles advertising the owner's products from general advertising ban); *Kotch v. Board of River Port Pilot Comm'rs for Port of New Orleans*, 330 U.S. 552, 67 S.Ct. 910, 91 L.Ed. 1093 (1947) (licensing scheme that disfavored persons unrelated to current river boat pilots justified by possible efficiency and safety benefits of a closely knit pilotage system). The laws challenged in the cases just cited were narrow enough in scope and grounded in a sufficient factual context for us to ascertain that there existed some relation between the classification and the purpose it served. By requiring that the classification bear a rational relationship to an independent and legitimate legislative end, we ensure that classifications are not drawn for the purpose of disadvantaging the group burdened by the law. See *United States Railroad Retirement Bd. v. Fritz*, 449 U.S. 166, 181, 101 S.Ct. 453, 462, 66 L.Ed.2d 368 (1980) (STEVENS, J., concurring) ("If the adverse impact on the disfavored class is an apparent aim of the legislature, its impartiality would be suspect.").

Amendment 2 confounds this normal process of judicial review. It is at once too narrow and too broad. It identifies persons by a single trait and then denies them protection across the board. The resulting disqualification of a class of persons from the right to seek specific protection from the law is unprecedented in our jurisprudence. The absence of precedent for Amendment 2 is itself instructive; "[d]iscriminations of an unusual character especially suggest careful consideration to determine whether they are obnoxious to the constitutional provision." *Louisville Gas & Elec. Co. v. Coleman*, 277 U.S. 32, 37–38, 48 S.Ct. 423, 425, 72 L.Ed. 770 (1928).

It is not within our constitutional tradition to enact laws of this sort. Central both to the idea of the rule of law and to our own Constitution's guarantee of equal protection is the principle that government and each of its parts remain open on impartial terms to all who seek its assistance. "'Equal protection of the laws is not achieved through indiscriminate imposition of inequalities.'" *Sweatt v. Painter*, 339 U.S. 629, 635, 70 S.Ct. 848, 850–851, 94 L.Ed. 1114 (1950) (quoting *Shelley v. Kraemer*, 334 U.S. 1, 22, 68 S.Ct. 836, 846, 92 L.Ed. 1161 (1948)). Respect for this principle explains why laws singling out a certain class of citizens for disfavored legal status or general hardships are rare. A law declaring that in general it shall be more difficult for one group of citizens than for all others to seek aid from the government is itself a denial of equal protection of the laws in the most literal sense. "The guaranty of 'equal protection of the laws is a pledge of the protection of equal laws.'" *Skinner v. Oklahoma ex rel. Williamson*, 316 U.S. 535, 541, 62 S.Ct. 1110, 1113, 86 L.Ed. 1655 (1942) (quoting *Yick Wo v. Hopkins*, 118 U.S. 356, 369, 6 S.Ct. 1064, 1070, 30 L.Ed. 220 (1886)).

Davis v. Beason, 133 U.S. 333, 10 S.Ct. 299, 33 L.Ed. 637 (1890), not cited by the parties but relied upon by the dissent, is not evidence that Amendment 2 is within our constitutional tradition, and any reliance upon it as authority for sustaining the amendment is misplaced. In *Davis*, the Court approved an Idaho territorial statute denying Mormons, polygamists, and advocates of polygamy the right to vote and to hold office because, as the Court construed the statute, it "simply excludes from the privilege of voting, or of holding any office of honor, trust or profit, those who have been convicted of certain offences, and those who advocate a practical resistance to the laws of the Territory and justify and approve the commission of crimes forbidden by it." *Id.*, at 347, 10 S.Ct., at 302. To the extent *Davis* held that persons advocating a certain practice may be denied the right to vote, it is no longer good law. *Brandenburg v. Ohio*, 395 U.S. 444, 89 S.Ct. 1827, 23 L.Ed.2d 430 (1969) (*per curiam*). To the extent it held that the groups designated in the statute may be deprived of the right to vote because of their status, its ruling could not stand without surviving strict scrutiny, a most doubtful outcome. *Dunn v. Blumstein*, 405 U.S. 330, 337, 92 S.Ct. 995, 1000, 31 L.Ed.2d 274 (1972); cf. *United States v. Brown*, 381 U.S. 437, 85 S.Ct. 1707, 14 L.Ed.2d 484 (1965); *United States v. Robel*, 389 U.S. 258, 88 S.Ct. 419, 19 L.Ed.2d 508 (1967). To the extent *Davis* held that a convicted felon may be denied the right to vote, its holding is not implicated by our decision and is unexceptionable. See *Richardson v. Ramirez*, 418 U.S. 24, 94 S.Ct. 2655, 41 L.Ed.2d 551 (1974).

A second and related point is that laws of the kind now before us raise the inevitable inference that the disadvantage imposed is born of animosity toward the class of persons affected. "[I]f the constitutional conception of 'equal protection of the laws' means anything, it must at the very least mean that a bare . . . desire to harm a politically unpopular group cannot constitute a legitimate governmental interest." *Department of Agriculture v. Moreno*, 413 U.S. 528, 534, 93 S.Ct. 2821, 2826, 37 L.Ed.2d 782 (1973). Even laws enacted for broad and ambitious purposes often can be explained by reference to legitimate public policies which justify the incidental disadvantages they impose on certain persons. Amendment 2, however, in making a general announcement that gays and lesbians shall not have any particular protections from the law, inflicts on them immediate, continuing, and real injuries that outrun and belie any legitimate justifications that may be claimed for it. We conclude that, in addition to the far-reaching deficiencies of Amendment 2 that we have noted, the principles it offends, in another sense, are conventional and venerable; a law must bear a rational relationship to a legitimate governmental purpose, *Kadrmas v. Dickinson Public Schools*, 487 U.S. 450, 462, 108 S.Ct. 2481, 2489-2490, 101 L.Ed.2d 399 (1988), and Amendment 2 does not.

The primary rationale the State offers for Amendment 2 is respect for other citizens' freedom of association, and in particular the liberties of landlords or employers who have personal or religious objections to homosexuality. Colorado also cites its interest in conserving resources to fight discrimination against other groups. The breadth of the Amendment is so far removed from these particular justifications that we find it impossible to credit them. We cannot say that Amendment 2 is directed to any identifiable legitimate purpose or discrete objective. It is a status-based enactment divorced from any factual context from which we could discern a relationship to legitimate state interests; it is a classification of persons undertaken for its own sake, something the Equal Protection Clause does not permit. "[C]lass legislation . . . [is] obnoxious to the prohibitions of the Fourteenth Amendment. . . ." *Civil Rights Cases*, 109 U.S., at 24, 3 S.Ct., at 30.

We must conclude that Amendment 2 classifies homosexuals not to further a proper legislative end but to make them unequal to everyone else. This Colorado cannot do. A State cannot so deem a class of persons a stranger to its laws. Amendment 2 violates the Equal Protection Clause, and the judgment of the Supreme Court of Colorado is affirmed.

It is so ordered.

Justice SCALIA, with whom THE CHIEF JUSTICE and Justice THOMAS join, dissenting.

The Court has mistaken a Kulturkampf for a fit of spite. The constitutional amendment before us here is not the manifestation of a "'bare . . . desire to harm'" homosexuals, *ante,* at 1628, but is rather a modest attempt by seemingly tolerant Coloradans to preserve traditional sexual mores against the efforts of a politically powerful minority to revise those mores through use of the laws. That objective, and the means chosen to achieve it, are not only unimpeachable under any constitutional doctrine hitherto pronounced (hence the opinion's heavy reliance upon principles of righteousness rather than judicial holdings); they have been specifically approved by the Congress of the United States and by this Court.

In holding that homosexuality cannot be singled out for disfavorable treatment, the Court contradicts a decision, unchallenged here, pronounced only 10 years ago, see *Bowers v. Hardwick,* 478 U.S. 186, 106 S.Ct. 2841, 92 L.Ed.2d 140 (1986), and places the prestige of this institution behind the proposition that opposition to homosexuality is as reprehensible as racial or religious bias. Whether it is or not is precisely the cultural debate that gave rise to the Colorado constitutional amendment (and to the preferential laws against which the amendment was directed). Since the Constitution of the United States says nothing about this subject, it is left to be resolved by normal democratic means, including the democratic adoption of provisions in state constitutions. This Court has no business imposing upon all Americans the resolution favored by the elite class from which the Members of this institution are selected, pronouncing that "animosity" toward homosexuality, *ante,* at 1628, is evil. I vigorously dissent.

I

Let me first discuss Part II of the Court's opinion, its longest section, which is devoted to rejecting the State's arguments that Amendment 2 "puts gays and lesbians in the same position as all other persons," and "does no more than deny homosexuals special rights," *ante,* at 1624. The Court concludes that this reading of Amendment 2's language is "implausible" under the "authoritative construction" given Amendment 2 by the Supreme Court of Colorado. *Ibid.*

In reaching this conclusion, the Court considers it unnecessary to decide the validity of the State's argument that Amendment 2 does not deprive homosexuals of the "protection [afforded by] general laws and policies that prohibit arbitrary discrimination in governmental and private settings." *Ante,* at 1626. I agree that we need not resolve that dispute, because the Supreme Court of Colorado has resolved it for us. In *Evans v. Romer,* 882 P.2d 1335 (1994), the Colorado court stated:

> [I]t is significant to note that Colorado law currently proscribes discrimination against persons who are not suspect classes, including discrimination based on age, § 24-34-402(1)(a), 10A C.R.S. (1994 Supp.); marital or family status, § 24-34-502(1)(a), 10A C.R.S. (1994 Supp.); veterans' status, § 28-3-506, 11B C.R.S. (1989); and for any legal, off-duty conduct such as smoking tobacco, § 24-34-402.5, 10A C. R.S. (1994 Supp.). *Of course Amendment 2 is not intended to have any effect on this legislation, but seeks only to prevent the adoption of antidiscrimination laws intended to protect gays, lesbians, and bisexuals. Id., at 1346, n. 9 (emphasis added).*

The Court utterly fails to distinguish this portion of the Colorado court's opinion. Colorado Rev. Stat. § 24-34-402.5 (Supp.1995), which this passage authoritatively declares not to be affected by Amendment 2, was respondents' primary example of a generally applicable law whose protections would be unavailable to homosexuals under Amendment 2. See Brief for Respondents Evans *et al.* 11-12. The clear import of the Colorado court's conclusion that it is not affected is that "general laws and policies that prohibit arbitrary discrimination" would continue to prohibit discrimination on the basis of homosexual conduct as well. This analysis, which is fully in accord with (indeed, follows inescapably from) the text of the constitutional provision, lays to rest such horribles, raised in the course of oral argument, as the prospect that assaults upon homosexuals could not be prosecuted. The amendment prohibits *special treatment* of homosexuals, and nothing more. It would not affect, for example, a requirement of state law that pensions be paid to all retiring state employees with a certain length of service; homosexual employees, as well as others, would be entitled to that benefit. But it would prevent the State or any municipality from making death-benefit payments to the "life partner" of a homosexual when it does not make such payments to the long-time roommate of a nonhomosexual employee. Or again, it does not affect the requirement of the State's general insurance laws that customers be afforded coverage without discrimination unrelated to anticipated risk. Thus, homosexuals could not be denied coverage, or charged a greater premium, with respect to auto collision insurance; but neither the State nor any municipality could require that distinctive health insurance risks associated with homosexuality (if there are any) be ignored.

Despite all of its hand-wringing about the potential effect of Amendment 2 on general antidiscrimination laws, the Court's opinion ultimately does not dispute all this, but assumes it to be true. See *ante*, at 1626. The only denial of equal treatment it contends homosexuals have suffered is this: They may not obtain *preferential* treatment without amending the state constitution. That is to say, the principle underlying the Court's opinion is that one who is accorded equal treatment under the laws, but cannot as readily as others obtain *preferential* treatment under the laws, has been denied equal protection of the laws. If merely stating this alleged "equal protection" violation does not suffice to refute it, our constitutional jurisprudence has achieved terminal silliness.

The central thesis of the Court's reasoning is that any group is denied equal protection when, to obtain advantage (or, presumably, to avoid disadvantage), it must have recourse to a more general and hence more difficult level of political decisionmaking than others. The world has never heard of such a principle, which is why the Court's opinion is so long on emotive utterance and so short on relevant legal citation. And it seems to me most unlikely that any multilevel democracy can function under such a principle. For whenever a disadvantage is imposed, or conferral of a benefit is prohibited, at one of the higher levels of democratic decisionmaking (*i.e.*, by the state legislature rather than local government, or by the people at large in the state constitution rather than the legislature), the affected group has (under this theory) been denied equal protection. To take the simplest of examples, consider a state law prohibiting the award of municipal contracts to relatives of mayors or city councilmen. Once such a law is passed, the group composed of such relatives must, in order to get the benefit of city contracts, persuade the state legislature—unlike all other citizens, who need only persuade the municipality. It is ridiculous to consider this a denial of equal protection, which is why the Court's theory is unheard-of.

The Court might reply that the example I have given is *not* a denial of equal protection only because the same "rational basis" (avoidance of corruption) which renders constitutional the *substantive discrimination* against relatives (*i.e.*, the fact that they alone cannot obtain city contracts) also automatically suffices to sustain what might be called the *electoral-procedural discrimination* against them (*i.e.*, the fact that they must go to the state level to get this changed). This is of course a perfectly reasonable response, and would explain why "electoral-procedural discrimination" has not hitherto been heard of: a law that is valid in its substance is automatically valid in its level of enactment. But the Court cannot afford to make this argument, for as I shall discuss next, there is no doubt of a rational basis for the substance of the prohibition at issue here. The Court's entire novel theory rests upon the proposition that there is something *special*—something that cannot be justified by normal "rational basis" analysis—in making a disadvantaged group (or a nonpreferred group) resort to a higher decisionmaking level. That proposition finds no support in law or logic.

II

I turn next to whether there was a legitimate rational basis for the substance of the constitutional amendment—for the prohibition of special protection for homosexuals.[1] It is unsurprising that the Court avoids discussion of this question, since the answer is so obviously yes. The case most relevant to the issue before us today is not even mentioned in the Court's opinion: In *Bowers v. Hardwick*, 478 U.S. 186, 106 S.Ct. 2841, 92 L.Ed.2d 140 (1986), we held that the Constitution does not prohibit what virtually all States had done from the founding of the Republic until very recent years—making homosexual conduct a crime. That holding is unassailable, except by those who think that the Constitution changes to suit current fashions. But in any event it is a given in the present case: Respondents' briefs did not urge overruling *Bowers*, and at oral argument respondents' counsel expressly disavowed any intent

---

1. The Court evidently agrees that "rational basis"—the normal test for compliance with the Equal Protection Clause—is the governing standard. The trial court rejected respondents' argument that homosexuals constitute a "suspect" or "quasi-suspect" class, and respondents elected not to appeal that ruling to the Supreme Court of Colorado. See *Evans v. Romer*, 882 P.2d 1335, 1341, n. 3 (1994). And the Court implicitly rejects the Supreme Court of Colorado's holding, see *Evans v. Romer*, 854 P.2d 1270, 1282 (1993), that Amendment 2 infringes upon a "fundamental right" of "independently identifiable class[es]" to "participate equally in the political process." *Ante*, at 1624.

to seek such overruling, Tr. of Oral Arg. 53. If it is constitutionally permissible for a State to make homosexual conduct criminal, surely it is constitutionally permissible for a State to enact other laws merely *disfavoring* homosexual conduct. (As the Court of Appeals for the District of Columbia Circuit has aptly put it: "If the Court [in *Bowers*] was unwilling to object to state laws that criminalize the behavior that defines the class, it is hardly open . . . to conclude that state sponsored discrimination against the class is invidious. After all, there can hardly be more palpable discrimination against a class than making the conduct that defines the class criminal." *Padula v. Webster*, 822 F.2d 97, 103 (1987).) And *a fortiori* it is constitutionally permissible for a State to adopt a provision *not even* disfavoring homosexual conduct, but merely prohibiting all levels of state government from bestowing special protections upon homosexual conduct. Respondents (who, unlike the Court, cannot afford the luxury of ignoring inconvenient precedent) counter *Bowers* with the argument that a greater-includes-the-lesser rationale cannot justify Amendment 2's application to individuals who do not engage in homosexual acts, but are merely of homosexual "orientation." Some courts of appeals have concluded that, with respect to laws of this sort at least, that is a distinction without a difference. See *Equality Foundation of Greater Cincinnati, Inc. v. Cincinnati*, 54 F.3d 261, 267 (C.A.6 1995) ("[F]or purposes of these proceedings, it is virtually impossible to distinguish or separate individuals of a particular *orientation* which predisposes them toward a particular sexual conduct from those who actually *engage* in that particular type of sexual conduct"); *Steffan v. Perry*, 41 F.3d 677, 689–690 (C.A.D.C.1994). The Supreme Court of Colorado itself appears to be of this view. See 882 P.2d, at 1349–1350 ("Amendment 2 targets this class of persons based on four characteristics: sexual orientation; conduct; practices; and relationships. Each characteristic provides a potentially different way of identifying that class of persons who are gay, lesbian, or bisexual. These four characteristics are not truly severable from one another because each provides nothing more than a different way of identifying *the same class of persons*") (emphasis added).

But assuming that, in Amendment 2, a person of homosexual "orientation" is someone who does not engage in homosexual conduct but merely has a tendency or desire to do so, *Bowers* still suffices to establish a rational basis for the provision. If it is rational to criminalize the conduct, surely it is rational to deny special favor and protection to those with a self-avowed tendency or desire to engage in the conduct. Indeed, where criminal sanctions are not involved, homosexual "orientation" is an acceptable stand-in for homosexual conduct. A State "does not violate the Equal Protection Clause merely because the classifications made by its laws are imperfect," *Dandridge v. Williams,* 397 U.S. 471, 485, 90 S.Ct. 1153, 1161, 25 L.Ed.2d 491 (1970). Just as a policy barring the hiring of methadone users as transit employees does not violate equal protection simply because some methadone users pose no threat to passenger safety, see *New York City Transit Authority v. Beazer,* 440 U.S. 568, 99 S.Ct. 1355, 59 L.Ed.2d 587 (1979), and just as a mandatory retirement age of 50 for police officers does not violate equal protection even though it prematurely ends the careers of many policemen over 50 who still have the capacity to do the job, see *Massachusetts Bd. of Retirement v. Murgia,* 427 U.S. 307, 96 S.Ct. 2562, 49 L.Ed.2d 520 (1976) (*per curiam*), Amendment 2 is not constitutionally invalid simply because it could have been drawn more precisely so as to withdraw special antidiscrimination protections only from those of homosexual "orientation" who actually engage in homosexual conduct. As Justice KENNEDY wrote, when he was on the Court of Appeals, in a case involving discharge of homosexuals from the Navy: "Nearly any statute which classifies people may be irrational as applied in particular cases. Discharge of the particular plaintiffs before us would be rational, under minimal scrutiny, not because their particular cases present the dangers which justify Navy policy, but instead because the general policy of discharging all homosexuals is rational." *Beller v. Middendorf,* 632 F.2d 788, 808–809, n. 20 (C.A.9 1980) (citation omitted). See also *Ben-Shalom v. Marsh,* 881 F.2d 454, 464 (C.A.7 1989), cert. denied, 494 U.S. 1004, 110 S.Ct. 1296, 108 L.Ed.2d 473 (1990).

Moreover, even if the provision regarding homosexual "orientation" *were* invalid, respondents' challenge to Amendment 2—which is a facial challenge—must fail. "A facial challenge to a legislative Act is, of course, the most difficult challenge to mount successfully, since the challenger must establish that no set of circumstances exists under which the Act would be valid." *United States v. Salerno,* 481 U.S. 739, 745, 107 S.Ct. 2095, 2100, 95 L.Ed.2d 697 (1987). It would not be enough for respondents to establish (if they could) that Amendment 2 is unconstitutional as applied to those of homosexual "orientation"; since, under *Bowers,* Amendment 2 is unquestionably constitutional as applied to those who engage in homosexual conduct, the facial challenge cannot succeed. Some individuals of homosexual "orientation" who do not engage in homosexual acts might successfully bring an as-applied challenge to Amendment 2, but so far as the record indicates, none of the respondents is such a person. See App. 4-5 (complaint describing each of the individual respondents as either "a gay man" or "a lesbian").[2]

III

The foregoing suffices to establish what the Court's failure to cite any case remotely in point would lead one to suspect: No principle set forth in the Constitution, nor even any imagined by this Court in the past 200 years, prohibits what Colorado has done here. But the case for Colorado is much stronger than that. What it has done is not only unprohibited, but eminently reasonable, with close, congressionally approved precedent in earlier constitutional practice.

First, as to its eminent reasonableness. The Court's opinion contains grim, disapproving hints that Coloradans have been guilty of "animus" or "animosity" toward homosexuality, as though that has been established as Unamerican. Of course it is our moral heritage that one should not hate any human being or class of human beings. But I had thought that one could consider certain conduct reprehensible—murder, for example, or polygamy, or cruelty to animals—and could exhibit even "animus" toward such conduct. Surely that is the only sort of "animus" at issue here: moral disapproval of homosexual conduct, the same sort of moral disapproval that produced the centuries-old criminal laws that we held constitutional in *Bowers*. The Colorado amendment does not, to speak entirely precisely, prohibit giving

---

2. The Supreme Court of Colorado stated: "We hold that the portions of Amendment 2 that would remain if only the provision concerning sexual orientation were stricken are not autonomous and thus, not severable," 882 P.2d, at 1349. That statement was premised, however, on the proposition that "[the] four characteristics [described in the Amendment—sexual orientation, conduct, practices, and relationships] are not truly severable from one another because each provides nothing more than a different way of identifying *the same class of persons*." Id., at 1349–1350 (emphasis added). As I have discussed above, if that premise is true—if the entire class affected by the Amendment takes part in homosexual conduct, practices and relationships—*Bowers* alone suffices to answer all constitutional objections. Separate consideration of persons of homosexual "orientation" is necessary only if one believes (as the Supreme Court of Colorado did not) that that is a distinct class.

favored status to people who are *homosexuals;* they can be favored for many reasons—for example, because they are senior citizens or members of racial minorities. But it prohibits giving them favored status *because of* their *homosexual conduct*—that is, it prohibits favored status *for homosexuality.*

But though Coloradans are, as I say, entitled to be hostile toward homosexual conduct, the fact is that the degree of hostility reflected by Amendment 2 is the smallest conceivable. The Court's portrayal of Coloradans as a society fallen victim to pointless, hate-filled "gay-bashing" is so false as to be comical. Colorado not only is one of the 25 States that have repealed their antisodomy laws, but was among the first to do so. See 1971 Colo. Sess. Laws, ch. 121, § 1. But the society that eliminates criminal punishment for homosexual acts does not necessarily abandon the view that homosexuality is morally wrong and socially harmful; often, abolition simply reflects the view that enforcement of such criminal laws involves unseemly intrusion into the intimate lives of citizens. Cf. Brief for Lambda Legal Defense and Education Fund, Inc., et al. as *Amici Curiae* in *Bowers v. Hardwick,* O.T. 1985, No. 85-140, p. 25, n. 21 (antisodomy statutes are "unenforceable by any but the most offensive snooping and wasteful allocation of law enforcement resources"); Kadish, The Crisis of Overcriminalization, 374 The Annals of the American Academy of Political and Social Science 157, 161 (1967) ("To obtain evidence [in sodomy cases], police are obliged to resort to behavior which tends to degrade and demean both themselves personally and law enforcement as an institution").

There is a problem, however, which arises when criminal sanction of homosexuality is eliminated but moral and social disapprobation of homosexuality is meant to be retained. The Court cannot be unaware of that problem; it is evident in many cities of the country, and occasionally bubbles to the surface of the news, in heated political disputes over such matters as the introduction into local schools of books teaching that homosexuality is an optional and fully acceptable "alternate life style." The problem (a problem, that is, for those who wish to retain social disapprobation of homosexuality) is that, because those who engage in homosexual conduct tend to reside in disproportionate numbers in certain communities, see Record, Exh. MMM, have high disposable income, see *ibid.;* App. 254 (affidavit of Prof. James Hunter), and of course care about homosexual-rights issues much more ardently than the public at large, they possess political power much greater than their numbers, both locally and statewide. Quite understandably, they devote this political power to achieving not merely a grudging social toleration, but full social acceptance, of homosexuality. See, *e.g.*, Jacobs, The Rhetorical Construction of Rights: The Case of the Gay Rights Movement, 1969–1991, 72 Neb. L.Rev. 723, 724 (1993) ("[T]he task of gay rights proponents is to move the center of public discourse along a continuum from the rhetoric of disapprobation, to rhetoric of tolerance, and finally to affirmation").

By the time Coloradans were asked to vote on Amendment 2, their exposure to homosexuals' quest for social endorsement was not limited to newspaper accounts of happenings in places such as New York, Los Angeles, San Francisco, and Key West. Three Colorado cities—Aspen, Boulder, and Denver—had enacted ordinances that listed "sexual orientation" as an impermissible ground for discrimination, equating the moral disapproval of homosexual conduct with racial and religious bigotry. See Aspen Municipal Code § 13-98 (1977); Boulder Rev. Municipal Code §§ 12-1-1 to 12-1-11 (1987); Denver Rev. Municipal Code, Art. IV §§ 28-91 to 28-116 (1991). The phenomenon had even appeared statewide: the Governor of Colorado had signed an executive order pronouncing that "in the State of Colorado we recognize the diversity in our pluralistic society and strive to bring an end to discrimination in any form," and directing state agency-heads to "ensure non-discrimination" in hiring and promotion based on, among other things, "sexual orientation." Executive Order No. D0035 (Dec. 10, 1990). I do not mean to be critical of these legislative successes; homosexuals are as entitled to use the legal system for reinforcement of their moral sentiments as are the rest of society. But they are subject to being countered by lawful, democratic countermeasures as well.

That is where Amendment 2 came in. It sought to counter both the geographic concentration and the disproportionate political power of homosexuals by (1) resolving the controversy at the statewide level, and (2) making the election a single-issue contest for both sides. It put directly, to all the citizens of the State, the question: Should homosexuality be given special protection? They answered no. The Court today asserts that this most democratic of procedures is unconstitutional. Lacking any cases to establish that facially absurd proposition, it simply asserts that it *must* be unconstitutional, because it has never happened before.

[Amendment 2] identifies persons by a single trait and then denies them protection across the board. The resulting disqualification of a class of persons from the right to seek specific protection from the law is unprecedented in our jurisprudence. The absence of precedent for Amendment 2 is itself instructive. . . .

It is not within our constitutional tradition to enact laws of this sort. Central both to the idea of the rule of law and to our own Constitution's guarantee of equal protection is the principle that government and each of its parts remain open on impartial terms to all who seek its assistance. (*Ante*, at 1627–1628)

As I have noted above, this is proved false every time a state law prohibiting or disfavoring certain conduct is passed, because such a law prevents the adversely affected group—whether drug addicts, or smokers, or gun owners, or motorcyclists—from changing the policy thus established in "each of [the] parts" of the State. What the Court says is even demonstrably false at the constitutional level. The Eighteenth Amendment to the Federal Constitution, for example, deprived those who drank alcohol not only of the power to alter the policy of prohibition *locally* or through *state legislation*, but even of the power to alter it through *state constitutional amendment* or *federal legislation*. The Establishment Clause of the First Amendment prevents theocrats from having their way by converting their fellow citizens at the local, state, or federal statutory level; as does the Republican Form of Government Clause prevent monarchists.

But there is a much closer analogy, one that involves precisely the effort by the majority of citizens to preserve its view of sexual morality statewide, against the efforts of a geographically concentrated and politically powerful minority to undermine it. The constitutions of the States of Arizona, Idaho, New Mexico, Oklahoma, and Utah *to this day* contain provisions stating that polygamy is "forever prohibited." See Ariz. Const., Art. XX, par. 2; Idaho Const., Art. I, § 4; N.M. Const., Art. XXI, § 1; Okla. Const., Art. I, § 2; Utah Const., Art. III, § 1. Polygamists, and those who have a polygamous "orientation," have been "singled out" by these provisions for much more severe treatment than merely denial of favored status; and that treatment can only be changed by achieving amendment of the state constitutions. The Court's disposition today suggests that these provisions are unconstitutional, and that polygamy must be permitted in these States on a state-legislated, or perhaps even local-option, basis—unless, of course, polygamists for some reason have fewer constitutional rights than homosexuals.

The United States Congress, by the way, *required* the inclusion of these antipolygamy provisions in the constitutions of Arizona, New Mexico, Oklahoma, and Utah, as a condition of their admission to statehood. See Arizona Enabling Act, 36 Stat. 569; New Mexico Enabling Act, 36 Stat. 558; Oklahoma Enabling Act, 34 Stat. 269; Utah Enabling Act, 28 Stat. 108. (For Arizona, New Mexico, and Utah, moreover, the Enabling Acts required that the antipolygamy provisions be "irrevocable without the consent of the United States and the people of said State"—so that not only were "each of [the] parts" of these States not "open on impartial terms" to polygamists, but even the States as a whole were not; polygamists would have to persuade the whole country to their way of thinking.) Idaho adopted the constitutional provision on its own, but the 51st Congress, which admitted Idaho into the Union, found its constitution to be "republican in form *and . . . in conformity with the Constitution of the United States.*" Act of Admission of Idaho, 26 Stat. 215 (emphasis added). Thus, this "singling out" of the sexual practices of a single group for statewide, democratic vote—so utterly alien to our constitutional system, the Court would have us believe—has not only happened, but has received the explicit approval of the United States Congress.

I cannot say that this Court has explicitly approved any of these state constitutional provisions; but it has approved a territorial statutory provision that went even further, depriving polygamists of the ability even to achieve a constitutional amendment, by depriving them of the power to vote. In *Davis v. Beason,* 133 U.S. 333, 10 S.Ct. 299, 33 L.Ed. 637 (1890), Justice Field wrote for a unanimous Court:

> In our judgment, § 501 of the Revised Statutes of Idaho Territory, which provides that "no person . . . who is a bigamist or polygamist or who teaches, advises, counsels, or encourages any person or persons to become bigamists or polygamists, or to commit any other crime defined by law, or to enter into what is known as plural or celestial marriage, or who is a member of any order, organization or association which teaches, advises, counsels, or encourages its members or devotees or any other persons to commit the crime of bigamy or polygamy, or any other crime defined by law . . . is permitted to vote at any election, or to hold any posi-

tion or office of honor, trust, or profit within this Territory," is not open to any constitutional or legal objection. (*Id.*, at 346-347, 10 S.Ct., at 302 (emphasis added))

To the extent, if any, that this opinion permits the imposition of adverse consequences upon mere abstract advocacy of polygamy, it has of course been overruled by later cases. See *Brandenburg v. Ohio,* 395 U.S. 444, 89 S.Ct. 1827, 23 L.Ed.2d 430 (1969) (*per curiam*). But the proposition that polygamy can be criminalized, and those engaging in that crime deprived of the vote, remains good law. See *Richardson v. Ramirez,* 418 U.S. 24, 53, 94 S.Ct. 2655, 2670, 41 L.Ed.2d 551 (1974). *Beason* rejected the argument that "such discrimination is a denial of the equal protection of the laws." Brief for Appellant in *Davis v. Beason,* O.T. 1889, No. 1261, p. 41. Among the Justices joining in that rejection were the two whose views in other cases the Court today treats as equal-protection lodestars—Justice Harlan, who was to proclaim in *Plessy v. Ferguson,* 163 U.S. 537, 559, 16 S.Ct. 1138, 1146, 41 L.Ed. 256 (1896) (dissenting opinion), that the Constitution "neither knows nor tolerates classes among citizens," quoted *ante,* at 1623, and Justice Bradley, who had earlier declared that "class legislation . . . [is] obnoxious to the prohibitions of the Fourteenth Amendment," *Civil Rights Cases,* 109 U.S. 3, 24, 3 S.Ct. 18, 30, 27 L.Ed. 835 (1883), quoted *ante,* at 1629.[3]

---

3. The Court labors mightily to get around *Beason,* see *ante,* at 1628-1629, but cannot escape the central fact that this Court found the statute at issue—which went much further than Amendment 2, denying polygamists not merely special treatment but the right *to vote*—"not open to any constitutional or legal objection," rejecting the appellant's argument (much like the argument of respondents today) that the statute impermissibly "single[d] him out," Brief for Appellant in *Davis v. Beason,* O.T. 1889, No. 1261, p. 41. The Court adopts my conclusions that (a) insofar as *Beason* permits the imposition of adverse consequences based upon mere advocacy, it has been overruled by subsequent cases, and (b) insofar as *Beason* holds that convicted felons may be denied the right to vote, it remains good law. To these conclusions, it adds something new: the claim that "[t]o the extent [*Beason*] held that the groups designated in the statute may be deprived of the right to vote because of their status, its ruling could not stand without surviving strict scrutiny, a most doubtful outcome." *Ante,* at 1628–1629. But if that is so, it is only because we have declared the right *to vote* to be a "fundamental political right," see, *e.g., Dunn v. Blumstein,* 405 U.S. 330, 336, 92 S.Ct. 995, 999–1000, 31 L.Ed.2d 274 (1972), deprivation of which triggers strict scrutiny. Amendment 2, of course, does not deny the fundamental right to vote, and the Court rejects the Colorado court's view that there exists a fundamental right to participate in the political process. Strict scrutiny is thus not in play here. See *ante,* at 1627. Finally, the Court's suggestion that § 501 of the Revised Statutes of Idaho, and Amendment 2, deny rights on account of "status" (rather than conduct) opens up a broader debate involving the significance of *Bowers* to this case, a debate which the Court is otherwise unwilling to join, see *supra,* at 1625–1627.

This Court cited *Beason* with approval as recently as 1993, in an opinion authored by the same Justice who writes for the Court today. That opinion said: "[A]dverse impact will not always lead to a finding of impermissible targeting. For example, a social harm may have been a legitimate concern of government for reasons quite apart from discrimination. . . . See, *e.g.*, . . . *Davis v. Beason*, 133 U.S. 333 [10 S.Ct. 299, 33 L.Ed. 637] (1890)." *Church of Lukumi Babalu Aye, Inc. v. Hialeah*, 508 U.S. 520, 535, 113 S.Ct. 2217, 2228, 124 L.Ed.2d 472 (1993). It remains to be explained how § 501 of the Idaho Revised Statutes was not an "impermissible targeting" of polygamists, but (the much more mild) Amendment 2 is an "impermissible targeting" of homosexuals. Has the Court concluded that the perceived social harm of polygamy is a "legitimate concern of government," and the perceived social harm of homosexuality is not?

IV

I strongly suspect that the answer to the last question is yes, which leads me to the last point I wish to make: The Court today, announcing that Amendment 2 "defies . . . conventional [constitutional] inquiry," *ante,* at 1627, and "confounds [the] normal process of judicial review," *ante,* at 1628, employs a constitutional theory heretofore unknown to frustrate Colorado's reasonable effort to preserve traditional American moral values. The Court's stern disapproval of "animosity" towards homosexuality might be compared with what an earlier Court (including the revered Justices Harlan and Bradley) said in *Murphy v. Ramsey,* 114 U.S. 15, 5 S.Ct. 747, 29 L.Ed. 47 (1885), rejecting a constitutional challenge to a United States statute that denied the franchise in federal territories to those who engaged in polygamous cohabitation:

> [C]ertainly no legislation can be supposed more wholesome and necessary in the founding of a free, self-governing commonwealth, fit to take rank as one of the co-ordinate States of the Union, than that which seeks to establish it on the basis of the idea of the family, as consisting in and springing from the union for life of one man and one woman in the holy estate of matrimony; the sure foundation of all that is stable and noble in our civilization; the best guaranty of that reverent morality which is the source of all benef-

icent progress in social and political improvement." (*Id.*, at 45, 5 S.Ct., at 764)

I would not myself indulge in such official praise for heterosexual monogamy, because I think it no business of the courts (as opposed to the political branches) to take sides in this culture war.

But the Court today has done so, not only by inventing a novel and extravagant constitutional doctrine to take the victory away from traditional forces, but even by verbally disparaging as bigotry adherence to traditional attitudes. To suggest, for example, that this constitutional amendment springs from nothing more than " 'a bare . . . desire to harm a politically unpopular group,' " *ante*, at 1628, quoting *Department of Agriculture v. Moreno*, 413 U.S. 528, 534, 93 S.Ct. 2821, 2826, 37 L.Ed.2d 782 (1973), is nothing short of insulting. (It is also nothing short of preposterous to call "politically unpopular" a group which enjoys enormous influence in American media and politics, and which, as the trial court here noted, though composing no more than 4% of the population had the support of 46% of the voters on Amendment 2, see App. to Pet. for Cert. C-18.)

When the Court takes sides in the culture wars, it tends to be with the knights rather than the villeins—and more specifically with the Templars, reflecting the views and values of the lawyer class from which the Court's Members are drawn. How that class feels about homosexuality will be evident to anyone who wishes to interview job applicants at virtually any of the Nation's law schools. The interviewer may refuse to offer a job because the applicant is a Republican; because he is an adulterer; because he went to the wrong prep school or belongs to the wrong country club; because he eats snails; because he is a womanizer; because she wears real-animal fur; or even because he hates the Chicago Cubs. But if the interviewer should wish not to be an associate or partner of an applicant because he disapproves of the applicant's homosexuality, then he will have violated the pledge which the Association of American Law Schools requires all its member-schools to exact from job interviewers: "assurance of the employer's willingness" to hire homosexuals. Bylaws of the Association of American Law Schools, Inc. § 6-4(b); Executive Committee Regulations of the Association of American Law Schools § 6.19, in 1995 Handbook, Association of American Law Schools. This law school view of what "prejudices" must be stamped out may be contrasted with the more plebeian attitudes that apparently still prevail in the United States Congress, which has been unresponsive to repeated attempts to extend to homosexuals the protections of federal civil rights laws, see, *e.g.,* Employment Non-Discrimination Act of 1994, S. 2238, 103d Cong., 2d Sess. (1994); Civil Rights Amendments of 1975, H.R. 5452, 94th Cong., 1st Sess. (1975), and which took the pains to exclude them specifically from the Americans With Disabilities Act of 1990, see 42 U.S.C. § 12211(a) (1988 ed., Supp. V).

*   *   *

Today's opinion has no foundation in American constitutional law, and barely pretends to. The people of Colorado have adopted an entirely reasonable provision which does not even disfavor homosexuals in any substantive sense, but merely denies them preferential treatment. Amendment 2 is designed to prevent piecemeal deterioration of the sexual morality favored by a majority of Coloradans, and is not only an appropriate means to that legitimate end, but a means that Americans have employed before. Striking it down is an act, not of judicial judgment, but of political will. I dissent.

Index